PRACTICAL COUNTRY LIVING

PRACTICAL COUNTRY LIVING

Guy N. Smith

THE BOYDELL PRESS

First published 1988 by The Boydell Press
an imprint of Boydell & Brewer Ltd
PO Box 9, Woodbridge, Suffolk IP12 3DF
and of Boydell & Brewer Inc.
Wolfeboro, New Hampshire 03894–2069, USA

ISBN 0 85115 495 6

British Library Cataloguing in Publication Data

Smith, Guy N.
Practical country living.
1. Farms, Small – England 2. Farm Life
– England
I. Title
630.92′4   S522.G7
ISBN 0 85115 495 6

Library of Congress Cataloging-in-Publication Data

Smith, Guy N.
   Practical country living.
   1. Home economics, Rural—England.   I. Title.
TX57.S64   1988   640′.941   87-22394
ISBN 0-85115-495-6

Jacket photograph by Rowan Smith

Printed in Great Britain by The Camelot Press Ltd, Southampton

Contents

Acknowledgements

Home Farm Magazine, Broad Leys Publishing Company, Widdington, Saffron Walden, Essex, CB11 3SP, for allowing me to reproduce various articles of mine hitherto published in this magazine.

Dalgety Agriculture Ltd, Dalgety House, The Promenade, Clifton, Bristol, BS8 3NJ for their helpful advice on milking goat feeds.

Philip & Carole Hockey, Newtown Farm, South Gorley, Fordingbridge, Hants, for their advice on organic poultry foods and 'real' meat.

Lance Smith, for taking the photographs used as illustrations in this book.

Dedications

This book is dedicated to all those without whose help we should not have succeeded. I can but mention a few by name:

Cyril Mason – for endless advice on goats

Ian Rowat – for milking our goats whilst we go on holiday

Jim Pinner – who knows what it's all about and showed us how to trim a donkey's feet

Sam Gillett, Percy Allwood and Lloyd Jones – three of the best vets around

Carol and Don Doyle – who supplied us with a turkey for Christmas after ours had been stolen

Charlie Matthews   countless jobs: help with the alterations, erecting sheds and making pools and ponds

Alice and Barry Stamp – for standing-in so that we could take a holiday each year

Rankin and Lilian Lewis – good friends and a valuable source of help and advice

Vic Grubb – who on more than one occasion has got a load of hay to us in arctic conditions

John Ford – who master-minded the plans for the alterations

Roger Grizzell – for helping with the alterations

Jeff Hannan – an exceptional plumber

Roger and Sheila Davies, Bert and Joan Bowdler and Members of the WRVS Transport Service – for providing an efficient and friendly school transport service, often in hazardous conditions

Guy and Jean Smith

Introduction

The early 1970s saw the beginning of a new era in rural lifestyle. Out of the towns and cities came disillusioned workers, 'nine-to-five' people in search of a new horizon, intent on obtaining their freedom long before retirement age when they would be too old to pursue an active role away from the connurbations in which they had been bred.

Derelict cottages with tracts of overgrown land adjoining, anything from two to twenty acres, were snapped up for a song. There were few books on the subject of self-sufficiency in those days and in most cases it was trial and error. This new breed of pioneers learned from their mistakes; often those mistakes were costly. Their Utopia was a land of free-range poultry and food from the land, where you needed little money because you had thrown off the shackles of civilization and had gone back to the basics.

For many it was a pipe-dream that faded, had them trudging back dejectedly to the urban areas in search of a job that provided a regular wage packet at the end of the week. Lack of experience, the sheer enormity of their task, had beaten them.

Consequently the self-sufficiency boom reached its peak and declined. But out in the few wild places remaining in Britain a handful of those poineers remained, eeking out a living of some kind, perhaps aided by a subsidiary income.

Total self-sufficiency is a near impossibility, one can merely hope to strike a happy medium which is where many of those who did not 'make it' failed. A compromise, the best of both worlds, is the answer – if you can find it!

The purpose of this book is an attempt to illustrate that compromise, finding the right smallholding and working it according to your capabilities and finances, creating a lifestyle which suits *you*, as opposed to a daily drudgery in order to survive. Therein lies the key to success.

Everything in this book has been attempted by my wife and myself with the help of our four children. There were failures, but by a process

ix

of trial and error we finally arrived at an organic smallholding which, in addition to making a small profit each year, provided us with that lifestyle of which we had dreamed of years before. *We have struck the right balance.* This is no over-loaded manual on self-sufficiency; rather it is a detailed account of what *we* found to be successful. Anything that is missed out is because we did not do it; we put our experimental failures behind us and concentrated on something that *worked*.

In 1978 we moved from the Midlands to the Black Hill on the Shropshire/Welsh borders. Although the possibility of a move had been talked over and carefully deliberated, we had not anticipated that telephone call one August evening informing us that the smallholding which we had casually looked at in the past, adjoining my rented Forestry Commission shooting rights, was for sale. The farmer had partically converted a stables, granary and wainhouse, thrown in seven and a half acres of rough upland grazing, registered it as a smallholding, and was asking twenty thousand pounds for a quick sale to help him with the purchase of an additional farm.

We moved in on 21 November, my thirty-eighth birthday, and stepped right out of a desirable housing estate with open-plan front gardens into a small unfinished cottage on a gale-lashed hillside. There was no garden, just a rough square of a quarter acre of grass that came right up to the front door. In due course we planned to convert the adjoining granary and wainhouse into additional living accommodation but for the moment we had to squash into those few rooms and sit out our first winter in the hills.

And when Spring came we determined that we would set about making some sort of garden and see what possibilities our land, some three hundred yards up the road, held. Little did we realise what it would all lead to!

It all stemmed from there and right from the start I kept copious notes and records. It is my fervent hope that these, reproduced in book form, will be of help to those who wish to do as we did, and that they may be spared many elementary mistakes.

Guy N. Smith, Clun, Shropshire

PART ONE: CHOOSING YOUR SMALLHOLDING

CHAPTER ONE

Finding the Right Smallholding

The most important step of all is to find the holding which is right for *you*. There are so many points to consider that it is well worthwhile sitting down and compiling a list before you actually begin your search. Whether you set out on a motor journey through the area of your choice to ascertain what property is for sale, or else you contact an estate agent direct, you must know what you are looking for.

Bear in mind what area of smallholding you are going into; cattle, sheep and goats will be fine on steep grassland but if your aim is cultivation of crops you will need land that is reasonably flat and sheltered. Altitude will play an important part, too, for market-gardening will be severely handicapped at a height of more than five hundred feet where the growing seasons are shorter.

The higher the land, the cheaper your property will be. In 1977 upland farms were selling at around one thousand pounds per acre, by 1985 they were fetching in the region of one thousand five hundred pounds, whilst on lower ground the price was five hundred pounds dearer. Wales has always been popular with self-sufficiency enthusiasts because of its mountainous terrain and the cheapness of property compared with elsewhere.

1986 saw a slump in the price of agricultural land. There were many factors affecting this, primarily over-production resulting in the EEC mountains of grain, milk and meat. Whereas previously farmers had received subsidies for everything they could produce, these products were not wanted in huge quantities any more.

As a result dairy farmers were forced to reduce their output by cutting their herds; therefore they no longer needed as much grazing land. Neither were they prepared to rear beef which nobody wanted. And with a reduction in corn growing then there was going to be surplus arable land too. So nobody needed to buy extra land for products which were not in demand.

Farmers with large bank overdrafts were hit hard. In almost every case the land was held as security by the bank but with the fall in the price of land the value no longer covered the extent of their borrowing. So the only alternative was to sell some land to bring the overdraft down. Which meant selling at a loss to finance a contracting business, whereas a few years previously they had been thinking in terms of expansion.

Land prices vary according to different regions but at the time of writing good lowland arable is worth about one thousand two hundred pounds an acre, with upland regions down to eight hundred pounds, less in some cases. Somehow a balance has to be found and we will look at the possibilities in the section on organic growing.

Reconnaissance

It is a good idea to spend a holiday in the area of your choice, preferably not in the height of summer when a more agreeable climate will influence you. Try a weekend in some holiday cottage around November; the owner will doubtless be amazed, quote a negligible rent and think that you are quite mad! But you will have a chance to get to know your surroundings at their worst. The disadvantages will outweigh the advantages and if you are disillusioned then it will have been money well spent.

In all probability you will experience gales and rain, the daylight hours will be short, and these are the conditions which you will have to work in. Farming is a 365 days a year lifestyle, livestock have to be tended in pouring rain and deep snow; the chores cannot be put off until tomorrow. Spend as much time out in the inclement conditions as possible for this is your initiation.

Your choice should be the type of dwelling place you are thinking of buying so that you can experience the snags. There will be innumerable draughts, you will need to keep the fire stoked and the available wood might well be wet or green. The roof leaks, every time you go outside and come back in you bring mud into the porch. There will be no home comforts, no convenient central-heating. Everything that needs to be done will have to be done by yourself.

Obviously your finances will dictate the type of smallholding you are looking to buy. In effect, you get what you pay for like everything else in life; there are no real bargains in this day and age. Anything which appears to be a bargain should be treated with suspicion for there may well be a hidden snag. Beware of estate agents' brochures! The term 'with panoramic views' is often a leading feature designed to divert a prospective buyer's attention away from other faults, whilst 'has great

4

potential' often means that the property is derelict and could be made desirable if it was rebuilt! An 'extensive kitchen garden and orchard' could well describe an area of wilderness and old fruit trees. Not always the case but look at the place objectively, the asking price could only be the start of your problems, you could well need to spend as much again to make it habitable according to your own standards.

If you have a house of your own to sell first then at least you have something to throw into the kitty. Building societies are reluctant to grant mortgages for anything other than conventional dwellings; they will not finance small farms and I have known prospective purchasers of houses with more than an acre of land attached be asked to sign a declaration, witnessed by a solicitor, to the effect that no income will be derived from the land. It seems strange that when lending money the societies do not want the mortgagee to make money to finance the repayments. And, of course, building societies insist on a very stringent survey; they do not like any dwelling that has been built or renovated by anybody other than a registered builder.

A survey is fine, it will throw to light any hidden faults and may save you costly repairs in the future, but with most old farmhouses or cottages the report will not be a satisfactory one. These places were built in the days before damp-proof courses were even heard of, previous occupiers have 'bodged', done repairs which suffice at the time but are unlikely to last; improvisation is paramount. However, the cost of a survey will at least let you know what expenses you will have to meet and whether major structural repairs will have to be undertaken. I heard some time ago of a vendor who refused to allow a prospective buyer to go ahead with a survey; certainly there was something suspicious about this.

If you need to borrow money then your bank manager is your best bet. Do not, under any circumstances, involve yourself with dubious finance companies for the sake of a fast loan; their interest rates will be high and they will not hesitate to foreclose on the loan and take possession of your home at the first opportunity.

Banks are in business to help their customers make a success of their venture and as long as the project is viable you can be sure of their co-operation. When we were faced with 'making the move' at very short notice I consulted my local building society as we needed a loan until our existing town house had been sold. Every obstruction was thrown in my way; they did not like the idea of the land that went with our rural home and tried to persuade me to sell the acreage off upon completion! Which is hardly encouraging to the budding smallholder! In the end I saw my bank manager and there was no problem. We did not even have a survey, primarily because we knew that there were a number of faults

5

with the property and we were prepared to rectify these anyway. As it turned out there were many more but these were overcome when finally we converted the adjoining wainhouse and granary into living accommodation. Of course, if you are a do-it-yourself person you will save a lot of expense; hired labour is expensive, builders and carpenters charge in the region of five pounds an hour and on top of materials this can be very expensive.

However, let us look in more detail at some of the major problems which the reader may come across.

Water

Water is a commodity which none of us can do without but unfortunately in the country there is no happy medium; you seem to have either too much or not enough.

A regular and adequate supply of water to any smallholding is imperative. Few remote holdings are connected to a mains supply, they are served by either a well or bore-hole, or a spring from which the water is pumped up by an hydraulic ram. Some farmers are reluctant to instal an electric pump because electricity costs money! Rams are fine but they need regular maintenance, a particle or rust or dirt can stop them and the first you know about this is when there is no water in your reservoir.

Perhaps if I explain how our own water supply works the novice will have some idea of what to expect. The ram is situated in a Forestry Commission plantation, in a small valley about half a mile from the furthermost part of our land, in a brick-built well about three feet deep. This device pumps up one gallon of water for every ten which it lets go on its way down a winding stream. The water is pushed uphill through plastic piping buried a foot or so in the ground; the farmer took advantage of a ploughed furrow, prior to the planting of the trees, which saved him an awful lot of digging.

The water travels about a mile to where two underground reservoirs are situated on the brow of a field about one hundred feet above the level of our house. The smaller reservoir, two hundred and fifty gallon capacity, is filled first after the pipe has fed a number of sheep troughs. This then overflows into our reservoir which when full holds about five thousand gallons. In other words, the stock drink before we do!

The snag is that in dry weather when the sheep are drinking heavily there is not enough water going into the small reservoir for it to overflow into ours so we are 'drawing on capital'. On more than one occasion we have found that there is no water coming out of our taps and emergency

6

plans have had to be put into force. The easiest way out is for the farmer to operate a 'float-switch' which directs the water piped up from the ram directly into our supply, by-passing the farm reservoir. That is fine for us but it means that he has to move his animals to another part of his farm where there is another source of drinking water.

Nowadays I check our reservoir weekly in the summer, fortnightly in the winter. If there is no water trickling in through the inlet pipe then in all probability the ram has ceased working and needs attention. At least by checking regularly we are forewarned and there is time to get the supply going again before we are completely dry.

One winter in the midst of a vicious freeze-up I discovered that the reservoir was not filling. The farmer made a difficult trek down to the ram through deep snow and discovered that a bit of rust had jammed it. All was well that ended well; we might have been frozen up without a drop of water for either ourselves or our animals.

Always ascertain that a supply of domestic water is incorporated in your deeds, particularly if you are dependant upon somebody else for it. But the clause may only refer to *domestic* and not farm water. There is no such provision for the latter in our deeds although there is an overflow pipe from our reservoir down to a trough in the field. But this is not likely to be much use if we are struggling to maintain enough water for household requirements. The tank only seems to fill in winter when we don't need it!

Consequently we have had to rig up our own rainwater supply system. This entails guttering on the poultry sheds which fill a fifty gallon drum. The drum is then drained off to fill an old bath. And if that is not sufficient then water has to be carried for the stock. This happened one very dry summer during our experiment with cattle (something which is dealt with in a later chapter) and I was transporting forty gallons a day from a village two miles away!

Bore-holes are fine providing there is water to feed them. The cost of drilling is enormous and some contractors do not guarantee anything more than a deep hole; if they don't find sufficient water below ground then that isn't their fault!

Wells can be very good or very poor. You will only find out in a dry summer whether they are adequate. The fact that there is water there when you inspect the property means nothing. An unscrupulous vendor might well have used his water cart to fill it up for your benefit!

Always have your water tested for purity. This is very important if you are to avoid stomach ailments. Generally, though, the type of dwellings we are considering are fine for cold clear spring water. Indeed, some of it is even collected, bottled and aerated, and sold in supermarkets for up to fifty pence a bottle!

In spite of the disadvantages of having your own private supply of water you will gain in as much as you will not be compelled to have fluoride added in the way that many towns-people have this forced upon them. All the same, there is no such thing as *free* water; at the best you will have to pay your local board the minimum fee for an extraction licence, which may be as little as ten pounds. Compare this with water rates running into hundreds of pounds!

Flooding

Many years ago I went to look at some property, a neat little black and white cottage set in a slight hollow about fifty yards from a river. It was idyllic, my dream home on a beautiful sunny day. I was so enthralled with it that on the following weekend I went back for another look. The weather had changed in the meantime, clear blue skies had turned to low cloud and there had been three days of torrential rain. Imagine my horror when I saw this hollow with its neat little garden under a foot of water which had also flooded the cottage! The owner was obviously dismayed, 'it's never happened before and it probably won't ever again!' They all say that! My advice is never to buy property situated below the level of a stream or river.

Having said that I would never have believed that it was possible to be flooded when one lives at a height of one thousand two hundred feet. Which is exactly what happened to us in our second winter on Black Hill.

After several days of incessant rain we awoke one morning to find an inch of water throughout the ground floor level of our house. Carpets were ruined, together with about two dozen bound volumes of magazines on a low shelf in my study.

Altogether we have had three floods, all for different reasons, the only common denominator being *rain*. The lane which passes our property is higher than the garden and the water flows towards the house. This should be no problem for we have a land-drain passing below and in front of the dwelling.

The first flood was due to this drain being silted up and broken so that the water flooded the drive and came in through the front door. The second was after a long hard winter when the ground had been frozen for weeks; the thaw came overnight with heavy rain and the solid ground could not absorb it; the drain was frozen so it all came in the house again.

We thought we had solved this by persuading the council to make a larger inlet point in the lane opposite, brick-built and with a grid. Then one June evening we had the worst thunderstorm which I have ever witnessed. The lane was flooded, a swirling torrent, washing down to the drain but bringing with it soil and rubble. Within minutes the grid was buried and we had the brunt of the floodwater from then onwards.

I don't think it will happen again(!) because I have constructed a small triangular-shaped rockery jutting out from the wall of the house and in theory this should push any floodwater on down the drive away from us. And if that does not work then I now have a 'storm-board' to slot on the front door. All this is is a three foot square of wooden board that drops flush with the bottom step. If any water does get through then it will only be a seepage which will give us time to mop up, whereas on all three previous occasions we have opened both the front and back doors and had a torrent flowing right through the house.

Always check the level of the land surrounding your prospective home. High soil banks can mean damp in the house if the earth is not kept away from the walls. If you are close to a road check the slope of the tarmac and make sure that the water does not flow on to your land. And if you know anybody who is a water-dowser it is a good idea to get them to see if they can detect underground water from *inside* the dwelling. Many old properties are built over springs and these can cause you trouble in wet weather; the least of your worries will be interior damp!

Most stone walls are damp to a greater or lesser degree anyway. The first step is to maintain the pointing. A coating of clear Aquaseal will protect the outside above ground level. Nowadays walls can be damp-proofed by means of injections and it is well worth consulting a reputable builder with regard to this.

The house

Let us now take a closer look at the property the reader is contemplating buying. Having scoured the countryside and visited every estate agent in the area, you are now about to make your big decision. I always think it is preferable to have your first viewing in bad weather; a lovely sunny day can lift the spirits and give a false impression. See the place at its worst, and if you like it then you will be even more favourably disposed towards it when you visit it in bright sunshine.

You are considering a stone-built farmhouse set in anything from six to fifteen acres of land. Once the dwelling was the residence of the farmer who owned one hundred acres of land, but he sold out to a neighbouring farmer who did not need the house so he has decided to sell it as a separate smallholding with a few acres.

9

Old property can harbour many unforeseen problems

My own priority would be the quantity and quality of the water supply (see the section on this), but you will need a sound and dry house to live in if you are to be successful in your venture. Don't rely just on a surveyor's report, examine it minutely yourself because there are many factors necessary to your comfort and well-being which are not covered by surveying.

Start at the top and have a good look at the roof. Are the rafters sound? Re-roofing can set you back anything up to three thousand pounds. Woodworm is not the bogey it is made out to be so long as it has not gone too far. You will certainly find signs of woodworm in most old property but it can be treated to stop the rot.

With the purchase price in mind, and let us say in this instance that it is fifty thousand pounds, bear in mind how much you are going to have to spend to make the dwelling habitable to your own standards. Check whether or not the former owner has received a grant for improvements or a conversion; the property could have been a farm building at one time which he has converted into a house, and if he has had a grant then you certainly will not get one.

You are unlikely to get a bargain these days but you do expect value for money, so you need to check up on everything which will want renewing or re-building and estimate the cost of this. Otherwise you could be in for a shock, moving into a place which you cannot afford to improve and you will be disillusioned with your new lifestyle right from the start.

If the windows are the existing ones it is a fair bet that they will need renewing, and this can set you back another thousand pounds. If they are new, see if they have been fitted properly. Our own windows were new ones, the snag being that they had been badly fitted and on two of them if you peeped through a hole in the stonework beneath the sill you could see daylight at the other end!

Often rooms will need re-plastering. This is not a serious defect but if you are not a competent plasterer then you are well advised to employ one. Check all the plasterwork because it will be cheaper to call the plasterer in for one big job rather than to have him two or three times. A professional works fast; you will be surprised how quickly he will complete the job.

Perhaps there are a number of beams which have been plaster-boarded over. If the beams are in a reasonable state then this is a sacrilege, for if anything really enhances a room then it is a beamed ceiling. Farmers are inclined to take the easy way out and cover them up simply because they have enough work to do tending their stock. Before you rip off all the boarding and then discover that the beams are in a bad state, expose a small section and then make up your mind whether or not it is worth going ahead. Sand them down, use a clear preservative *but do not paint them.* A lot of beams in old houses are spoiled by being painted black; their true colour is the natural one, either oak or pine.

The decorations are immaterial, almost certainly the lady of the house will want her own colour scheme, anyway.

Your available capital and your own standard of living will dictate what you consider to be a good buy. Remember that many old properties do not have damp-proof courses and the discerning viewer will doubtless find the odd patch of damp here and there. In many cases this can be rectified by having the walls injected with a substance to eliminate this by specialist firms.

Do examine the house thoroughly, though, and don't let your heart rule over your logic. Panoramic scenery doesn't count for much on a winter's night when there is a blizzard howling outside and snow is drifting into the attic and threatening to collapse the bedroom ceilings. Only you know what you want – make sure you get it!

You may be purchasing a small property with an extension in mind. It is a good idea to check first with the planning department whether or not this is possible in principle. In most rural areas any alterations have

11

The author's house before the move

to blend in with the original dwelling but your property may be restricted in floor space. It is a blow if you have moved from a four-bedroomed town house to a two-up, two-down cottage in the country and then discover that you are unable to extend.

Maintenance

Once you have bought your property and completed all the necessary structural work to your own satisfaction, that is not the end of your expenses. Maintenance is vital to any dwelling place and it needs to be carried out regularly.

Exterior decorations will not last as long on a windswept hillside as they will within the confines of a sheltered township. Whereas you have been accustomed to painting the outside of your property every five years in the past, you will need to do it every three now. Failure to keep the woodwork weatherproof will result in rotten window frames and warped doors that fail to close properly and let the rain in so that it rots your wooden porch floor.

Electrical wiring can present a hazard; if you have light switches which give a small flash every time you flick them or are sluggish, get them investigated without delay. Electricity is always a danger because the wiring is hidden and faults can go unnoticed until they start a serious fire.

Original floorboards will need renewing from time to time in old property. If you are undergoing any major structural work then it is cheaper to renew these at the time; we replaced two whole rooms with chipboard floors and resolved a recurring problem all in one go.

It is well worthwhile every couple of years or so checking the mortar in between your stonework or brickwork on the outside of your house. Rain and wind erodes and crevices are opened up through which the wet will seep in. To save a later damp problem or a crumbling wall, keep up to-date with the pointing and save yourself a major expense in the future.

There is always a maintenance job to be done somewhere around the house. In the past previous owners were usually negligent of these; if nothing actually fell down they left well alone! This is something you must take into consideration when making your move to the country, it is all part of the lifestyle and if you aren't a handyman then you will have to learn.

Electricity

Whereas I would resist mains water I would not be without mains electricity. Alternative means of heating and lighting sound fascinating;

The author's house today

free heat from the sun and wind. Fine, but there are often long spells when there is little or no wind nor sunshine.

Generators can prove a costly experiment. Windmills are not entirely free, either, because you need to buy a new battery every so often costing up to one hundred pounds, and on a stormy winter's night you could find yourself out on a gale-lashed hillside trying to repair your contraption.

Heating oil is costly and the experts tell us that our oil resources will run out at the end of this century – and that's only a little over a decade away! Our house was fitted with an oil-fired Rayburn when we moved in. After a year or so we replaced it with a woodburner (see chapter 2 for woodburning advice) but I think that overall calor gas is the cleanest, most efficient and cost competitive of the lot. But certainly you need electricity for your lighting and to power household devices.

CHAPTER TWO

Woodburning and Alternative Heating

Woodburning was a fashion that came to its peak around the middle of the 1970s. It was a natural progression for the self-sufficiency enthusiasts, a cheap means of heating and cooking, more natural than flicking a switch and paying for electricity. An understandable change to a natural source of energy. What better way to spend a day than gathering firewood in the forest, relaxing before a log fire and smelling the sweet scent of woodsmoke?

But fashions become commercial enterprises. Where once a landowner was glad of somebody to cart away his fallen trees he now sees it as a source of income. All kinds of woodburning stoves were being sold, there was a boom in firewood, not just amongst remote smallholdings but in the towns as well; a log-burning stove was a fitting central piece in a plush commuter-belt lounge. Wood was in demand, prices soared.

When we first came to Black Hill I bought a ton of wood for our lounge fire for seven pounds. Our heating-system was oil-fired, convenient and competitively priced against electricity, gas and coal. We were reasonably satisfied. Until oil-prices rocketed and as an added insult when I ordered six hundred gallons one day I was told I could only have two hundred; there was some dispute amongst tanker drivers and as a result I had to pay the full price, being forced to forego the bulk discount even though it was no fault of my own. It was then that we decided to change over to wood.

All went well in the beginning, and we were fortunate in being able to sell our oil-fired Rayburn and storage tank at the same time that we took delivery of our Tirolia and we managed the change-over for one hundred and eighty pounds. Having the shooting rights of the adjoining forest I was given permission to collect all the fallen wood I needed. I invested in a chainsaw costing around one hundred and fifty pounds but from now onwards all our heating would be free!

That first summer I carted and sawed up around ten tons of wood, mostly pine. By mid-winter our problems were beginning. All that

15

wood stacked in our backyard was gone; I had anticipated it lasting until the Spring. So I ordered a trailer load of wood from a local merchant. It arrived, huge chunks, wet and green! I spent hours splitting it. It fizzed and smouldered in the stove, we had difficulty in getting the water hot enough for a bath and our meals took ages to cook. So we fitted an immersion heater and resorted to cooking on the electric stove.

In addition to this I began to suffer back trouble. This had started originally with all those hours of chainsawing, now I seemed to have permanent lumbago. And unknown to us the chimney was tarring up. One day the stove began smoking back, ruined the kitchen decorations and we had to open all the windows in freezing conditions in order to disperse the smoke. I swept the chimney. Fortunately I had kept my brushes which dated back to the 1950s, my golden era of jobbing

This woodburning stove cooks, heats the water and runs ten radiators

16

gardening when I also swept chimneys for five shillings! The stove behaved itself for a week and then began smoking back again. I decided my worn brushes were beyond regular use and called in a chimney sweep. He used his vacuum, took less than ten minutes, and remarked as he was leaving that 'it's in a bad state up top'.

Our plumber is a jack-of-all-trades and servicing boilers incorporates sweeping chimneys, so I sent for Jeff. He climbed up on the roof, removed the cowl, which was so badly tarred that we needed a replacement, and discovered that there was a hole rougly the size of a tenpence piece for the smoke to escape through. Jeff scraped it out, swept the chimney again, returned a few days later and fitted a new cowl. But our problems were only just beginning!

One evening towards the end of January, Rowan remarked that the lounge wall was very warm. On going to investigate I discovered that the chimney breast was so hot that the wallpaper was furling and browning! I dashed back into the kitchen and opened the steel trapdoor just above the stove – and promptly slammed it shut again! There was a roaring inferno in the well behind the flue-pipe!

The fire-brigade arrived within a quarter of an hour and had to chip a hole in the lounge wall to reach the blaze, removing it in buckets and depositing it outside. It could have turned into a major disaster but we got away with having a builder to rebuild the hole in the wall and fit a larger inspection hatch. That, together with redecorating the lounge, cost more than our winter's wood supply.

Heatlogs and Peatheat

It was after this that we experimented with *Heatlogs*. This type of fuel comprises compressed waste wood, is octagonal in shape with a hole through the middle which assists burning. Truly it was the best fuel I had ever tried, capable of boiling a kettle on the stove in five minutes from a dead start. We discovered that the most economical way to use them was to get a good fire going with them and then to bank up with either a conventional wood log or a few blocks of Peatheat.

Peatheat is natural peat which has been dried and compressed into small bricks. They are slow burning and ideal on both stoves and open fires. Indeed, most mornings when I rake the ashes I find that they are still 'alive', often enough to start the day's burning just by adding a few sticks.

These alternative fuels were our salvation, they solved all our problems. They are so compact that it is possible to store several tons in a small shed; heatlogs must be kept in the dry but peatheat is fine stacked outside, preferably covered with a tarpaulin. As an experiment I left a block out in the snow for a fortnight and its quality was not impaired.

Which was why we became distributors for these fuels. I had no intention of delivering loads to customers, rather the odd bag or two and anybody who wanted a quantity could collect it themselves. Yet, as already stated, it was difficult to sell in a rural area where everybody was still wood-burning orientated in spite of tarred and smoking chimneys. Basically I think the customers themselves were to blame; I explained carefully to each one how to use the heatlogs for maximum heat and value but it appears that all they did was load up their stoves, let it blaze and then poke it. *One must never poke heatlogs*, they are designed to retain their heat intact; once they are broken up they crumble and burn quickly.

Neither heatlogs nor peatheat spit, they burn evenly and are the answer to the smallholder's comfort after a long hard day on the holding when all he wants to do is to relax in front of a real fire. In addition their ash is superb on the garden and it has certainly improved our soil.

Heatlogs – Solid Fuel Heat Values

Type	Volatile matter	Ash content	Carbon	Moisture	Approx. gross calorific value BTU/LBS
Heatlog (R)	77.93%	0.36%	15.04%	6.67%	8400
Peatheat	55.32%	2.57%	27.03%	15.08%	8000
Straw	65.82%	2.56%	17.67%	14%	6500
House coal	29.8%	7.5%	46.7%	16%	8500
Coalite	6.6%	9%	76%	8%	9750
Wood (seasoned	65.2%	.5%	16.3%	18%	7000

Above based on London Analytical and testing Laboratories figures. Calorific value estimated on basis of almost total burn of Heatlog (.36%–.43% ash) and Wood (.5% ash) to Household Coal/Coalite high ash content (7.5%–9% ash), i.e. incomplete burn.

The most important characteristics of the Heatlog are:

1. Low Ash – Therefore high heat value.
2. Dense compression – therefore low moisture content with complete slow burn and no expansion.
3. Cleanliness of fuel and ash.
4. Heatlogs are supplied by: Heatlogs Ltd, Thornhill House, Fisher St, Maidstone, Kent ME14 2SU. Telephone: 0622-690688.

Successful woodburning

Wood is no longer a cheap means of heating except where you have your own woodland or access to free supplies. For the benefit of those fortunate people let us look at the correct way to cut and store firewood for maximum efficiency.

Hardwood is always preferable to soft wood, avoid the latter wherever possible. The best trees to use are oak, ash, elm or beech. On no account use poplar; I bought a load once, it smouldered, smoked and gave off very little heat and left huge charred chunks in both the stove and the lounge grate which had to be thrown out.

Wood should be cut and stacked in a dry place twelve months before you need to use it. The logs you cut this year should be for next year's use. Split wood dries more quickly than unsplit.

Ideally you need a sawbench and a helper to put the boughs on it for you. It is time-wasting to keep having to put your chainsaw down whilst you load up again. Never become complacent with your saw, it is a lethal weapon. Do not wear a tie or any loose garments, wear a visor to protect your eyes from flying sawdust and always make sure that the guard is in place. The experienced woodcutter is more likely to have an accident than the amateur because familiarity breeds contempt; the latter's respect for his tool is to his advantage and it should always remain so.

Buying wood

You may find that you have no alternative other than to buy logs (until of course you are able to get fixed up with heatlogs and peatheat!) and unless you are discerning an unscrupulous woodcutter can take advantage of you.

When buying by *weight* always try and arrange for supplies to be delivered in *dry* weather. Wet wood weighs heavy and you will be paying for moisture. Don't buy green (freshly cut) wood either, for even if you are prepared to stack and dry it out yourself you will find that this, too, weighs heavier than seasoned wood. Ask for logs that have been cut from dead trees or timber that has been felled several months ago. And the smaller the logs, the less splitting you will have to do. If you are paying in the region of twenty-five to thirty pounds per ton then you do not want to have to spend hours splitting it. That way it is very costly fuel.

Off-cuts from sawmills

Sawmills can often be a valuable source of hardwood and softwood offcuts and it is well worth exploring the possibilities if you have one in your area. The waste chunks are usually piled up in the yard to be sold to anybody who cares to go and collect them. Some mills may sell them by the bag but often they are sold by weight, at around twenty pounds a ton, and are better value than you will buy from a log merchant.

You drive on to the weighbridge with your vehicle and the attendant weighs your van or Land Rover. You need to take as much as ever you can in order to make your trip worthwhile so rather than bag the wood, stack it and load as much as you can safely carry. Back on the weighbridge and you are charged for the difference between the empty and the full vehicle. Choose a dry day, if possible one after an absence of rain or you will be paying for moisture.

The offcuts are symmetrical, you will stack far more in your wood-shed than you will logs from the forest. Also you can include some smaller pieces and keep them separate for kindling; it will save you time chopping sticks.

Coal

Coal has been a traditional fuel for the fire ever since Man learned how to mine it. Needless to say it is expensive, but used in conjunction with wood or heatlogs it can be economical. Never buy cheap coal, you will get the best value from the best quality. For closed stoves phurnicite is best, you can bank it up at night and it will still be burning in the morning.

Recently we have been experimenting with coal briketts which we discovered on sale at our local supermarket. In fact, when I saw it stacked by the entrance I mistook it for peatheat, so similar was it in appearance. Smooth and shiny, the blocks are clean and convenient to handle, and long-lasting in both closed stoves and open fires. They are of uniform size, leave no clinker, are virtually smokeless, they don't spit and give an even heat distribution. I can recommend them.

Electricity

Like most forms of heating electricity can be either relatively cheap or expensive according to how you use it. Storage heaters are for use at off-peak times but if you use them during the peak times you will have an unpleasant surprise when you receive your next bill! A blow-heater is handy for instant warmth if you have been out and come home to a cold house. But only use it for a short time; prolonged use is expensive and creates a stuffy atmosphere.

If your premises are not connected to mains electricity you may well decide to do without it and invest in a generator. Some friends of ours had no electricity and contacted the board with a view to installation. The total cost was in the region of nine thousand pounds!

Paper logs

Some years ago we experimented with logs made from rolled-up newspapers. The kit comprised a tool resembling a pair of tongs and a packet of wire-ties. Six newspapers were laid out on the table, folded in half, and then, exerting maximum pressure, you rolled the papers as tight as they would go, held them in place with the tool and tied them. The finished product was remarkably professional, heavy, and burned for a considerable time although they did not give out the heat of other fuels. We used them for keeping the woodstove alight overnight or when we were away for the day.

It was some weeks before we discovered the main drawback though; the chimney had a residue of charred papers that also floated down and blocked the flue so that it smoked back.

This method is time-consuming, one can work for a couple of hours and at the end have only a small pile of logs to show for the effort. Only newspapers should be used, glossy magazines do not burn well.

There is also a device for making these logs whereby the papers are soaked first to solidify them. Useful, if you have the time; that is the criteria.

Paper firelighters are very successful, though. Simply, one rolls a few sheets of newspaper diagonally, twists them a few times and they will get the most stubborn of fires going. This is an ideal job to give the children on a wet day in their school holidays.

Chimney sweeping

If you burn solid fuel of any description then you must sweep your chimneys regularly. Failure to carry out this task could result in a costly chimney fire.

Good brushes are essential if you are to do the job properly. I know some people who get away with using a holly branch but your aim must be to scrape out *all* the soot and tar right up to the pot. You need good flexible rods (make sure that you screw them tightly together or else you could be dismantling your chimney in order to retrieve a length of rod that has come adrift!) and a stiff brush. We have a friend who claims that the most efficient way is to sweep the chimney *downwards*; he may be right, it all depends whether or not you mind going up on the roof.

Soot is useful for the garden but allow it to weather first or else you risk scorching your plants; it is especially beneficial to the onion patch.

Rather than make a mediocre job of chimney sweeping, call in the expert. A fiver a chimney is good insurance against a fire and he will certainly do the job much better than an amateur.

Heating oil

When we first moved to the Black Hill oil was thirty-three pence a gallon; on removal of our oil-fired Rayburn it had reached one pound.

Oil certainly has its advantages; it is clean and convenient, you don't have to stack or load it, and provided there are no industrial disputes or snow drifts a phone call will bring the tanker to your door within a day or two. All you have to do is to write out a cheque and turn a knob now and then. But, as I have said earlier, what happens when our oil supplies dry up in the early part of the next century as we are told they are going to do?

Calor gas

We once entered a competition in a magazine; the first prize was calor gas central heating, installed free of charge. We won a runner-up prize – a gas-match with which to light the burners! We still have it because one day we might change to calor. . . .

Calor gas appeals to me more than oil. Indeed, I run my Land Rover on gas at a saving of seventy pence a gallon against petrol. The engine runs well on it, there is a slight loss of efficiency on steep hills (you have to change down a gear), but the engine remains beautifully clean, plugs rarely need changing and you do not have to suffer choking exhaust fumes.

If it can run an engine as efficiently as that I am prepared to let it heat my house.

Solar heating

When we moved to Black Hill I considered the possibility of a solar panel in the roof but I feel that this method of heating is still in its infancy. A friend of mine had such a panel installed some years ago, and certainly it will heat up enough water for a bath, but if his wife requires a bath soon afterwards then they have to use the immersion heater. My own study of literature on the subject left me with the feeling that there is still an awful lot more to be learned about solar heating.

Whichever method you use to heat your house depends upon:

1. How much work you are prepared to put into cutting costs and whether or not you could be spending that time more profitably.
2. Whether or not you *enjoy cutting up and splitting logs*.

A neighbour of ours, whose job entailed an exacting week, used to spend the whole of every Sunday lugging wood from the forest with his Land Rover and trailer, wet or fine. Only *deep* snow prevented him. He claimed that it was relaxation after a week spent driving many miles with a mountain of paperwork at the end of it. If he enjoyed it, all well and good. The basis of this book is doing what you *want* to do, using your freedom from the shackles of a conventional lifestyle in the most rewarding way. There is no necessity to become a slave to woodburning.

CHAPTER THREE

Outbuildings and Land

Outbuildings

You will need more outbuildings than you envisage. However many you have, within reason, you will always manage to utilise them. Crumbling stonework, sagging roofs, rotted doors all cost time and money, and when you are smallholding you will have little time for building and repairing chores. Basically these places need to be warm and dry and situated conveniently for winter use.

However, if like ourselves, you buy an outbuilding which has been converted to a dwelling place then you are unlikely to have many additional outbuildings. So you will have to be prepared to erect these from scratch.

Stonework, brickwork and woodwork are costly and it will be many years before the income from your small farm pays for these. The alternative is corrugated tin-sheeting. This latter has a reputation for being ramshackle and unsightly but it need not be so.

Some years ago there was the possibility of a law being introduced whereby all tin sheeting had to be painted green which, ridiculous as it seems, was quite sensible for at least there would have been a neatness and rural uniformity throughout Britain. Consequently there are still stocks of tin to be purchased which have been sprayed green. If you cannot get hold of any of these then paint your sheets with bitumastic paint. I prefer green, the alternative, black, gives a funeral appearance as though you have a row of private mortuaries on your property!

Timber, as already mentioned, is costly but sometimes it is possible to buy reclaimed timber from a demolition site. In addition to this there will invariably be a few stout secondhand doors going for a fiver or so.

So buy up a stock of *quality* tin sheets, as much reclaimed timber as you can, and roofing felt. Unless you line the insides of your roofs your animals will be troubled with damp from condensation and your equipment will rust. A few pounds of springhead nails and you will

Suitable outbuildings can be erected cheaply out of re-claimed timber and corrugated tin sheets

have those outbuildings up in a very short time. And they will last you for a very long time, the only maintenance needed being a fresh coat of paint every four or five years.

Existing outbuildings

You will be very fortunate indeed if you purchase a smallholding which has existing outbuildings which entirely suit your requirements. The ideal situation would be a former stables with ample stalls to house your goats or even a previous smallholding where somebody else had already set everything up.

But beware! An enclosed building which is seemingly waterproof could prove to be your downfall. Farmers of the older generation were not too particular as long as they had buildings of some sort in which to house their stock. Goats, for example, don't like draughts or damp, they can stand any amount of cold provided they are *dry*. A brick or stone building could prove to be both damp and airless, a condition which is conducive to pneumonia in livestock.

See that there is air but not a draught and that if the floor is concrete there is an outlet for the urine. Check the roof carefully for in old buildings the rafters might be rotten and if there are slates missing, then renew them. Even if you have to re-roof the outbuilding it is cheaper than starting to construct one from scratch.

Ascertain that there are no protruding rusty nails on which a goat could rip its udder, nor holes in the floor where it could break a leg. And see that the doors fasten securely; stable doors are best where the top half can be left open, particularly in the winter months when the weather is unsuitable for the animals to go out to graze.

Your outbuildings complex should be as compact as possible. My own ideal is to be able to walk out through a garage to a covered walk, and to move from one building to the next under cover on a winter's morning when it is pouring with rain or there is a driving blizzard. But the important thing is to try and arrange your livestock housing with 'time and motion' in mind. The less you have to double back on your tracks, the quicker and easier your stock work will be.

An outside tap is a must, or at the very least some handy water butts. No housewife likes a husband in muddy wellingtons filling his buckets at the kitchen sink!

Poultry housing

Sectional poultry arcs are both expensive and rarely slot together as the directions claim they do. I think a good sound shed with a run-out on the lines of my 'fox-proof' enclosure (described in the poultry section of this book) is a far better proposition. You can get inside to muck-out, and collecting the eggs daily is far easier than reaching into virtually inaccessible dark recesses and groping around for them.

Beware of an existing dilapidated poultry shed on your new holding, though. Loose and rotten boards are little obstacle to a determined fox. Hens are much healthier and lay better in a nice dry house. They don't care for draughts at bedtime any more than goats do.

Fodder sheds

Your hay, like your livestock, requires a dry and airy store. The old-fashioned dutch barns are fine as, although the ends of the bales are wet in a rainstorm, the wind blows right through and dries them. Hay which is stacked in an airless, damp shed quickly goes mouldy; you are lucky if your livestock refuse to eat it for if they do their health can suffer.

It is fine to store hay in an ordinary shed but check, first that there is plenty of air, and secondly that the bottom bales are not on an earthen or concrete floor. I use old pallets on the floor of our shed and this enables an undercurrent of air to dry out the lower bales. Bales on a damp floor go black and rotten and are wasted.

The storage of straw, though not so important if you are using it for litter, should be much the same. Damp straw on the floor of your goatshed is little better than that which you have mucked out.

One other problem you might encounter with stored hay and straw is *rats*. With the onset of winter, rats move out of the fields and hedgerows in search of a warm, dry winter refuge, and what better place than a haystore! They will soon foul numerous bales and cost you money as well as the inconvenience of having hay or straw which is no use for anything other than mulching. It is best to keep a pan of rat-bait permanently in your hayshed during the winter months, ensuring that nothing other than these marauding rodents can get at it.

Land

You will need a minimum of two acres otherwise you will not qualify as a smallholding and will not be able to take advantage of farming benefits. Your first step upon completion of purchase should be to join the Small Farmers' Association and you will then be able to obtain all the information you require. There are numerous grants available through the Ministry of Agriculture; perhaps your land needs fencing and you will apply for a fifty per cent grant towards the cost of materials, provided you fence a minimum of five hundred metres. Or you may need drainage. Up until fairly recently a farmer could obtain a one hundred per cent grant for road-making so long as he provided the materials himself, i.e. stone, and most hill-farmers have somewhere on their land where they can quarry.

Check at the outset whether or not your land is a registered small-holding. If not, then consult your local Ministry of Agriculture office and get the necessary forms to apply for registration. You may also be eligible for a grant for renovating or repairing your dwelling place. And if you have not already got enough outbuildings then once you are classed as a smallholding you will be able to erect them, within reason, without having to go through the time-consuming and costly process of obtaining planning permission.

If you are going to rear cattle and sheep then there are hill subsidies available, but unfortunately not for goats. Only in recent times have goats been recognised as farm stock; perhaps eventually there will be goat subsidies!

Land is a valuable commodity and you should utilise it even if you think at the outset that you have more than you need. Even if all your capital has gone into the purchase of your holding and you cannot afford to stock it just yet, your acres can still bring you in an income. You can let the 'grasskeep' (grazing rights) but rents will vary from year to year and are also influenced by the type and size of terrain. A hundred acres of lowland pasture might let for one hundred pounds per acre; farmers who are overstocked often go for a larger acreage as long as it is in one block. A few acres here and a few more there is time-consuming, and they prefer to have all their sheep and cattle together so that they can check them quickly and then get on with the rest of their day's work.

The quality of the grass is generally not so good at higher altitudes because, like other crops, the growing season is short and if the letting covers the winter season also the farmer may have difficulty in reaching his animals if there is a sudden snowfall with drifting. If there has been ample rain and the grass is growing well, you might be able to let a few acres at around twenty-five to thirty pounds an acre. You may decide that it isn't worth the trouble of having someone coming onto your land daily. Maybe not, but if you neglect the grass, allow it to grow thick and coarse, it will not be suitable for when you want to use it yourself. So look upon it as a benefit, an improvement to your holding, and a few pounds in the bank into the bargain.

A couple of words of warning though: if you let your grazing be sure to have an agreement in writing and do not let it for a full twelve months. A ten-month letting, say March to December, completes the term of letting and if the tenant wishes to renew it a fresh agreement is needed. Just allowing a neighbouring farmer to graze your land can result in problems; you might have difficulty in evicting him when you need the ground for yourself. Often grasskeep is let by auction and providing you put a reserve on your land you may get more than you think for it, and you will also have the safeguard of the auctioneers drawing up the various agreements. Nevertheless, check them carefully before signing.

Revenue from grasskeep is classed as unearned income so you will be paying a higher rate of income tax on this. Bear this in mind before you rush out and spend the money!

So if the purchase price is right, and you can afford it, don't be dissuaded from buying a smallholding just because it has more land attached to it than you think you will require. On paper you could be a wealthy smallholder even if you are short of ready cash!

There are three main drawbacks with our own smallholding, snags which we did not realise at the time but ones which we now have to live with and perhaps my own mistakes will assist the novice purchaser:

1. The land is too far from the house. Our neighbours' fields surround our dwelling due to the way the original farm was split up and sold off. Consequently we have a walk of three hundred yards to see to our stock which is time-consuming many times a day, plus the inconvenience of carrying buckets, hot water to thaw out drinking troughs in the winter, and a vehicle often has to be used for transporting hay, etc. A needless expense plus the disadvantage of not being able to cast an eye over our livestock from the house at all times; a goatling might have its head stuck in some sheep-mesh and will remain there until one of us goes up there again. Anybody intent on stealing anything stands a fair chance of getting away unhindered (see the chapter on turkeys!).

2. The terrain is far too steep. One accepts some steep land on a hill-farm but not nearly all of it! In the beginning it did not seem to matter because it was ideal for sheep when we let the grasskeep and later it suited the goats, but when eventually we branched out into growing organic crops we were restricted to a small area of reasonably flat ground. There is no way we can expand.

3. We are too close to the road. Our many visitors shake their heads and smile in amazement when we tell them for perhaps only the odd car passes whilst they are here. On average we see maybe twenty vehicles a day but a percentage of these are irresponsible teenagers who have only recently passed their driving tests. They speed by in a cloud of dust or muddy spray, according to weather conditions. We have lost three cats, a goat and numerous feathered stock right outside the house! In addition I have been smashed up in the Land Rover (one thousand four hundred pounds worth of damage!) and a stretch of picturesque country lanes has become a nightmare. There is no solution apparently for speed limits are restricted to built-up areas, and the council inform me that we cannot have 'sleeping policemen' (raised ridges in the road) because the criteria for this is street-lighting. In addition to the daytime problems we have late-night pub traffic, drinkers who use our road in preference to the main roads where they stand a chance of being breathalysed.

CHAPTER FOUR

The Community

Having purchased your smallholding bearing these various disadvantages in mind (there are innumerable other snags, of course, some which I possibly have not encountered yet), you must accept that your entire lifestyle will change overnight. Living in the country is not always as idyllic as some of the coffee-table magazines would have us imagine. Gone are the amenities which you have taken for granted in urban life; you will probably get a refuse collection, maybe only once a fortnight, there will be no street-lighting, no newspaper deliveries. You will have to learn to do without a handy shop. But this is what it is all about; you want to be as self-sufficient as possible and do your own thing. Your aim is to shake off the shackles of petty town restrictions; mostly the rural dweller is left to his own devices; if the roads are in a bad state, well nobody much uses them anyway, is the council's attitude. People living 'out in the sticks' are an abandoned race. Treat it as a privilege, take full advantage of it.

However it is a good idea to find out what kind of social life you will have because it should not be your intention to make a hermit of yourself, and also you must consider your children, if you have any, and how they will adapt.

When we first moved here Rowan was nine (she is deaf and had to attend a partially-hearing unit in a school thirty miles away; a WRVS car was provided daily to transport her). Tara was four but she was immediately accepted into the village school, starting the following week! Gavin was three and Angus was eighteen months. By the first Christmas they all had double the number of friends which they had had in the town and party invitations were such that we could barely cope with the transport!

Overall you will be far busier than you would be living in a town. My wife, Jean, is an active W.I. member, belongs to a machine-knitting club, plays badminton, helps run the smallholding as well as the house; her day begins at 6.30 am and we finally get to bed sometime after midnight. We love every minute of it but our only regret is that we do not have time to savour every moment; there is always another chore waiting.

In the country you must be prepared for visitors dropping in on you at virtually any time of the day. However busy you are, spend time for a chat because that is how you will make your future friends. Life moves at a slower pace; there is more to do but it all gets done somehow. It is the *quality* of life that counts.

There is generally a disco or a dance to be found somewhere on a Saturday evening, you just have to be prepared to drive further than you have been accustomed to. But if you don't go out you won't meet people, and country folk like to mix.

Contacts are valuable, you cannot make an island of yourself. In remote areas everybody knows everybody else. In the beginning you will be at a disadvantage because they will all know you, indeed the 'jungle drums' will have sounded long before you move in. For a time you will be 'on trial'. Rural people are naturally suspicious and who can blame them? They have lived here all their lives, their fathers before them, they have their traditions and they are afraid that 'outsiders' will try to alter the community.

Without 'outsiders' remote areas would die. Indeed, many of the schools are already under threat, some have been closed. Falling pupil numbers is the excuse used by the education authorities to close village schools; perhaps they resent a way of life which is different from that in the towns, tuition which is virtually individual. It is a kind of plot to make everybody conform, I think, a fear of a privileged class living beyond the boundaries of the towns, a resentment towards the country dweller in just the same way that some would take away the traditional fieldsports which are his heritage.

In areas where small schools still survive, transport is provided. Often this is a farmer's wife who is glad of the opportunity to get out twice a day, have a brief chat with parents as she collects and returns their children. Another important facet of country life which keeps the community spirit alive. Often sincere friendships are brought about in this way through your children.

Weather

As I have already said, you should sample your proposed area outside the summer season before taking the plunge. The elements will be a major factor in your life from now on; you will watch those weather forecasts on television with a new interest, for the success or failure of the morrow will often depend on them.

You will be snowed in for varying periods most winters, which is why you must learn to be as self-reliant as you can. The freezer and the fuel store are a vital part of your life, they must not be neglected.

Our second winter was, so the experts tell us, the worst since 1947. We were completely snowed in for a fortnight, were granted a week's grace by a temporary thaw to replenish our stocks, and then we were cut off for another two weeks. In fact, it was one of the cosiest periods of our life; we found that our needs were modest, and as a professional novelist, I accomplished an enormous amount of work which left me free for farmwork once the spring arrived.

A telephone is an essential. You never know when a real emergency might arise. And rest assured, in the case of accident or illness, a helicopter would reach you. But to have that safety cushion you must have a means of instant communication.

I discovered an interesting fact only fairly recently; councils are obliged to remove all litter from highways, *including snow*! Usually when there is a snowfall the ploughs are out in force clearing the main roads first so the rural dweller must be patient. However, usually the Highways Department only snowplough side roads when requested to do so and it is policy to ask them to do this otherwise you may remain snowed in unnecessarily for some time. In most cases the smaller roads are cleared by contractors; you may be lucky and have one of the modern 'snow-blowers' open up your road, but more likely it will be a local farmer earning himself an extra few pounds with a blade on the front of his tractor.

Arctic conditions on upland smallholdings

I think it is only fair to explain in detail to those readers contemplating buying a smallholding at a height of one thousand feet above sea-level just what they will have to expect during the winter months. I would like to illustrate this by describing our daily routine during January when snow has fallen, not sufficient to cut us off, but the temperature has fallen to around -15°C and the steep lanes are compact snow and virtually impassible except by 4 wheel-drive vehicles and tractors.

Jean rises first at around 6.45 am. Rowan's WRVS taxi will pick her up in the village sometime after 7.30 and the school bus taking Gavin and Tara to Ludlow school is due at 8 am. This means a wait of around half an hour which will be spent in the warmth of the newsagents' shop.

Jean leaves and I begin by taking the ashes out of the stove and scattering them on the drive. Next it's filling the goats' hayracks because they are becoming impatient; the dogs' food is prepared, the free-ranging silkies let out, together with the peafowl, and some corn scattered on the lawn to keep them happy.

Today is going to be much harder than usual because in every shed the drinking water will be frozen and has to be thawed out. This is done by filling a can with hot water from the sink tap and a little is given to each batch of creatures, just enough to thaw the ice and enable them to drink.

Now it is time to go up the field and take the donkeys their buckets of sugar beet pulp. I take Muffin with me, Hobbit will have her walk later. Two spaniels at feeding time for the other animals are more than I can manage!

The donkeys are fed and their hayracks filled, the turkeys let out into the enclosure and the poultry sheds opened up. I let the ducks and geese out and see if I can open up a patch of water on the pool for them, but no such luck! This means another trip back to the house and up here again with a couple more cannisters of hot water.

The dogs are fed and I see Jean is back. Tara and Gavin are with her because the school bus is not running; the diesel is frozen. Right, they can give me a hand now!

Jean milks the goats and puts them back in their shed, they won't be going up to the field today. I snatch a quick plate of muesli and a cup of coffee; I'm going to take Jean to work today where she is helping a friend restore antique furniture; normally I would let her go on her own but I shall be needing the Subaru as the roads are not suitable for the van. There is heavy snow forecast for tomorrow and I am going to drive into Knighton, seven miles away, and top up our supplies; another bag of sugar beet pulp, a couple of bags of corn, four hundredweight of coal and anything else which we might need.

I spend a fairly relaxing couple of hours in town, treat myself to lunch at the café and arrive back about two o'clock. Tara is making bread and Gavin has gone to visit a friend on the next farm. Now it's time for the second round of feeding and thawing out the animals' drinking water. By 3.30 most of the hens have gone to roost and the ducks and geese are lining up on the bank of the frozen pool, ready to be driven into their shed, for once they are not objecting to an early night! Tara has gone out to exercise the dogs and we should be through by about 4.15.

Now it's time to fetch Jean back. Shortly after five o'clock there is a phone call from Rowan. Her voluntary driver cannot make it up the hills in his car so it's an icy drive down to the village and back to pick her up.

Teatime and then I milk the goats. But the day is not over yet. During the particular winter which I am writing about, we had trouble

33

with our water supply; the drive-pipe of the ram needed renewing and although the neighbouring farmer, from whom we have our water, ordered a replacement pipe in November, it did not arrive until December – and then he discovered that the firm had sent the wrong fittings! He ordered the correct ones; they did not arrive by Christmas, and as virtually everybody (except farmers and smallholders) were closing down until the first week in January, we could not expect it before then. Now, in the second week in January, it still has not arrived and we are on the verge of a big freeze which will make outside work on water systems virtually impossible.

The farmer has obliged us by tipping water carts of water into our reservoir to keep us going until he can do the repairs, but four hundred gallons every now and then does not go far. No baths or showers, and the washing-machine uses too much water, so tonight Jean is off to a friend's to do some washing; we rotate this, along with scrounged baths, so that we do not become too much of a nuisance to one household.

Which is what living in the country is all about, helping and being helped, improvising and always trying to be one move ahead. The septic tank needs emptying, too, and we are wondering how the sludge firm are going to make it up here. But we'll leave that one until tomorrow. . . .

Village schools

Village schools have always been the heart of rural communities. Their various functions served to bring people together in a scattered area, one meets friends which otherwise one would hardly see from one year to the next; they promote a spirit of comradeship, and almost everybody, whether they have children at the school or not, attend carol services, Christmas concerts, jumble sales and coffee evenings.

The schools themselves often provide an education on a parallel with a private school; pupils receive individual attention, as classes are smaller than in larger comprehensive schools, and teachers form a relationship with their pupils which promotes learning, respect and discipline.

Sadly, many village schools are being forced to close. Such was the fate of our own village school; we put up a sterling fight but it was as though the education authorities had some kind of vendetta against it. The reason for closure was given as falling numbers of pupils yet, with new people moving into the area, Chapel Lawn school was merely undergoing a temporary decline.

It closed and we all experienced a deep sense of loss. Our regular

34

meeting place had been taken from us.

I would strongly urge anybody with children moving into a rural area to send them to the village school. Don't be dissuaded by rumours that the school might be closing soon due to lack of pupils. If everybody believed these damaging whispers then the school would surely close because there would be no new children attending it.

The school is a vital part of the community – do everything possible to prevent it from being closed!

Holidays

Possibly the reader has always been accustomed to taking an annual break away from it all. No problem, you put the dog or cat into a boarding kennels, lock up the house and forget everything for a week or a fortnight. Unfortunately with your new smallholding lifestyle you will not be able to do that quite so easily. However, holidays are not out of the question, they just take more arranging.

In the early years we boarded our goats out at a nearby goat farm and arranged for a neighbour to feed and water the poultry. That is fine where you have only a few head, and you might manage it for the first couple of years, but as you expand the work involved in transporting livestock to a boarding establishment, and then fetching them all back again, is time-consuming, not to mention the daily cost per head throughout their stay.

In effect, if you want to go on holiday then you have to find somebody *reliable* to come and look after your farm whilst you are away. If one looks in the classified columns of smallholding magazines one will see advertisments by others seeking to run a small farm in such circumstances. This may be the answer to your problems but before you make any arrangements 'vet' the advertisers. The majority are genuine, people who would like a holding of their own but for various reasons are unable to own or rent one. What you need to discover is the limitations of their experience; are they merely seeking a free holiday in the countryside at your expense? It is your animals and your livelihood which will suffer in such circumstances. If they are genuinely keen to learn it is even then a risky business for their mistakes could cost you dearly. Invite them over for a weekend beforehand, spend the Saturday showing them the chores which have to be done and on the Sunday let them do the work with you supervising. You will soon learn whether or not they can cope. They need to be able to milk a goat *properly*, strip her right out, not simply squeeze the teats until they have a pint or two of milk in the bucket, or else by the time you return from holiday your milk-yield will have dropped drastically. Can you rely on them to remember to shut the poultry up each night? Make a list of all the jobs, go through them individually and be absolutely sure that you are satisfied with your visitors' performance. Any niggling doubts will ruin your holiday.

We are fortunate in that we have two superb friends whom we can rely upon implicitly. They do not have a smallholding of their own but they do have an acre of land which they are developing into a 'mini-farm' with poultry, turkeys and geese. They are one hundred per cent reliable and without them I doubt very much whether we should get a family holiday. In all probability we should settle for Jean and the children going away and myself remaining at home.

Whilst we are away I make a point of ringing up Alice and Barry every evening. At the outset I felt slightly embarrassed about this in case they thought that I did not have faith in them but in actual fact they prefer me to call them. One year a goat broke into the cultivation area and gorged herself on peas to the extent that they could barely get her back in through the shed door that evening. I explained on the phone how to drench a goat, left them to it and rang back two hours later by which time they had managed to treat her and she was fast returning to normal size.

Visiting farm 'minders' can manage to squeeze some sort of holiday in between the jobs. They are only expected to do the basics and by ten o'clock in the morning, once the goats have been milked and put out to graze, they should be free until early evening. They have time for a day out somewhere, and for office workers and urban dwellers it can be a total change of lifestyle.

In fact, it is the best way to learn small farming. If you fancy a week as 'minders' then you will almost certainly learn what smallholding is all about. But go and try a farm holiday first, learn how to look after livestock, because it is not fair to those whom you relieve if you are totally without experience.

Rented smallholdings

I would not advise anybody to give up their regular job and take the plunge on a rented basis. Very soon financial problems will arise and, however successful you might be, most of your profits will go on paying the rent and ultimately your efforts will not be your own. Any improvements you carry out will be for the benefit of your landlord. There is a very true saying that 'don't do anything for nothing but if you do, do it for yourself'.

I have attempted to set out the pro's and con's of a lifestyle which is but a dream for many. I want the town dweller to be under no illusions concerning life in the country; if I have discouraged you, then perhaps I have saved you much heartbreak. If you still decide to go ahead then at least you have some idea of what is in front of you.

Dedication is what it is all about; dedication to animals, the country-side and everything that goes with it. There are no set working hours, your day begins soon after daylight and goes on until darkness, and there are times when you will have to get up in the middle of the night to tend a sick animal or assist with a birth. The rewards will be small in terms of money but rich in job-satisfaction. Only *you* can make a success of it.

But if I have helped the reader to make up his or her mind, to stay in the town or pack up and head for rural parts, then the writing of this book will have been more than worthwhile, and hopefully our mistakes will be avoided.

PART TWO: LIVESTOCK

Introduction

The responsibilites of keeping livestock

Every smallholding will have livestock in some form or other even if it is only a few hens and the family pets. But the important thing to do is not to rush into buying innumerable animals and birds as soon as you move to your smallholding.

Which species to keep is a matter for careful deliberation. You need to visit a few neighbouring farms and have a look at what livestock they have got, give them a hand at feeding times and find out at the outset how tied you will be. I find it sad after every Christmas to read of the number of unwanted pets which have been handed in to animal welfare centres or, worse, abandoned in the countryside. Livestock of any kind entails *work* and the more animals you have the busier you will be. There will be no 'days off' apart from those special occasions when you have arranged for a friendly neighbour to cover for you, and you can't do that every weekend.

I would advise starting with a few hens, a dozen or so point-of-lay birds, as an initiation. They will need letting out first thing in the morning and shutting up at dusk; to neglect the latter might mean losing your stock to a prowling fox. You have to develop a routine and ensure that it is religiously adhered to.

Once your hens begin to lay you will experience a burst of enthusiasm – don't get carried away by it! In the meantime you should be reading magazines and books concerning livestock and learn a few basic facts about the various animals and birds, the rest will come with experience but you need to know what you are in for.

Whatever you move on to next, I firmly believe that animals and birds should be kept in pairs at least, a single creature becomes very lonely and is inclined to stray in search of company. *But start slowly*, perhaps a couple of khaki campbell ducks to increase your egg supply, and if one of your hens goes broody you might utilise her to rear a few

41

chicks or ducks and thereby build up your numbers.

Avoid cross-bred stock where possible. If you have several varieties of hens, and a cockerel of mixed origin, then you will surely breed some hybrids, which may not be conducive to productive laying. Likewise you will be unable to sell pure-bred stock. Choose your feathered varieties with care, either for egg production or for meat for the table, and if your early efforts prove successful then stick to the tried and proven.

Don't overcrowd, and ensure that you have ample housing. If you try and keep all your different varieties in one shed then you will surely encounter a disease problem before long.

You can always introduce a few free-ranging varieties of birds which will cause you a minimum of work. Guineafowl are a good example for they will range quite happily over your land, and if they can be encouraged to roost in a tree they will solve a housing problem. A few handfuls of corn, night and morning, and they will be quite happy.

Ducks and geese need water, a pool on which to swim and dabble, and if you have such a pond then utilise it. But they will still need shutting up in a shed for safety each night; they may roost on the water, safe from foxes, but at first light they will come ashore to feed and that is when they are most vulnerable.

Moving on to larger stock I think the ensuing chapters should give a basic guide to the requirements of animals kept on the smallholding but once you progress to these your freedom will be limited. Asking a friend to shut up the hens and ducks for you is one thing, but goats, for example, need more than that. They need milking morning and evening, hayracks filling in the winter months when they are stall-fed and water buckets changing.

We progressed in gradual stages and I think that is the only way for the beginner, otherwise you will be over-worked and overwhelmed. You lose *conventional* freedom but you gain a lot more in becoming your own boss. And the odd day out is not out of the question. For instance, during a rare spell of *real* summer you might decide to take the children to the sea for the day. So you rise an hour earlier, see to the poultry, milk the goats and put them out to graze, and get off by nine o'clock. Provided you are not too far from the coast you could well be basking on the beach by 11.30. Ensure that you start back promptly at, say, 5.30 and you will be home by eight, plenty of time to see to the goats and shut up your birds.

But allow for any unforeseen delays; you might run into heavy traffic trekking back from the coast or even breakdown; one has to be realistic and look on the black side. We have a very obliging neighbour who would always help us out in an emergency and a phone call would ensure that those daily chores would be done.

You don't have to make a martyr of yourself. Only take on that which you can handle and be patient in the early days. Before you expand consider carefully how much of your time you are giving up, and are you prepared to make further sacrifices. Likewise you will need to work out whether or not additional stock will be profitable. Nobody likes working for nothing and there is a limit to the amount you can do without monetary reward.

If you have a subsidiary income, or even a job which is the main bread-winner, then you will possibly like to keep a few animals and birds just for the pleasure of having them around the place. But don't overdo it and become a slave needlessly for there is no surer way to lose interest and find yourself heading back for suburbia.

You need to build up a relationship with your birds and beasts otherwise there is little point in keeping them. Few smallholding animals show a high profit so you must enjoy their company and at first be content if they pay for their own keep. You are not in it for money but to enjoy an improved lifestyle, so make sure that your farming enterprise is a happy one, for that is why you made the change and cast off the mantle of convention.

CHAPTER FIVE

Conventional Farm Livestock

Of course it is entirely up to the reader what type of livestock he runs on his holding. If I were to attempt to dictate to him then I should be hypocritical and on the same footing as those who dictate national farming policies with total disregard for those who work the land. This book is all about doing your own thing and enjoying your freedom.

However, before we discuss the possibilities of conventional small farming let us first look at the type of pastureland which we have at our disposal. We must pause for a moment to consider why goats, for example, are much healthier, hardier and less prone to the innumerable diseases which affect sheep and cattle.

One answer lies in the factory-type farming designed to produce a quantity of meat at all costs, regardless of the ever-increasing surplus in cold storage, hormones and steroids and other nasties which are serving to swell the ranks of the vegetarian army year after year. We have learned to reduce our consumption of animal products for health reasons but farmers are still being subsidised to rear more and more meat. Animals are dogged by ill-health, almost every lambing and calving has its problems.

The other reason which has been discreetly swept under the hedge-rows is that the continual application of chemicals on the land has served to reduce the valuable minerals, trace elements, vitamins and beneficial herbs which were once prolific on grazing land. Consequently livestock rely on injections from birth without which they would die.

The value of old pastureland is only too obvious, however much modern farmers may try to refute it. A ministry official who called one day to measure up our fencing so that we might claim a grant remarked upon this. At my invitation a Nature Conservancy Council representative inspected our land to help and advise us with our efforts to improve the environment. Wild flowers and herbs were in abundance, whereas on a neighbouring field there was nothing to be seen except grass. That is the difference; our neighbour will cut a lucrative hay/harvest or graze it to

44

A bull can present a very real danger

the maximum, but proportionally our pasture will provide the greatest benefit per grazing animal. Even in the early years we had achieved that much.

Cattle

It had never been my intention to run cattle on our land but it was the children who persuaded me to give it a try. Some of their friends, farmers' children, apparently made a few pounds from having calves of their own and, on the face of it, it seemed easy money to buy in a few three month-old calves in the spring, run them on the grass for six months and then sell them again in the autumn. All it cost, apparently, was a few bags of concentrates.

So we tried it. Frankly, it seemed just too easy. If one reared calves from birth then there was a decided element of risk but if you bought healthy stock when somebody else had already done the difficult part, barring a catastrophe it was money for old rope. Or so I thought!

I made the children a loan of four Friesian x Herefords, bought-in in

Cattle can present a problem where there is not an adequate water supply

April and then re-sold at a local sale of store cattle in October. According to my hazy records they made a profit of one hundred and sixty-eight pounds. I had my outlay back and paid the children their profit, forty-two pounds each, and they were already pressing me to do the same again next year. With some reluctance I agreed; but next time I was determined to keep accurate records and find out how other smallholders seemingly made a sizeable profit out of a few calves with a minimum of work involved.

This time I bought five Charolais, one of which was markedly smaller than the others but their age was supposed to be four to five months. I paid a total of seven hundred and fifty pounds for them and when I wrote out the cheque I had a decidedly uneasy feeling. But I was committed and I'd have to see it through.

The children did their share; buckets of calf-mixture morning and evening, and the shed mucked out a couple of times during the summer. Unfortunately we had one of the driest July and Augusts this century, and not having an adequate water supply for large stock I was carrying twenty gallons of water a day (sometimes forty if we were going out the following day) for ten weeks, but that's by the way. It wasn't the children's fault but it wouldn't have happened if I'd stuck by my hunch and kept to goats and poultry.

Consequently I was relieved when October arrived and our five

46

Charolais heifers were loaded on to the lorry for market.

However, my relief turned to horror a few hours later when I learned the results of my experiment with cattle. *I had made a total net loss of one hundred and twelve pounds and seven pence!*

The figures which, to the best of my belief, are accurate to the last penny are made up as follows:

Expenditure

Purchase of five Charolais calves	£750.00
Transport: from vendor	£10.00
to market	£17.00
Feedstuffs	£10.10
Water carrying (petrol for Land Rover)	£10.00
Bank charges on overdraft April–October	£68.97
	£866.07

Income

Sale of five Charolais calves	£754.00
LOSS	£112.07
	£866.07

Cattle can prove to be an expensive summer luxury

47

Having recovered from the initial shock I re-checked my figures, found them to be correct, and tried to determine where I had gone wrong. Undoubtedly the one small animal had pulled the sale price down, but even if it had made the one hundred and sixty-one pounds which the other four made we would still have ended up with a loss. Had I paid too much for the calves in April? One or two of my farmer friends thought that I might have bought them a bit cheaper but not enough to make a considerable difference. Some advised that it would have been better to have kept them over the winter, but at a weekly feed cost of fourteen pounds I cannot see much profit in that.

One factor must surely be the decline of the meat market; a butcher told me that his beef sales have fallen drastically and the average housewife seems to prefer chicken for the weekend.

Basically I think a lot of smallholders do not keep accurate records. On a mixed smallholding profits and losses are on the swings and roundabouts, and often when they are overjoyed with an auctioneer's cheque for a few hundred pounds, they overlook the initial outlay which has already become swallowed up in a multitude of different dealings. Which isn't good business but, there again, most smallholdings are a part-time income and a hobby, supported by a labour of love.

All the same I could think of a much easier way of losing one hundred and twelve pounds and seven pence!

So for us cattle are definitely out from now onwards. We never buy beef anyway, so even as a self-sufficiency project the exercise is pointless for us. We stopped eating red meat many years ago, primarily for health reasons, but I personally have never been much of a carnivore although I enjoy a little poultry and game.

Sheep

Just as some farmers don't like goats, I don't like sheep. In quantity, anyway. They do not have the individual personalities of goats, and they seem incredibly stupid. In the light of my experience with cattle I costed out the keeping of sheep on our seven and a half acres and estimated that if everything went well, with a minimum of disasters, we might show a profit of three hundred pounds. To earn this we should have to cope with lambing, shearing, dipping, feet-trimming, etc.

Possibly the best way to make a few pounds from sheep is to buy in four year-old ewes in the autumn as cheaply as possible, let them lamb and then sell both ewes and lambs the following year. But even so I feel that sheep are something which I would not enjoy keeping and it would spoil the enjoyment derived from the rest of our small farming venture.

48

The bleating of newly-born lambs is music

Coincidentally I am writing this in the midst of the lambing season. Our neighbours are working twenty-four hour shifts and we rarely have time for a chat. The lambing is going badly, a number of different problems; prolapses, scouring, the weather bitterly cold.

All the same I feel that some of the problems are unnecessary and would not have happened years ago. We are paying the price for the boom in chemical farming, the animals have little resistance. I note also with some dismay that where bottle-feeding is necessary, in the case of lambs which have either lost their mother or else the ewe does not have sufficient milk, that some farmers do not sterilise the feeding bottles. They may argue that they don't have time but it is all a question of whether you want your lambs to live or die.

Last week we had occasion to milk an ewe; Gavin's guinea pig which has just given birth to four young, has mastitis and we have to bottle-feed the babies. I have always wanted to try sheep's milk and so I poured some on to my bowl of muesli. It was absolutely delightful. I have, of course, eaten fetta cheese which is mostly made in Greece, but I feel that there is a market for the home-produced sheep dairy products which is being ignored. Perhaps one day we might experiment with a milking ewe, or even a Jacob's sheep which are renowned for their fleeces.

Sheep farmers have a problem when they turn the ewes and lambs

49

out on to pasture. Every field needs to be securely fenced and it is necessary to check this meticulously beforehand. A few don't seem to care if their stock does stray but, nevertheless, you are required to fence against your own stock.

The work is far from over once the ewes and lambs have been turned out and from now onwards regular supervision is a must. Lambs will frequently get their heads stuck in mesh fencing, sickly ones will be prey to corvines and foxes. And in the hills there is always the risk of a late spring snowstorm with drifting; the worst I have known was on 27 April 1982, drifts of up to six feet, the lanes filled in from hedge to hedge. It had all melted within three or four days but it was disastrous for ewes and lambs caught out in the open.

Sheep-rustlers present an every-growing menace. Only a couple of fields away from our own land four lambs disappeared one night. The borders and Wales are particularly vulnerable, as is Scotland, where sheep graze on unfenced roads and theft is easy after nightfall. Only constant vigilance by farmers and police, plus severe deterrents, will combat this type of crime.

Pigs

We have never actually kept pigs although we are all immensely fond of them, particularly the Tamworth breed; I was born in Tamworth (I am told therefore that I am a 'Sandyback'!) and there is a possibility that one day we might invest in a pair, selling the litter to breeders, not for meat. I have always been allergic to any meat from the pig and, anyway, I would not want such a fine breed to go for slaughter.

Many smallholders keep pigs and claim that they are profitable. I will take their word for it until I do a costing of my own one day and perhaps prove otherwise. Small scale pig breeding became popular during the war years when even urban householders kept a pig in their back yard to supplement food rationing. There is little or no waste, 'only the grunt' one pig keeper told me and I believe him. In the days before refrigeration it was a common sight in most farm kitchens to see sides of ham and bacon, frosted with salt, hanging from the beams. Nowadays these are not in evidence but the freezers are well-stocked with chops and joints.

Pigs are not dirty animals; if you see a filthy sty then blame the owners. They are affectionate creatures and quickly become pets and if you have an area of rough ground which you are considering turning over to cultivation, then put some pigs on it for a week or two. They surpass any motorised cultivator!

Bees

I am including bees in this section because about a year ago I read in a farming journal that bees were a possible alternative to sheep and cattle now that the whole structure of farming is changing.

So far we have resisted the temptation to instal a few hives, primarily because bees are an immense amount of work contrary to what the layman may think. I know because a neighbour of ours has several hives and she finds it almost a full-time occupation. Her shelves are stocked with jars of delicious pure natural honey yet the profit margin is small. However, honey is a very marketable commodity and if you can manage to fit a few hives into your busy smallholding schedule then I am sure that you will have no difficulty in selling your surplus.

'Real Meat'

In line with today's trend in healthy eating, a number of farms are specialising in meat that is free from additives; no hormones are injected into the animals, they are reared naturally and, in some cases, organically. This move is proving popular and in time may well go a long way towards saving the meat trade. If you decide to keep conventional farm animals then this prospect is well worth exploring for the day will come, I am certain, when our discerning public rejects all manner of factory farming and intensively reared meat. It is as well to be established in this line well in advance.

Goats integrate well with cattle

*A mischievous goat who found a way into the peas and
bloated herself on fourteen rows*

CHAPTER SIX

Goats

You either like goats or you don't, it is as simple as that. They have more intelligence than either cattle or sheep and seem to spend their entire existence working out innumerable ways of causing you inconvenience and annoyance. Yet they are fascinating creatures, love the company of humans and other animals (do not run them on the same pasture as sheep, though, because sheep will give them worms) and are more like pets than farm livestock.

When you buy your first goat you must decide whether to purchase a) a nanny in kid, b) a nanny who has already kidded and is giving milk, c) a nanny goatling in its first year which will not be put to the billy until twelve months next autumn.

We chose to buy a nanny in kid. This gave us time to get used to Abby for a few months, learn a bit about goat-keeping, before we were faced with kidding and subsequent twice-daily milking.

Do not under any circumstances buy a billy goat for a pet unless it has been castrated. A billy won't be worth its keep for stud purposes unless you have a herd of your own, but a billy goat is the equivalent of having a bull in your field except that the former is more agile, and you will not be able to dodge its charge. I would not risk having a billy because of the children, also they are troublesome and their perpetual smell is likely to taint your milk.

Feeding

A goat needs pasture to graze from spring until autumn; they are also browsers and will ravage a hedge, eat their way out of a field if you let them. They are fond of briars, virtually any green vegetation, but foxgloves are poisonous. In actual fact I have never known a goat eat foxgloves and there are so many on our land that it would be impossible to keep them away from them except by confining the goats to their

A billy goat can be a nuisance and a danger to children

stalls for 365 days of the year. Poisonous plants are unpalatable, a goat might nibble one but that is all, once it has sampled the bitter flavour. Ivy is beneficial to a sick goat but only in small quantities.

Goats will generally only eat nettles towards autumn when the plants are beginning to die down. Nettles are full of iron and very beneficial; if you want your animals to eat nettles then scythe a patch down, let it wither, and I guarantee the goats will devour it in a day or two. If you have the time make a few bales of nettle hay to vary their diet in the winter months; cut the nettles, allow them to dry on the ground and then, wearing a pair of thick gloves, pack the plants into a large box and tread down until you have a fairly compact bale which you can tie with string. You can also make conventional hay in this way but if your fodder store is limited you will not be stocking up to full capacity, for whilst you will fill the building the bales will be loose and will not have the quantity of a machine-compressed block although taking up the same amount of room.

I once tried making silage with disastrous results. I used lawn-mowings packed into black plastic dustbin liners, squeezed the air out and tied the neck. When I opened the first bag about December it smelled superb so I fed it to my goats. Two of them sniffed it and turned away, the third ate sparingly. Two days later Gubbins was desperately ill and it was only due to the skill of our excellent vets that she was saved. She had entero-toxaemia which is generally fatal. I blame the silage, for a change of diet sometimes causes this condition. I may be wrong but I have not risked silage since.

A few more plants which are generally poisonous; rhododendron, laburnum, privet and laurel (my goats usually sneak a leaf or two of the latter from a neighbour's bush on their way back from grazing; it has never harmed the goats but I make sure that they do not consume any quantity), hemlock, Dog's Mercury, White Bryony, rhubarb, ragwort, water dropwort and cowbane. Of course there is always the danger of any of the smaller poisonous herbs being baled up in hay. Sometimes we make hay from the grass verges after the council grass-cutter has paid us one of its twice-yearly visits but we generally check before we bale; turning the hay is a good opportunity to examine it. On the other hand 'natural' hay, as opposed to that from a farmer's field which has been sprayed, is richer in medicinal herbs.

So much for natural feeding but once winter comes and the goats are confined to their sheds you will need to feed dry feedstuffs; hay for bulk, concentrates (which must be fed to all milking goats throughout the year, anyway) to give them a balanced diet, maintain the best health for those in kid and promote maximum milk yield for those being 'carried through'. We generally put our goats to the billy every other autumn.

Concentrates

We used to make up our own concentrates years ago, using a mixture of bran, rolled oats and flaked maize which were sufficient. However, we opted in favour of buying commercial mixes simply for convenience; as we expanded and stocked up with a variety of other birds and animals we had so many different types of feedstuffs to store that we did not have room enough for all the bins.

Coarse Calf Mixture or Ewe and Lamb Mixture were fine except for one drawback, the goats would not eat the pellets in the mixture. Few free-ranging goats will eat pellets of any kind, mostly because they have a bitter taste, so in effect prepared commercial mixtures are wasteful because a proportion has to be thrown to the hens who aren't keen on it either!

Imagine our delight one day when we went to the mill to pick up our weekly collection of animal feed to discover that Dalgety Agriculture Ltd, had brought out a Milking Goat Mixture. This open-textured feed for milking goats is based on rolled and flaked cereals with wholesome vegetable proteins added. Correctly balanced vitamins, minerals and trace elements are incorporated in the pelleted fraction where special attention has been paid to palatability to avoid rejection. Intake for high yielders is encouraged by the addition of kibbled locust bean and sufficient molasses to make the mixture dust free.

Our goats devoured this mixture ravenously – for about a fortnight and then began rejecting the supposedly palatable pellets! Back to square one. I wrote to Dalgetys but by this time they were aware of the pellet problem and had already solved it by crumbling the pellets in the mixture so that fussy goats were unable to sort them out and leave them.

The goats ate the next bag without any residue and from then onwards everything has been fine. So I decided to experiment with the Milking Goat cubes.

Our goats investigated the contents of their feed buckets and moved to their hayracks! So I passed the bag on to another breeder. His goat ate the cubes for three days and then refused them. Again Dalgetys provided an answer to the problem.

To quote from their reply to my letter 'our experience seems to show that goats which have always been given a wide variety of feed, varied from season to season, are much more prone to reject a standard (and by their experience monotonous) diet than those which have never had any alternative. Certainly most of our output of cubes goes to commercial herds where we have to date had no rejection problems and where repeat business has followed the initial order without exception.'

So, the Mixture is for the smallholder and the Cubes are for the commercial breeder. I now use the Mixture daily with the exception of the first fortnight following kidding.

A local goatkeeper showed me how to make these cubes palatable so that goats will eat them; soak the cubes in water, add some flaked maize and stir it into a 'porridge'. Nevertheless, there is little point in buying this product unless your supplier has sold out of everything else.

A salt lick is an essential as it is with all ruminants. Ensure that one is hanging in the goat shed at all times.

Housing

A goat's coat is not waterproof like a sheep's or a cow's, consequently shelter should be available at all times, especially on the grazing field. Hedgerows will not suffice; at the advent of rain your goat seeks cover and some sort of hut should be available. Also they need shade in hot weather.

Goats do not mind the cold but they suffer from damp and draughts.

So ensure that the goathouse is dry, draught-proof, but well-ventilated. During the winter months keep them inside with the exception of mild, sunny days when they will benefit from an airing. The essentials are plenty of hay and fresh water, a salt lick, concentrates night and morning. In addition to this I collect the waste from a greengrocery shop in the village and give them a *few* cabbage leaves daily; too many will cause them to scour.

Goats should be wormed a couple of weeks after kidding and again in the autumn. Their feet must be trimmed regularly; learn to do this by watching another experienced goatkeeper or else consult your vet. On no account attempt it by trial and error.

Overall, goats are healthy, much more so than conventional farm animals. The criteria mostly is if they go off their food; an animal which does not eat is sick. Consult a vet immediately, delay could cost you your goat.

I prefer free-range grazing to tethering. Unless they are within regular supervision goats can get into a tangle when they are tethered and they can even hang themselves when stretching up to browse overgrowing branches. I have, on occasions, tethered them on the lawn but they seem intent on doing everything possible to reach the flower borders. In a well-fenced pasture they can come to little harm and cause no damage.

Kidding

You will be only too aware when your nanny goat comes into season! Usually this begins at the outset of autumn and happens about every three weeks right through to the New Year. She will bleat incessantly, wag her tail and generally be disturbed; she is desperate to visit the billy. Take her as soon as these signs show and if the mating has been successful she will not come into season again that year; if she does then she is not pregnant and you will have to take her again.

The gestation period is five months, so if she has been mated about the middle of October you can expect kids during the second week of March. Kidding generally does not have all the problems associated with lambing or calving, the majority of ours have been straightforward affairs. However, you need to keep a strict eye on her and once the water bag starts to come away she should give birth in a very short time. If nothing has happened within the hour call the vet.

A first kidder may only have one kid; the normal is two, sometimes triplets. The nanny will eat the after-birth, she needs it. From now onwards she must not have concentrates, we give ours rolled-oats mixed with black treacle or molasses. A drink of luke-warm water will be acceptable.

Mother and young will need to remain in the goathouse for a week to ten days. The kids must not be exposed to cold winds or wet in the early stages, and likewise you must be careful about putting them straight out on to lush grass or else they may scour.

I have never been in favour of de-horning; certainly goats with horns can be dangerous, if they fight amongst themselves they can damage one another but on the other hand horns are useful 'handles' to catch and hold an animal by. Basically, though, I think that removing the horns interferes with nature, the creature is supposed to have them so who are we to decide that they must not? It is a matter of personal choice, but if you decide to de-horn then consult your vet.

It is vital that kids have *colostrum* at the outset. This first milk is very important if they are to survive and thrive. Watch them carefully to see if they are suckling and if not then put them on to the teats. If this fails then milk some colostrum off and bottle feed them.

Often the nanny has so much milk after giving birth that unless she has hungry triplets they are unable to take it all. She will be uncomfortable and there is a risk of mastitis, so milk her and freeze the surplus colostrum. It will keep until next year because you might then have a nanny with no milk and you will need it for the kids. In any case it is a useful standby; every year we are approached by farmers at lambing time who have ewes with no milk and they are grateful for some colostrum.

Disposal of kids

These days everybody seems to have a surplus of goatlings. Gone are the days when you could advertise and sell them quickly. If you get twenty pounds for a three-month old nanny then consider yourself very fortunate.

Nobody wants young billies, though. Really there are only two alternatives open to you: knock them on the head at birth or rear them for meat. Apart from the fortunate males kept for stud purposes, the billies are destined for the chop sooner or later.

Goat meat is very tender and on a par with best English lamb but we could never bring ourselves to eat it because we have too much of a personal relationship with our goats. On occasions we have taken them to the cattle market at three months; once they made twelve pounds each but on the last occasion only four pounds. One year we were contacted by somebody who was looking for week-old billies to bottle-feed and rear for meat, and this was absolutely marvellous because we cleared out our unwanted billies and were able to have the benefit of the extra milk. One of our goats had triplets, all billies, so we let two go and left her with one for a couple of weeks rather than upset her right away by removing all her offspring.

I accept that billies must go for meat but I am particular whom I sell them to. Their short life must be a humane one.

When we first went into goats, a nanny in milk was selling for sixty to eighty pounds. No longer, there are too many goats available these days and on more than one occasion we have been offered them free of charge. Nowadays a milking goat is worth around thirty pounds. Demand dictates the price as with everything else.

Milking

Once the kids begin to grow it is best to separate them from the mother at night which means that you can take a full quota of milk from the nanny each morning. Once you have either disposed of the kids or else weaned them then you will be on to peak milking aided by the lushness of the summer grass, and you should be taking about a gallon a day from each goat.

However, the novice must learn to milk properly or else the yield will fall. Before you even contemplate having a goat of your own go and

Newly born goat kids

practise on somebody else's. A friendly goatkeeping neighbour will be only too pleased to show you. There is a knack, a rhythm, but once you have mastered it, like swimming or cycling, you never forget.

Jean and I learned on a neighbour's goats, a couple of docile animals who made it very easy for us. But when we came to milk Abby for the first time it was a different story!

Abby was always intent on obstructing you in anything you wanted to do. We knew we were going to have problems so we decided to bring her into the kitchen to milk her; she fought us all the way from the back porch and deliberately waited until she was inside the kitchen before releasing a shower of pellets which bounced all over the floor like dried peas. I held her by her horns, Jean attempted to squeeze the teats; Abby bucked, somehow got free of me and bounded through to my study were she crouched and squirted a gallon or so of steaming, smelling urine all over the floor.

We grabbed her, held her and telephoned our friend at the goat farm. 'How the dickens are we going to milk this goat?' I asked him.

'Get rough with her,' he laughed, 'pin her up against the wall with your knee, show her who's boss.'

Which was precisely what we did and milked almost three pints. After that Abby was no trouble; she knew that she would be milked eventually whatever she tried to do to thwart us so she stood and surrendered.

You will from now onwards have a daily surplus of milk and you must take steps to dispose of it profitably for that is what goat farming is all about.

The milk trade

Remember that your milk will drop in quantity with the approach of autumn when the grass is no longer lush, so from May onwards you will need to store as much frozen milk as possible. I was rather concerned at the end of our first season because our freezer was crammed with milk, but by Christmas it was all gone and we were grateful for the two pints a day which Abby was still giving us.

Your trade will depend upon your location. If you are reasonably close to a town, or on a main road, then you should sell plenty of fresh milk. However, if you are isolated as we are then you will sell very little fresh and your trade will be mostly frozen milk, principally from October through to February when fresh milk is scarce. In any case it will not pay you to deliver a few pints of fresh daily; almost all our customers buy frozen, even in summer, collecting it in quantities to store in their own freezer and replenishing when they are running low.

This works out nicely for us and consequently we charge the same for frozen as fresh, otherwise we might lose out to goatkeepers living nearer the towns. We have customers as far as seventy miles away and have established a reputation for good quality milk.

The reader will already be saying to himself that milk is milk wherever it comes from. Certainly it is much the same when it is squeezed from the udder but from thereon quality can change.

Always use a stainless steel milking bucket and sterilise it after each milking. Plastic may be convenient but you can never really sterilise it properly. Boil your bucket always.

The secret of good frozen milk is to cool and freeze it within twenty minutes of milking. If it has been left standing longer, or is bagged and frozen when still warm, it will separate upon thawing and look rather revolting. Everybody gets the odd pint which separates and there is a simple remedy, stir it with a spoon or else use a whisk to restore it. But the customer can be put off by the sight of a pint of separated milk and may not come back for more.

Frozen goats' milk will keep perfectly in the freezer for up to six months. If you are selling it then you need to mark your bags with the date, stack them in rotation, and you are also required by law to have your name and address on the product. Rather than have time-wasting sessions writing on the polythene bags with an indelible pen, have a small stamp made and use a Trodat ink, obtainable from good stationers. It will not rub off and you can stamp up five hundred bags in a very short time.

Your product should look professional, there is a lot of competition these days. Freeze the bags flat, it is convenient for both yourself and your customers to be able to stack them neatly in the freezer. Bags resembling humbugs waste an awful lot of space.

It may take you some time to establish a market but with an increasing supply of milk in the freezer this is a good thing because you may be lucky enough to persuade a shop to take your product, and if they ask for an initial one hundred pints then you want to be in a position to supply that quantity. Shops soon tire of suppliers who cannot meet their demands and look elsewhere.

In the beginning you might need to advertise but don't spend a lot of money on costly newspaper classifieds, rather rely upon a card in the windows of a few shops throughout the district. We took some coloured photographs of our goats with their kids (townspeople can't resist baby animals!) and made up our own displays on postcards. We covered five towns in a radius of fifteen miles and found all the customers we needed.

Customers come and go without warning as you will find out soon enough. A car will pull up, a woman loaded up with empty cartons will come in through the gate. 'Have you got any frozen goats' milk? Oh, thank goodness for that, I'll take twenty-five pints now and I'll have the same again next week.'

You load her up and then you never see her again. Possibly she has found a supply nearer to her home or else it is a sudden whim and she has discovered that she prefers cows' milk after all. Dog breeders will often take large quantities; I began supplying a pet shop for that purpose and we did an unbelievable trade – not to dog owners but to customers who found out that our milk was cheaper than that supplied by the health food shop in the next street!

Price your milk competitively; as a guideline it should be slightly dearer than cows' milk but cheaper than the commercial brands which most delicatessens stock. Don't be greedy, remember you have only six months in which to turn your stock over. In actual fact milk will keep frozen much longer but this you must use yourself. It comes in handy where you have a number of farm cats.

When delivering milk more than a few miles from home transport it in 'cool-boxes', obtainable from most camping shops. They are expensive but will earn their keep by enabling you to deliver milk to your long distance customers as hard as though it had just come out of your freezer. Milk which has begun to thaw out may well separate after it has been re-frozen and thawed again.

Cheese and yoghurt

Cheese and yoghurt are very popular, more so with some people who would not otherwise buy goats' milk. However, you can only afford to make it to order because any unsold will either have to be consumed by yourself or else wasted. Again, demand depends upon where you live.

We only make cottage cheese because hard cheese requires equipment costing over one hundred pounds and we do not do enough trade to make it worthwhile. I would advise the reader to invest in a good dairying book and to experiment with a number of recipes until a satisfactory product is arrived at. We find that a number of customers ask for 'sharp' cheese; sharpness depends upon how long it is kept.

Sometimes we are asked for 'vegetarian' cheese. Well, there is no such thing as vegetarian cheese, only cheese substitutes made from soya etc., but what the customers require is cheese made from non-animal rennet. It took an awful lot of searching before we actually found this rennet. Customers having difficulty in obtaining vegetarian cheese rennet should contact Lotus Foods Ltd, 29/31 St Luke's Mews,

London, W11 1DF. The ingredients of this product are: non-animal enzyme, salt and organic preservative.

Cheese and yoghurt are barely worth making as a commercial enterprise, only when you have a surplus of milk which you cannot sell. For instance, if you have a supply of frozen milk in the freezer which is nearing the end of its 'sell-by' date, then thaw it out and make cheese and yoghurt. You can also make delicious ice-cream but again I would recommend a dairying book rather than limit the reader to our own basic recipe.

We always display a goats' milk sign at the gate. It is worth going to some trouble to produce an attractive eye-catching sign; a chalked blackboard will wash clean in a shower of rain and the casual motorist may not trouble to read it even if it is still legible. He has already passed numerous egg and vegetable signs and is more interested in admiring the countryside.

Tara painted a very attractive sign for us, a goat against a meadow background. Many motorists slow up just to admire it, and if it serves no other purpose than to slow down the speeding cars then it has served its purpose!

You are not allowed by law to sell cows' milk at the gate. If you have a cow and wish to sell your milk then it has to go to the milk marketing board where it will be subjected to stringent testing. Even if it passes, tankers will only collect a minimum quantity daily, certainly much more than the average smallholder would be able to supply, so you are faced with having to deliver it to a depot several miles away. Which will prove uneconomical.

The System provides for the large farmer, the smallholder is a nuisance. Fortunately the authorities do not class goats' milk as 'milk'. Hence you are still allowed to sell it privately. If ever legislation is passed to control goats' milk then most goatkeepers will go out of business. Your best line of defence is to join the Small Farmers' Association; we must unite if we are to preserve our way of life and not be amalgamated into the Great Britain Farm which will stretch from John o' Groats to Land's End. Our freedom is always under threat; taking the plunge and, to coin a popular catch-phrase 'opting out of the rat-race', is not enough in itself. Fortunately today we have a large sector of the public crying out for natural foods, campaigning against chemicals on the land and demanding organic produce. Agriculture is faced with having to make a change and we on our few acres are the poineers. But this is something which will be dealt with in greater detail in the chapter on organic growing.

CHAPTER SEVEN

Poultry

Virtually every smallholding has poultry of some kind; they may be pure bred, a mixture of 'barnyarders' or bantams. Yet the birds are not utilised to their maximum capacity, a few handfuls of corn thrown out to them morning and evening and if there are a few eggs to be found then that is a bonus.

In total contrast we have the intensive poultry farms where laying birds spend their entire life in cages; there were forty million battery hens in Great Britain in 1983 according to a survey at that time. Undoubtedly the number has risen since then. The factory farmer will vehemently argue that there is no difference between his eggs and those off a free-range smallholding, the yokes are paler but so what? He will go on to tell us that the birds are in the warm and dry in the winter months. They are fed on high protein pelletted feed, they know neither darkness nor daylight, just perpetual artificial light which keeps them laying. They have one thing in common with the town-dweller living in a block of high-rise flats; they are deprived of their freedom. In short, it is cruelty.

The smallholder is aiming to strike a happy medium, to run free-range poultry which produce eggs with deep yellow yokes whilst at the same time attempting to show a small profit, or at least break even. Of all the species on a smallholding hens are the most difficult to make any kind of profit out of unless they are managed efficiently.

Feedstuffs are expensive, averaging over five pounds for a twenty-five kilogram bag of best quality layers' pellets. A few handfuls of corn are mere subsistence level, the birds will only lay the odd egg outside the peak laying period. In short, you have to spend on feed to reap maximum egg yield; in the long run those handfuls of corn will prove even more costly because over the months you will have used several kilos for hardly any eggs.

Next to protein hens require daylight, which is why the free-range birds lay many more eggs in summer than in winter. Unless you are

64

prepared to be unscrupulous and shut your birds up in wire cages with electric light twenty-four hours a day, you must persuade them to lay enough during the lighter period of the year to compensate for those days of gloom and early darkness.

I am not in favour of artificial feedstuffs because some of those birds will be destined for the table and our aim is to produce everything as naturally as possible. Consequently I was delighted to come across a supplier of 'Real Meal', an organic poultry food supplied by Philip Hockey of Newtown Farm, South Gorley, Fordingbridge, Hants. This should give your laying hens everything they require and the break-down is as follows:

        0.50% Barley
       30.00% Wheat
       30.00% Maize
        2.50% Fish Meal
        5.00% Meat & Bone Meal
        3.75% Soya Bean Meal
        2.50% Milk Powder
        2.50% Grass Meal
        2.50% Dried Yeast
        2.50% Dried Whey
        1.00% Codliver Oil
        7.25% Oystershell

Analysis: 3.5% oils
            15%   protein
             4%   fibre
            12%   ash

At all times poultry should have access to fresh water and oystershell grit. We are attempting to give them a balanced diet, fresh air and freedom, and in return hope that they will reward us by laying eggs. That is our goal but first it is necessary to buy the right breed to suit you and your environment.

Which breed?

Our first batch of hens were supposedly pure-bred Rhode Island Reds and came in a package deal with a small poultry house and run. The latter came in sections; the firm assured me over the telephone that anybody, even if they had no knowledge whatsoever of carpentry, could

This cockerel is suffering from bumble-foot hence the bandage

erect it in half an hour. BRS delivered it at 2.30 on a sunny spring afternoon and I decided to erect it right away. By 5.30 I would have reduced it to a pile of handy kindling wood had not it cost in the region of ninety pounds! Instead I phoned Charlie, a friend and local builder-cum-carpenter. Charlie came up straightaway and two hours later he had not had a lot more success than I had. 'I'll come back tomorrow,' he concluded, 'and I'll have to do some improvisations.'

The following day, having cut the perches to size, shaved the pop-hole door so that it fitted into its grooves and made some of the slatted flooring slide into place, we were all ready to go.

Those birds were fine, I would probably have stuck with them had not a combined effort by a poultry-killing dog and a fox reduced their numbers. We learned the perils of free-ranging and decided to compromise.

Two corrugated-tin sheds were erected, surrounded by six-foot high mesh fencing incorporating some fifty square yards of pastureland. This was our first attempt at *fox-proof fencing* of which I have written extensively in several journals. The mesh is buried six inches deep in the ground, which prevents Reynard from burrowing beneath it, and the top is left floppy. A fox is reluctant to leap over anything which hangs loose; a rail would give him the necessary leverage both ways. Thus our birds were ninety-nine per cent safe, we did not shut them up at night which meant that they went to roost when they were ready and came outside at first light. They were given the maximum amount of natural daylight in this way and certainly our egg-production increased as a result.

Our next step was to replace the original birds and now we could accommodate three times as many. I confess that I went for the cheapest and easiest. I purchased twenty-four ex-battery hens, one year-old 'throw-outs' from the local intensive poultry farm. They cost eighty pence each (the Rhode Islands had cost two pounds and forty pence per bird) and some of them even laid in the back of the Land Rover when I fetched them.

Angus's remark summed them up the first time he saw them. 'Dad,' there was sheer amazement on his face, 'somebody's *plucked* all those hens!'

They certainly had not got many feathers on them. They spent the first fortnight huddling in a corner of the shed until I decided that they really had to go outside, and I gradually persuaded them to do this by moving their food and water out into the enclosure. They stopped laying for about a week and then built up to a prolific rate until I sold them the following spring for one pound each and bought another batch.

Free-range Rhode Island Reds

I had obviously been lucky with the first lot. Birds direct from cages are a gamble, the only consolation is that you have given them belated freedom. I was disappointed with these hens and resolved to try another species. Warrens are fine but the battery farm has had the best out of them, so weighed against the cost of your feedstuff they are not such a bargain after all.

Old breeds

I decided to go in for Rhode Island Reds again but to concentrate on pure-breds rather than the hybrid variety which is so popular today. Twenty years ago most farms had RIRs running free-range but they disappeared in favour of birds which are supposed to be better layers. Locating some of the original breed was not easy; it was also very expensive.

I managed to track down some hens in a Welsh commune and they cost me seven pounds each including carriage by rail. Finding a cockerel was even more difficult. I was quoted twenty-five pounds and decided I could find one cheaper, which I eventually did, paying ten pounds for a magnificent bird which came by rail from the north of England.

In the long term rare breeds are a better investment. Now that many smallholders have experienced the drawbacks with hybrid birds they are seeking to establish flocks of the old varieties. So if you can rear these and sell breeding birds then your surplus eggs for the table will be a bonus.

Marans are another worthwhile breed; they are large, lay beautiful brown speckled eggs, which the passing tourist will pay an extra twenty pence a dozen for, and a broody will cover a sizeable clutch of fertile eggs.

Free-range eggs

A few years ago there was a high court case over a smallholder who had advertised free-range eggs for sale in much the same way that others were doing throughout Britain; his hens roamed freely by day but were fed in their shed and shut up at night. The judge ruled that as they did not glean their entire living with just supplementary feeding, they were not deemed *free-range*.

Consequently most smallholders, including ourselves, removed the 'free-range' from our egg signs and substituted the wording with 'real

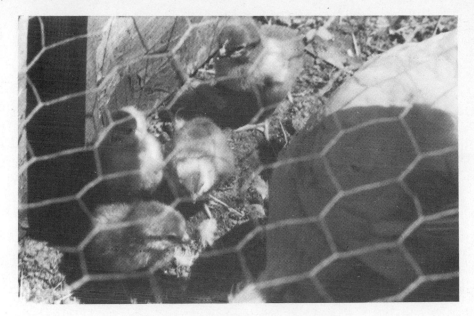

Day-old pure-bred Rhode Island Reds

eggs' or 'farm eggs'. Now, thankfully, we have a definite guideline on what constitutes free-range egg:

1. hens must have continuous access to runs in the open air.
2. the area must be *mainly* covered with vegetation.
3. there must be no more than one hen to every ten square metres or one thousand hens per hectare.

So even if you have an enclosure such as ours, provided that you stock accordingly then you can produce free-range eggs. At least the EEC, with all its restrictions for the farmer, has at last laid down a definition and we all know where we stand.

Breeding

Up until 1986 we used broody hens solely for hatching our various chicks. Of these we found Silky hens to be by far the best mothers. Admittedly they are small, and can only cover about six ordinary hen eggs, but they make up for this with reliability.

Years ago when I used to rear pheasants under broodies we were always short of hens to sit and the only way to find any was to tour the countryside, calling at farms and smallholdings. Most claimed to have a broody 'about the place'. You were shown a glimpse of the intended bird scuttling across the yard, but I never bought any bird other than one which crouched down tightly when you put her down on the ground. And even then the journey home was likely to upset her; she would sit reluctantly for maybe a couple of days and then scatter the clutch of eggs so that you had to try and find a replacement very quickly before those eggs cooled.

The snag with broodies is that you never seemed to have one ready at the right time. They also entail a lot of work, they have to be fed and watered daily, and at the height of the season you could be attending to a dozen different coops. On the other hand, once the chicks are hatched the broody will do all the work for you.

If you invest in an incubator then shop around and find a good one. It must be electric; I had one years ago that was heated by oil and it was difficult to regulate the temperature. On cold days the thermometer would fall and if you had a heatwave you were doing everything you could to prevent the eggs from cooking! The results were mediocre.

However, most smallholders will use a broody hen when there is one

Rhode Island chicks

70

available. Ideally put her in a coop with a wire run and let her sit a few dummy eggs for a day or two just to make sure she is really broody. Then, preferably after dark, substitute the crock eggs for real ones and leave the rest to her.

Disease is your worst enemy. Never use the same ground for rearing within three years. Always ensure that there is *fresh* water available in a shallow container in which the young chicks cannot drown themselves.

As we free-range when the time comes to turn the poults into our enclosure I let the mother hen run with them. She is protection against rats to some extent. One of the main threats comes from winged vermin unless you have a roof over the enclosure. Sparrow-hawks will swoop and take a chick and I have had first-hand experience of a buzzard attempting to fly off with a fully-grown hen. Eventually the large hawk could not manage its burden and dropped the bird. Buzzards are a threat and they are also protected by law; a rogue one will keep on fetching your birds and I have heard of a stack of decomposing corpses being found in an old nest.

Staggered hatchings are best; that way you will almost always have a supply of point-of-lay hens to sell or else have birds coming into lay. Don't sell cheaply, either eggs or birds. When you are rearing old breeds they are much more expensive than hybrids and to keep up with current prices it is a good idea to send for catalogues from leading breeders. Don't undercut their prices too much because that way you will only devalue a species and relegate it to ordinary poultry prices.

You will invariably find that you have a much higher proportion of males to females, it is always the case. The reason is that the male chick is much stronger and is able to chip its way out of a tough eggshell whereas the female may fail. Most of those unhatched eggs with chicks dead inside them are female.

Winter

Winter is a dismal unproductive time on the smallholding. Egg production will be at its lowest during the short days and your birds will spend most of their time huddling inside the shed. You will be feeding and watering them for very little return.

In hard weather you will need to thaw out the frozen drinking water with boiling water. And when there is deep snow your birds are better off shut inside their shed. Those drifts spilling up over the perimeter fence and freezing hard by night could be offering access to a prowling fox. My greatest worry, though, is that a hunting polecat might discover my poultry. One killed seven Silkies close by the house one afternoon within a matter of minutes. Jean and I had both popped out and when we returned our first intimation that something was wrong was when we saw all the guineafowl bunched on the patio making a terrible noise. It was almost dark but they made no move to go up to roost in their favourite elder bush beneath the bedroom window; they finally retired for the night by the light of the porch light long after dark. Next morning I discovered the remains of my birds in our neighbours' field. I feared for the rest of the livestock which free-range around the house and set a tunnel-trap. But that villainous polecat never came near again; Gavin caught sight of it at dusk in the adjoining field a few nights later but it never troubled us again and we have not seen it since.

Specialising

If you decide to enjoy the best of both worlds with rare breeds of poultry as opposed to conventional ones, then specialise in no more than two or three varieties. *Become known for a particular breed.* It will also save you a lot of work because you will have to keep the varieties separate anyway; never mix breeds, nobody wants cross-bred birds except for backyard laying at backyard prices.

CHAPTER EIGHT

Ducks and Geese

Before you contemplate keeping ducks or geese you must have a pond, even if it is only a fairly small one. As we had no water on our smallholding, we either had to forego the idea of waterfowl or else make a pool. We decided to make one.

But there was one big hurdle which had to be overcome; our only stretch of level ground had been taken up with vegetable cultivation, the remainder was a steep slope. There was only one feasible way to make a pool, a shelf had to be cut out of the hillside; it was going to prove costly and there was no guarantee that it would work.

We employed a bulldozer driver with nerves of steel to level half an acre and then scoop the bed of the pool out with a JCB, piling all the rubble on the lower side to make a high bank. So far, so good!

We then spread eight tons of builders' sand on the bed, levelled it and covered it with thick polythene. There was a problem at every stage; although we could buy rolls of polythene of sufficient length it seemed that nowhere could we purchase the required *width*. Our proposed pool was to be forty yards long by ten yards wide, so we had to settle for three rolls and overlap them; I was already envisaging a slow seepage which would empty the pond! Anyway, we were well past the point of no return so we rolled out our liners, over-lapped them by about a foot, and then spread another eight tons of sand on top to weigh them down. We were aiming at a depth of no more than a foot to eighteen inches because ducks and geese do not like deep water, they prefer shallows in which they can dabble.

At last we were finished and our end product resembled an excavation on a building site! Viewed from the bottom of our land it was something akin to the lost plateau in Conan Doyle's 'Lost World'; at any moment one expected to see some scaly prehistoric monster peering over the edge! One of our neighbours called by and enquired if we were going to build another house on the field as we appeared to have dug out the foundations!

73

Ducks like shallow water, no more than a foot deep, to dabble in

Of course a drought followed and we suffered a nail-biting three weeks before it finally rained. There was only one way in which our pool was going to be filled and that was with rainwater for there was no other source of supply, the small stream down below mostly dried up in the summer anyway.

At last the heatwave ended with a torrential thunderstorm, an hour of deluging rain. We hardly dared to go and look as the skies cleared, in all probability there would be a big puddle in the middle which would either drain away or else evaporate. Imagine then our surprise and delight when we saw that our artificial pool was full, a sheet of level muddy water stretching from bank to bank, and we performed our own version of the rain dance. But would it hold?

It did. The pond remained full right through autumn and winter, froze solid and thawed out again. We could now proceed with the rest of our plan.

The half acre was fenced on much the same lines as the poultry enclosure described in the previous chapter, six foot high mesh buried in the ground, as near fox-proof as it was possible to get without going to the expense of weldmesh. We enclosed ample pastureland for the geese to graze and planted a windbreak of spruce trees together with a few scrub bushes for shelter for our birds. In addition a friend gave us a very nice shed which he had no further use for and this we erected inside the enclosure. Things were really working out!

Once the banks began to grass over the whole scene took on a different setting, unless you looked carefully and saw the odd piece of polythene everything was completely natural. All we needed now was to stock our pool with wildfowl.

Ducks

Our pool was to serve a dual purpose, a combination of domestic and ornamental birds. It would earn its keep from eggs and birds for the table as well as being a sanctuary for wild duck and providing a breeding area for something more exotic. It was going to be an investment in a variety of ways.

Our first ducks were a pair of young mallard purchased from a game farm. I did not pinion them nor cut their flight feathers because I wanted to encourage them to remain of their own free will. Which they did, the female flying off sometimes but returning eventually. The drake was quite happy to remain and even stayed during that first winter when the pool was frozen, roosting on the ice with the geese. Eventually he left but the fact that wild duck flight into our pool is reward enough. They are not shot for this is our private sanctuary, birds

The author's man-made pool

75

Khaki Campbell ducks

for the table are taken from the other rented pools on adjoining land.

Mallard are encouraged by feeding, and if there are resident ducks on the water then often they will remain as they do on hundreds of recreation parks elsewhere in the country. Mallard are easily tamed and are happy to be semi-domesticated. At present we have a pair of mallard hybrids on our pool; they are black with white markings on the breast, the drake's head bottle green. I think that at some stage mallard have mated with a domestic species and these are the result.

Of all the laying varieties Khaki Campbells are undoubtedly the best. They begin laying in the early spring and often produce an egg every day almost up until Christmas if the weather is mild, possibly averaging three hundred eggs a year. These birds are, in fact, the farmyard cousin of the mallard and make superb eating, although they are on the small side, and as a result are often overlooked as a table bird.

In a set-up such as ours breeding is not easy simply because the area does not offer the privacy which waterfowl like to sit their eggs. There are ample bushes and undergrowth, indeed most days in the summer we have to search for the eggs but the birds will not sit a clutch. As a result any fertile eggs have to be hatched either under a broody hen or in the incubator. The pool itself is not extensive enough to install nesting rafts.

In recent years we have housed our flock of Rhode Island Reds in the

76

pool enclosure, adding a small henhouse to the existing shed. The poultry love it, they have integrated with the ducks and geese, but the outcome of this is that every night the hens go into the sheds to roost and the water birds follow them. It is ludicrous having Canada geese sharing the same home as hens, and has in some ways defeated the idea of having waterfowl roosting on the water at night, but it has its advantages because in prolonged spells of severe weather all the birds can be shut in. In the winter of 1985/6 the birds were shut in the sheds for a period of six weeks; boring as it must have been for them they were safe there, they had plenty of food and water and when eventually they were released they were in superb condition.

Khaki Campbells are the finest possible decoys to encourage wild duck to use a pool. However, if you hatch any ducklings they need to be protected for the first few weeks against vermin. Rats are the worst offenders, I have known them to take a six week-old gosling, and many hatches of ducks on lakes and rivers fall prey to these rodents. Corvines will take a young duckling, too. Bait extensively for rats and shoot as many crows as you can.

Too many drakes can be a nuisance on a small pool. In the spring they will fight and disturb the females, they will also sometimes kill young ducks by drowning them. Regard your drakes as fare for the table and thin them out in the autumn. One drake to five or six ducks is ample.

If you are rearing ducks for meat then Aylesburys should be your choice for they grow to a good weight. However, we prefer mallard, meat that is lean with a marked absence of fat. Also I am not keen on killing domestic birds; it is inevitable that over the months when you are feeding them regularly that you build up a relationship, and it is little short of treachery to grab a bird and pull its neck one day when it has been coming to you for food. Far rather sport and food from the wild, the unsuspecting pheasant or duck killed outright; the meat will be healthier, too, with an absence of fat, low in cholesterol, and the adrenalin will not have had time to pump.

Ducks, wild or tame, are gluttonous feeders and should be fed twice a day, morning and evening. Throw the corn into the shallows rather than scattering it in the open, for if you don't there will be a number of uninvited guests; magpies, crows, starlings, moorhens, rats, the list will be unending. Ducks love to dabble in shallow water and they will enjoy searching for their food on the bottom.

Ducks are easy to rear, the eggs having a high rate of fertility. In my boyhood I once came across a deserted mallard's nest by the river. I took the eggs home, put them under a broody hen and hatched the lot. Ten out of ten, although one duckling did die a few days later.

77

Our first experiment was with farmyard geese for Christmas. Right from our first venture into self-sufficiency we had always kept a goose simply for its eggs. Geese will begin laying in early March, and if the eggs are taken away (i.e. they are not allowed to sit) they will continue laying right into the summer. The Chinese goose will often lay until October.

Our resident goose died and we decided to replace her, phoned a farmer's wife who breeds geese. Of course we could have a goose, she would be delighted to supply us with one, but we would have to take six goslings with her which had hatched the previous week.

So we became the proud owners of a goose and goslings. The latter grew at an incredible rate, consumed an amazing amount of grass (we did not have our big pool in those days), and then we were faced with disposing of them. There was only one solution, a goose for Christmas, one for a friend and the rest in the freezer.

I did not fancy killing them myself and shopped around for a willing executioner. I abhor the old country way of killing geese; the birds are stunned, hung up by their legs, their throats slit and the blood drained

Part of the author's wildfowl collection: From left to right – Chinese goose, Khaki Campbell ducks, Canada goose and Greylag goose

into a bucket. I managed to find a man who was prepared to 'neck' them which he did most efficiently. The six birds were killed in almost as many minutes, swiftly and humanely.

There is no quick method of plucking geese. You cannot dip them in boiling water as their feathers are waterproof and this only makes the task harder. Every feather has to be pulled out by hand and you often have to use a pair of pliers to remove some of the larger quills. Fortunately our friend plucked her own so that left us with five. Jean and I started at 1.30 pm and with a short break for tea finished at 8.30!

By domestic standards the birds were superb but for us there was too much thick yellow fat. We filled three carrier bags with that which we cut off and I was already convinced that farmyard geese were not for us. Next time it would be a Greylag or a Pinkfoot shot on the Solway!

Possibly the only way to rear reasonably lean geese is to feed them solely on grass, but if you are looking to the Christmas market then there won't be much grazing after September and you will have to supplement their feeding with corn. As a commercial enterprise they are worthwhile so long as you do not mind the work involved in plucking and dressing. As with everything else you cannot cost your own labour and if you employ a plucker the profits will be drastically reduced. Certainly if you price them competitively you will not be left with any on your hands because the goose is once again festive fare and very much in demand.

We now have a Chinese goose which we keep solely for her eggs. Goose eggs are ideal for cooking and make superb omelettes. Chinese are noisy birds, excellent watchdogs and are sufficiently attractive to run with more ornamental species.

Canada geese

Canada geese, with their distinctive black and white heads, are a common sight on most lakes and park pools. They breed prolifically and in recent years have become an agricultural pest, damaging growing crops and grazing pastureland; four of these birds will eat as much grass as one sheep!

There are no truly wild Canadas in Britain although flocks do frequent our marshland, mostly breeding on lakes and rivers. In my opinion the feral Canada is the finest eating bird of all geese; I once shot one weighing fourteen pounds which would have graced any Christmas dinner table.

My experiments with Canada geese go back many years to the time when I reared a variety of birds on my grandmother's rough orchard. A local gamekeeper sold me a pair, which myself and three friends had to go and catch. I constructed a mesh enclosure with a small pond, built them a house of straw bales and left them to it. All should have been fine but when no eggs appeared I began to have my suspicions.

Then I was offered some Canada goslings by another gamekeeper who had been instructed by his employer to reduce the population on the lake. Another catching-up expedition resulted in three Canadas which had not yet grown their flight feathers. These I put in the enclosure with the others and minutes later bedlam broke out. The old geese were trying to kill the young ones, chasing them, pecking them, pinning them up against the wire. Even a hastily constructed partition did not stop them trying to get to the young, so I removed the goslings without delay and gave them to a friend who had a flooded marlpit on his land. A few weeks later they flew off and were not seen again.

Then one morning my Canadas began to fight, trumpeting like angry elephants and charging each other, pecking and battering with their wings. I knew then that my earlier suspicions were correct and these birds were not a pair but *two males*! They were caught up, crated separately and sent by rail to a waterfowl farm in the south of England.

Now with my pool on Black Hill I was determined to try again. I purchased a pair of Canadas and most certainly they were a pair. They did not mate but at least the female laid eggs! One word of warning to the beginner on rendering birds flightless for the purpose of keeping them in captivity. There are two methods; you can either pinion them or else you can remove the flight feathers from *one* wing with a pair of strong kitchen scissors. But if you do this remember that you will have to cut those feathers again the following year after the annual moult when they will have grown once more. Failure to do this will undoubtedly result in your birds flying off.

At least the Canadas were ornamental, even if they did not breed, and enhanced the population of the pool enclosure. But even birds with their flight feathers removed are not totally grounded. In a very strong wind they are able to become airborne up to five or six feet, and in the case of our pool by using the high bank they can just make it over into the field. Not that they go anywhere when they have jumped the enclosure; they walk along the fence trying to get back inside!

But if they escape during the hours of darkness then they are easy prey for a fox. Flightless geese do not have the same aggression as those which still have their powers of flight; often a Canada goose is too fierce even for a fox but not so mine and all I found next morning was a pile of feathers.

The following summer we took the children to a holiday camp where they have a large flock of resident Canadas on their lake. On the morning of our departure the head gardener arrived at our chalet and said that the boss had instructed him to catch up a pair of Canadas for me! It was a marvellous gesture of an established friendship except that both the Land Rover and the Subaru were loaded up to the roof with luggage. Nevertheless, I didn't look a gift horse in the mouth and a pair of Canadas came home with us amidst the luggage, their feet and wings tied with string! They settled in within a few hours of being released on to our pool and have made no attempt to leave.

The Wildlife and Countryside Act, 1981, makes it illegal to rear Canada geese and release them into the wild. So bear this in mind if, like us, you have Canadas in semi-captivity. Not that ours have shown any signs of breeding yet!

Greylag geese

Once the pool was found to be a success I was determined to have a pair of Greylags on it. Having been a keen wildfowler for many years one of my ambitions has been to be able to hear the cry of wild geese close to my home. Not wishing to live in a coastal area I did the next best thing, I bought a pair of Greylags.

Like the Canadas they didn't do much apart from sit on the bank most of the day and go for an occasional splash in the pool. The female laid but made no attempt to sit her eggs. And then one night she just disappeared. There had been a blizzard in the night which left an inch or two of snow on the ground. When I went to feed the pool birds there was no sign of the Greylag goose and the gander was obviously very distressed. I checked the perimeter fencing but there were no marks, no feathers nor footprints. A more intensive search revealed no sign of the missing bird and all I can conclude is that her pinion had come off and she had used the gale to lift herself into the air and had gone far afield. I would not be surprised if her instincts had taken her back north to answer the call of the wild. Perhaps she joined the migratory flocks that spring and returned to the mountains of Greenland or Spitzbergen to breed. Wherever she is, I wish her well, and may she enjoy her freedom at my expense.

Geese, barring accidents and ill-health, are long-lived birds. I once heard of a Greylag locally who remained on a smallholding after the flock had been forced to land in thick fog. It joined up with the domestic geese and remained happily in a paddock. And when the owner retired and went to live in the village a quarter of a mile away, this goose turned up on his doorstep one morning in search of its usual crust of bread. This journey became a ritual, the Greylag walking unconcernedly up the main street to its previous owner's house. Sadly, one night a fox got it. The bird in question was at least fifteen years old, it may have been older depending upon its age when it arrived that foggy afternoon.

The wild goose is the traditional quarry of the wildfowler. In no way are the wintering population diminished by this sport for only about two per cent of all the geese which winter on our shores are killed; indeed, their numbers are increasing. Man has pursued them long before guns were invented, the old Fenland decoymen trapping them in decoys built from netting, and before that our ancestors hunted them with bows and arrows and slings. The true wildfowler is a conservationist; he will only shoot what he needs for the pot, and the well-being of the skeins which flight to and from the mudflats, filling the skies with their wild chorus, is often more important to him than a bird in the bag. But the culling of the species is necessary if its numbers are prolific, something which is vital to the survival of a healthy stock which will breed and flourish.

CHAPTER NINE

Turkeys

When I was a small boy my grandmother reared turkeys every year in the big shed at the bottom of her garden; huge dark coloured birds and a stag that used to ruffle his feathers and chase me if I dared to go near him. It was something we grew up with as children, and after my grandmother died we used to go and choose our Christmas turkey from a neighbouring farm, but these were not the once-familiar American Bronze birds but white characterless creatures. It was not the same any more.

For myself turkeys lost their seasonal appeal. Then the farmer ceased rearing them and my father bought the festive bird from the local butcher, oven-ready so you had no idea what their plumage had once been. After that we sometimes bought frozen turkeys, pre-packed virtually flavourless birds and the old Christmases were slipping further and further away.

When I moved with my family to our smallholding I was determined to have a go at rearing turkeys again, for old time's sake. A friend fixed me up with six twelve-week old birds that autumn, nervous white ones that fluttered up to the roof of the shed every time you went to feed them. I was determined to wean them off their artificially-manufactured food and eventually I persuaded them to eat mixed poultry corn; it was several days before they realised that grain was edible!

They did not fare well; the heaviest was eleven pounds and when we came to dress them a couple of days before Christmas their livers were scored and they showed signs of suffering from coccidiosis. We had only just made it! However, they were quite good eating but weighing up the cost of getting them on to the table (around fifty pounds) I honestly did not think that they were worth the hassle. I had seen for myself just how 'artificial' commercial white turkeys are, needing to be kept indoors and pumped full of steroids and anti-biotics to keep them alive. They were a far cry from the old Bronzes!

The following year I was half-heartedly thinking about turkeys again

American Bronze turkeys

when I chanced to pick up a specialist breeder's list. American Bronze turkeys were offered at thirty-five pounds a pair and at once my enthusiam was resurrected. I would invest in a pair, keep them through the winter and the next spring, hopefully, rear our own flock of 'proper' turkeys.

A pair of turkeys arrived by rail in due course and sure enough they looked just like they used to look when I was a boy although I could not make up my mind which of them was the stag. By December I still was not sure although one did seem to be *slightly* larger than the other. By February I knew without any doubt that they were both hen birds!

I phoned the breeder and he promptly despatched me a fully grown stag for a nominal ten pounds, inclusive of carriage, and I began to feel more confident. I made up two nestboxes in the shed and became optimistic again.

Hatching eggs under Silkies

On 4 April we had our first turkey egg, and from then onwards there was an egg, sometimes two, daily. I removed them, decided to wait until we had a dozen and then I would put them in the nests for the birds to finish laying and, with luck, to sit them.

However, by the time I had a dozen eggs ready I had made up my mind to hedge my bets. Suppose the turkeys didn't sit . . . I would hatch the first batch under Silky hens, collect more eggs and then give the turkeys their chance. The only problem was that we did not have a broody Silky at the time when we needed one. So I arranged with a friend forty miles away to have the eggs sat by his Silkies, and took him a dozen on 20 April.

On 30 April I put a dozen turkey eggs in each of the nestboxes in our shed; the birds continued laying, and then, to my annoyance, both decided to sit in the same nestbox! Rarely are eggs hatched by two birds sitting the same clutch but I decided to let them carry on and hope for the best.

I had a phone call from my friend on 20 May to say that his Silkies had hatched nine of the twelve eggs which I had taken him. I drove over, collected a Silky hen and nine chicks and installed them in one of our sheds.

In the meantime both our turkey hens were still sitting tightly in the

*An American Bronze
turkey stag*

same nestbox. The day for hatching arrived but I saw no sign of activity and I did not wish to disturb the birds. Surely something had to hatch out before long.

On 8 June we decided that enough was enough and Jean and I removed the turkeys from their nests with some difficulty. Only four eggs remained and two of those were broken! A valuable lesson had been learned – don't let more than one bird sit eggs in the same nest.

Rearing

Anyway, we still had nine growing poults and I was determined to rear them. We lost one at six weeks for no apparent reason but the others were healthy enough and thriving. We now had to introduce them to the adult birds because we did not have the space for two sheds of turkeys.

I remembered that day many years ago when those Canada geese had tried to kill the goslings but in fact this time there was no problem. The introduction of offsprings to parents was achieved with remarkable ease, simply by putting Silky and poults into the shed next to the parent turkeys and leaving both doors open. The poults left their foster mother at the rate of two a day and by the end of that week we had all our turkeys happily under one roof.

The first fourteen weeks is the crucial period. After that you can heave a slight sigh of relief (but not too loudly!) but with turkeys you can never be certain. A friend of mine lost an apparently healthy bird (white variety!) a couple of days before Christmas. There was a freak thunderstorm in the night and next morning the bird was lying dead in the shed. The only feasible explanation is that it had had a fright at an overhead clap of thunder and had had a heart attack.

It is important that during the first four months turkeys are fed the correct food. Chemically-prepared feedstuffs do have their benefits; years ago entire flocks were wiped out by blackhead but nowadays there is a means of preventing this. For the first five weeks I feed them turkey chick crumbs, and then go on to growers' pellets; these have all the preventitives necessary to enable the birds to survive. At the outset of my turkey-rearing I used to go to finisher pellets at nine weeks, but the danger here is that you are putting too much weight on your birds and where you are keeping or selling some for breeding stock you could make them infertile. Anyway, my aim is to get the birds off the artificial food long before it is time to slaughter those destined for the Christmas market. Consequently I now feed them growers' pellets up to fourteen weeks and from then onwards nothing but whole oats. Oats produce the real *turkey flavour* which we have almost forgotten.

The other essential is to add Emtryl to their drinking water as a further precaution against blackhead. Never use the same ground within a space of three years for turkeys and always give them *fresh* water daily.

Turkeys are avid eaters of vegetation and free-ranging will supplement their oats diet as well as cutting your feeding costs. I ensure that they have an ample supply of waste fruit and vegetables from my source in the village and when I have time I also cut them a few barrowloads of nettles.

Your aim should be a natural bird and you will only achieve this by natural feeding.

Breeding stock

I reared five stags and three hens that year. As with most species one ends up with a higher proportion of males to females as we have already discussed. Which goes to defeat my real objective; the selling of breeding pairs and trios.

Our local butcher informs me that Bronze turkeys are now becoming popular again with the surge towards more healthy eating. One of the reasons for the decline of this species was that the white turkey was much easier to pluck, a white quill overlooked does not show but a darker one can spoil the appearance of the bird. Also whites are better for intensive rearing, they put on more weight when pumped full of all kinds of artificial 'nasties'. The fact that the flavour is inferior to that of the original breeds doesn't matter. Basically it is the commercial rearer who benefits, the profit margin is much greater, they say, so the customer must take what he is given. No longer, I'm delighted to say. American Bronze, British Buff, Norfolk Black, any of the old breeds reared naturally will fetch a higher price. I found that out when I began offering my surplus stags to Christmas buyers.

Currently there is a ready market for breeding birds at around fifty pounds per pair but this will not last as the old breeds become more common. Consequently I know that I have to look to the festive market if we are to show a profit on our birds. Which means that hatching under broodies is not going to provide enough turkeys to meet demand.

One year a friend of ours expressed a desire to breed his own turkeys and we made a deal. I would provide the eggs and he would rear them up to ten weeks for me; I would pay the cost of the food and as his remuneration he would keep a trio of his choice, free of charge. It worked splendidly; he put thirty eggs in his incubator, hatched and reared twenty-two (losing only one the night before I was due to collect my birds!) and I had eighteen. During the same period one of our hen turkeys sat fourteen eggs and hatched seven. This determined me to invest in an incubator and brooder.

Ideally one needs to retain a breeding stock of five hens and a stag in order to provide an adequate supply of fertile eggs for the small rearer.

Free-ranging

A quarter of a century ago most of the farmers who reared turkeys did so on a free-range basis, the birds wandering in a paddock or orchard close to the house. We strike a compromise; the turkey sheds are enclosed by our fox-proof fencing but they rarely stay in there all day. After an initial feed they fly up on to the roofs and then hop down into the field. They are strong fliers and sometimes a few of them make it down to the pool enclosure and join the grazing Canada and Greylag although the ducks do not seem keen on the idea!

Turkeys are stupid birds and seem to have no idea how to fly back into the enclosure, walking round the fence, poking their heads through the wire and gobbling loudly.

It is therefore essential to drive them all back into their compound at least an hour before dusk otherwise they will fly up to roost in the hedgerows, usually perching on low branches where they would be easy prey for a prowling fox. Like geese, they drive-in easily. I could, of course, cut a few flight feathers out of one wing and keep them confined to the enclosure but I have no wish to do this. Apart from my objective of producing *natural* birds, I am reluctant to sell birds to other breeders looking like the dog has grabbed them!

Turkey eggs for eating

There is also a market for turkey eggs for the table. From time to time I am asked for them but will only sell them if we have a surplus. Currently fertile eggs fetch up to five pounds a dozen and if you are selling them at, say, one pound fifty a dozen for eating then there will be a lot of cheap turkeys being hatched! The yoke is much paler than that of either hen, duck or goose but is absolutely delicious.

Herbert, the British Buff turkey stag who was stolen

Turkey thieves

This is possibly the hardest part of this book for me to write. One reads of wholescale poultry thefts, sympathises with the unfortunate victims, but you always think it will never happen to *you*.

1985 had been our record turkey year so far. We had sold a number of breeding pairs and trios in September and October, and were left with a surplus of twelve stags; we could have sold these three times over! The order book was full, we had reserved a day during Christmas week for plucking and dressing. In fact, this was going to be one of our most successful smallholding ventures so far.

As I have already stated, our ground is several hundred yards from our house. On the morning of 4 December, after a night of severe gales,

I was walking up the lane to let my birds out and feed them when I heard a turkey gobbling in the field opposite. I could not understand it for there was no way they could have got out; I am meticulous about shutting them up and I also had a gas-filled burglar alarm fixed to the gate of the enclosure.

It was one of our turkeys all right, a very distressed Bronze hen. And then I saw the shed doors swinging open and knew that the worst had happened.

My first reaction was to try and catch that hen bird which had obviously escaped the clutches of the nocturnal thieves. With hindsight I would have left her there, gone back home and phoned the police and then caught her. But it was obviously our only remaining turkey, the family Christmas dinner in fact, so I climbed into the field after her. She was badly scared, ran and then took to the wing, glided down to the forestry plantation bordering our land. I never saw her again although twice I made a trip down there with the gun, determined to secure our family dinner if I could only get within range of her.

The rest of the day was taken up with the police, the local press and also a television crew who happened to be in the area filming a news item on poaching and thought that turkey stealing would fit the bill nicely. Once the police were aware that the turkeys were not just ordinary commercial birds they spared no effort in their investigations. The CID took samples of fibres from the intruders' clothing off the mesh fence, established what they were wearing and also that the vehicle used was a dark blue transit van.

It was a professional job; the thieves had obviously done their homework well, knew that there was an alarm on the gate and had entered by means of a thick hawthorn roadside hedge and pulled the wire-mesh netting down on the other side. One had caught the birds in the shed and had handed them through the hedge to his companion who stuffed them into plastic coal sacks (we found the top of one of these), and the whole job probably took no more than a quarter of an hour.

It was planned to perfection; a windy night so that even had the alarm gone off then we would not have heard it. Even the guineafowl roosting in the elder tree beneath our bedroom window never murmured.

Four hundred and fifty pounds worth of birds were gone overnight and we did not have a penny in compensation. No insurance company will insure turkeys kept in a shed away from a dwelling place. Even my breeding birds were gone, including Herbert, the stud stag, a majestic specimen who was fully grown when I bought him and we had had him three years; so somebody, somewhere, was going to have a very tough old turkey on their plate that Christmas!

No clues, nothing. I was faced with starting from scratch again the next year. Fortunately I had given Barry and Alice, our stand-in holiday helpers, a pair of turkeys the previous October and they told me that I could have all the eggs I wanted. At least, then, I had not lost the strain which I had spent three years developing.

Just how do you prevent such criminal acts without investing in sophisticated alarm systems which cost a fortune and thereby render a project uneconomical? A poultry-keeping friend gave me his solution. 'Get an old blanket and stitch some fish-hooks into it and then hang it up inside the shed door,' he winked, 'and when you go up next morning the devils'll still be there!'

The weekend following our loss I was idly perusing the local paper when I came across a firm of poulterers advertising venison, grouse, pheasant, quail, mallard and *goose*. Now, in my reasoning, goose listed among game birds could only mean wild goose and the sale of wild geese has been banned since the Protection of Wild Birds Act, 1968. I decided to do some detective work and I phoned the suppliers to 'check on a few prices'. We went down the list and when we came to 'goose' I remarked that I did not care for fatty farmyard geese.

'Oh, these are *wild* geese, sir,' the other assured me.

I reported the matter and the police investigated, but they were unable to find any evidence of the vendors supplying wild geese. Nevertheless, it was an interesting exercise.

However, my faith in human nature was restored shortly before Christmas. Earlier in the summer I had swapped a few turkey eggs for a Maran broody and our friend, Carol, had been delighted to rear three turkeys. I had not heard from her for months and then she phoned to commiserate and told me that she had a Christmas turkey for me if I would like to go over and collect it.

It was some consolation to have one of our own turkeys on the table after all. But I have learned the hard way and next time I shall be prepared for any gang who might come and try to reap the full benefit of my year's turkey rearing.

One final word on this which anybody reading this book would do well to consider. My turkeys were stolen three weeks prior to Christmas so there is no way that they could be offered as fresh birds legitimately. What in all probability happened was that they were dressed and frozen and then thawed out a day or two before the peak festive poultry sales. Unwitting customers in search of fresh turkeys would buy these birds. They had been tricked but would come to no real harm provided they did not decide to freeze the remains of their turkey for perhaps the New Year or Easter.

It is highly dangerous to re-freeze any meat and one runs the risk, a very real one, of salmonella poisoning! Which is why you should never buy

91

game or poultry from anything other than a reliable source. If everybody adhered to this rule then the trade in stolen and poached birds would die overnight. Unfortunately, it won't, because there will always be thieves and unscrupulous dealers, and a section of the public whose only concern is a bargain. You get what you pay for in this life, and where meat is concerned you might end up in hospital. Or worse.

CHAPTER TEN

Guineafowl

Some years ago I agreed to sell a young nanny goatling to a neighbour. The young man scratched his head and said somewhat hesitantly that 'there was a slight problem'. No, it wasn't a question of money, simply of accommodation for his goat because his only shed housed six guineafowl which he did not particularly want anyway. On the spur of the moment I said that I would swap the animal for the birds. A smile of relief spread across his features. 'On one condition,' I added, 'and that is that you cut their flight feathers before you bring them here.'

There was no delay. The following evening this customer arrived with a crate of birds which he put into our poultry shed in the enclosure and departed well satisfied with his goatling.

Next morning I let the guineafowl out into the enclosure and threw them a few handfuls of corn. They were wary, nervous of me, which was only to be expected. However, when I went up to the field later in the day to check on them they were nowhere to be seen. I realised what had happened; their previous owner had cut their flight feathers all right, on *both* wings! Consequently the birds were not unbalanced and still had their power of flight. Well, that was that, I decided, I should have done the job myself.

To my astonishment at dusk that evening the guineafowl returned from wherever they had spent the day gleaning. They did not fly back into the shed to roost, though, but preferred the topmost branches of the roadside hawthorn hedge. That was fine by me, they could stay around the place and if I did not have to provide them with housing that was a bonus. The guineas could look after themselves.

There is a belief, an erroneous one, that guineafowl will ward off a prowling fox with their deafening alarm cry. Not so; two of these birds fell victim to Reynard, presumably when they dropped down from roost at first light. All I found were two piles of feathers.

The remaining four survived the winter, often roosting on top of the tall enclosure gate in tearing gales and blizzards. Then, with the advent of spring, three disappeared. I found out some weeks later that they were living wild in the adjoining forest. One stayed behind, a hen bird that occasionally laid an egg out in the field; probably it laid most days but the magpies found the eggs before I did. Then this bird, too, vanished,in all probability caught by a fox.

However I was fascinated by these strange birds and decided to buy some more. The Pearl or Grey guineafowl is the most common one seen in this country, although Lavender or white ones are to be found occasionally. They are of the same species as turkeys, pheasant, grouse and farmyard hens and originate from Africa. Adaptable to a variety of climates they are to be found in most countries of the world, including Siberia. They are superb eating, indeed I would put them at the top of my list of table birds, not so gamey as a pheasant but more so than a cockerel. Their flavour is excellent, an adult bird weighing up to four pounds are sought after by high-class restaurants.

Their constant calling is distinctive, it resembles a creaking farmyard gate and at the approach of a stranger or a four-footed foe this screech becomes a 'get-back, get-back, get-back'.

For the smallholder they are incomparable watchdogs. However, they are rarely silent throughout the daylight hours and one has to learn to differentiate between their various notes in order to recognise the genuine warning cry. Often, it seems, they just make a noise for the sake of it! Which is why you need to be in a fairly remote location or else there will surely be complaints from the neighbours.

I persuaded a game-farmer friend to rear me twenty poults which he did with some difficulty. Guineafowl are unpredictable when free-ranged. First you have to find the eggs which could be anywhere within a half-mile radius. They are fond of laying in a bed of nettles, laying an egg each day until they have a clutch of a dozen or so and then sitting them. You may not even notice that one of your hen birds is missing if you have a sizeable flock until she turns up with a brood of chicks. Unfortunately when sitting in the wild guineafowl often fall prey to foxes. Buzzards are a menace also in hilly regions and one year we lost a dozen six week-old poults to these birds of prey.

Rearing

You can either rear intensively within the confines of a shed or else free-range your birds. I prefer the latter in spite of the risks although the former would be a better commercial enterprise. First of all, though, you must decide what you are going to rear for. Do you want guineafowl merely to roam your land (and your neighbour's!) simply as

Guineafowl roosting in the elder tree

a convenient alarm system or are they strictly for the pot? If you can find a market for them locally then you would do well to provide a shed and encourage them to use it for, apart from shooting them, you will have extreme difficulty in catching them when they roost in bushes and trees. Even in pitch darkness it is almost impossible to grab more than one bird without the whole flock taking to the wing.

My own experience is that fertility in eggs is inconsistent and this may be due to having a surplus of cock birds. The male is recognisable by the longer wattles; sexing is not always easy at first glance. Ideally you need one cock to seven or eight hens; a surplus of males results in constant squabbling and little mating!

Collect your eggs (always supposing that you can find them!) and turn them daily until you have enough for a sitting. If you do not turn the eggs the embryo will become stuck and it won't hatch. Note how hard the shells are; sometimes these stupid birds lay on their perches and I have known eggs drop from a height of seven or eight feet on to stony ground and be unbroken.

The incubation period is twenty-three to twenty-six days. Again, Silkies make ideal foster mothers if you are hatching under broodies but the guineafowl herself is the best mother if she is allowed to sit her eggs. The chicks are known as *keets* and need to be kept dry in their early life.

95

They will grow quickly and soon learn to fly. It is better to confine them with their mother for the first four weeks for they are easy prey to rats and winged vermin. Give them chick starter crumbs followed by growers' pellets; I usually use pheasant food and have had good success with it. Mostly my failures have been attributed to allowing the keets to free-range too early; once we had a marauding sparrow-hawk which had discovered an easy source of regular food. Every day there was a fresh pile of feathers where it had killed.

If you hatch and rear the birds in a shed then they will regard it as home and return to it each night. As already described, my first guineafowl deserted a safe roost because I let them out the day following their acquisition.

In the summer months they will mostly glean for themselves and until the surrounding stubbles are ploughed-in you hardly need to feed them at all. From November through to April a few handfuls of corn scattered on the yard will suffice.

Guineafowl can do immense damage to growing crops. I have watched them feeding in a field of growing corn. They jump up, pull the stalks to the ground and ravage the ears of grain. Also they seem to work fairly systematically, clearing a patch at a time, which makes their depredations only too evident.

Guineafowl feeding on the patio

96

Pheasants and partridge are attracted to guineafowl and regularly I see a cock pheasant running with them.

Guineafowl as sporting birds

As I have already said, far better to shoot a bird stone dead in flight than to wring its neck. As a sporting bird the guineafowl's potential is vastly under-rated. They are strong fliers . . . once they can be persuaded to take to the wing!

We have little choice other than to shoot any birds needed for the pot. The procedure follows much the same pattern each time; I await my chance until the flock is feeding in one of the adjoining fields and then with gun and dog I go in pursuit of them. It must be rather confusing for Muffin, our Springer spaniel, not to be allowed to touch the guineas in the yard yet to be sent to put them on the wing, and hopefully to retrieve a brace, in the fields.

It is best to wait until the birds have gleaned their way up on to a rise and then I send Muffin after them, making sure that I am standing between the guineafowl and home, for that is the direction in which they will always fly. With a deafening clamour they are on the wing, testing shots, but if everything goes according to plan and my aim is true, then a couple thud and bounce on the turf. By the time I arrive back at the house, a brace in my bag, the rest of the guineas are perched on the gate voicing their welcoming cry. They seem totally unaware of what has happened a few minutes ago, whereas birds killed in the conventional way in a shed would be terrified of any human-being for days to come.

Yet even shooting them has its difficulties. One Christmas we decided to give oven-ready guineas as presents. I did not envisage any problems, the birds would be shot and dressed a couple of days beforehand and I made a note of this chore in my diary. But on the day of the intended cull an obstacle occurred to me. After the flock have been put up by the dog, and shot at, they return to the farmyard and although not un-nerved by the experience they do not venture far afield for the rest of the day. Their foraging has been interrupted, they cannot be bothered to go out again, it seems. So how was I going to shoot a few brace? With one hundred per cent marksmanship the most I could hope for would be a brace and no way could I discharge the gun amidst the goatsheds.

There was only one solution, I decided. I had read of the moonlight techniques of poachers, the stealthy stalk through woodlands with a high-powered air-rifle and a torch, knocking roosting birds off their perches. Well, I would do the same with the guineafowl which roosted in the elder tree beneath the bedroom window.

Gavin was only too eager to operate the torch for me and as soon as darkness had fallen we went outside. The tree was full, at least twenty birds weighing down its branches and chattering in their own peculiar way amongst themselves. The beam picked one out, I sighted the head and fired. A barely audible 'ping' was followed by the thud of a falling bird. A moment of silence followed and then my smug sense of satisfaction was shattered as the branches above me burst into life. There was a terrible din as the guineas took to the wing; they flew heedlessly into the darkness, some landing in the lane and walking up and down, voicing their displeasure. So much for night-poaching and those writers who seek to romanticise it. They should give it a try!

I went back inside and swapped the .177 for the single-barrelled .410 shotgun. A brief word with my neighbour gave me the necessary permission to shoot up on to his roof, and with Gavin's help I set about the high-perching birds. This time there were no snags, the guineafowl sat tight as I fired and reloaded, fired again until I had the required number for our festive gifts. And the next night the guineas were back roosting in their usual tree!

Selling breeding birds

There is a market for stock birds. I have sold them to gamekeepers, farmers and people who just want a resident flock of guineafowl like ours. But the greatest difficulty, as the reader might already have gathered, is in catching the birds. Not only do you somehow have to secure two live and extremely wary ones but you have to catch a *pair*. Identification is not always easy even when you have them pecking corn around your feet. You must single out a cock bird with longer wattles than the hens; usually cocks are slightly larger but size is not always the criteria. You may be lucky and with the help of a companion grab a pair before the rest take off in alarm, which was what Jean and I tried to do one day when we had a customer on the way to purchase a pair.

She caught one, I made a hash of mine, and I told the customer that I would catch the other as soon as I could and deliver it to him. In fact, it took me a fortnight!

I constructed a large frame and covered it with nylon netting, propped it up with a stick with a length of string attached to it that led into the house. I spent hours watching behind a partly open window as the flock of guineafowl pecked about in the yard. There was corn beneath the trap but they went off free-ranging in the fields. They even deserted their favourite tree and took to roosting on the roof! As a boy I had been fairly successful at catching sparrows and starlings using a similar device but guineafowl were a different proposition.

Then one day I discovered the secret of catching them. Up until now the weather had been mild with scarcely a breath of wind even up in the hills. Then it changed overnight to gales and lashing rain and I noted that the birds were hugging the shelter of the sheds in the yard. So I propped open the woodshed door and threw handful of corn inside. Hardly had I had time to return to my lookout post before half-a-dozen guineas were feeding amidst the logs.

I crept outside, made a detour along the sides of the sheds and had those elusive birds shut up before they even realised what was happening. Even then it was no mean feat to catch one for they flew crazily in the pitch darkness. A fortnight to the day our extremely patient customer got his bird!

Guineafowl in the garden

It is not easy having a vegetable garden in close proximity to a flock of free-range guineafowl. We had had Silkies for some time but they never troubled us unduly; they seemed to prefer feeding on patches of chickweed which was very convenient for us. But the guineafowl were a different proposition!

We found we had to net anything that showed green foliage with the exception of parsnips. We were sure that they would not touch potato tops. They didn't, they merely harvested a crop of earlies about a month before they were ready, unearthing the tubers so that the daylight turned the potatoes green and dangerous for human consumption!

In effect you have to protect all growing crops, even garlic and onions for the birds will scratch them up, not to eat but merely to dust-bath in the soil.

But in spite of all the drawbacks I would not be without my flock of guineafowl, even when they start up a conversation beneath the bedroom window in the dead of night for no apparent reason. We erected a section of perches at one end of the hayshed in an attempt to persuade the birds to roost further away from our own sleeping quarters. It took them six months to give it a try and even now they only use this sheltered roost on very windy nights. They prefer the swaying branches, do not seem to mind a covering of snow.

One very useful purpose they serve is to grit on the road outside our house and halt speeding traffic! I am always afraid that some irresponsible speeding motorist will plough into them but over the years we

99

have only had one bird killed, and that was at a time when I was going to shoot one for the pot anyway. The corpse was unmarked and was delicious eating.

The law concerning guineafowl (or any other domestic birds for that matter) is quite clear. The owner of land upon which the birds are doing damage may kill them but he is not entitled to the corpses; they must be returned to the owner of the birds. If he keeps them then it is theft and the offender would be liable to prosecution.

Noise is a different matter and far more complex. I have heard of a guineafowl breeder being ordered by the county council to confine his flock in a shed between 6 pm and 8 am. Which is quite ridiculous for no way are you going to get guineas into a shed (even if they are accustomed to roosting in one) at six o'clock on a summer's evening. They will go to bed when they are ready and not before.

Noisy as they are, guineafowl are part and parcel of the countryside. Anybody who objects to their continual 'get-back, get-back' should go and live in a town.

CHAPTER ELEVEN

Ornamental Breeds

Silkies

As already stated, the theme of this book is to do what you *enjoy* doing, not to undertake a chore simply for a monetary reward. Consequently you do not have to choose your livestock simply because 'they pay'. Often the pleasure of having a certain species about the place far outweighs whatever small return, if any, they might bring you. And if it costs you a few pounds for the privilege of their company then it is money well spent. And Silky hens can hardly be termed as a paying proposition.

Some people are inclined to confuse Silkies with bantams. The Silky is a friendly fluffy little bird, a regular layer of small eggs and probably

Silky hens make the best mothers

101

the best mother of all. We have had our best hatching results under Silkies and they are extremely useful on the smallholding. One has to search for their eggs, often to be found in some corner of the hayshed or in the goats' hayracks.

Many of the so-called Silkies around farms and smallholdings are bantam crosses which is only to be expected where there are numerous birds running together. The Silky is easily identifiable by its 'feathery' legs and its blue flesh, the latter in its flavour for whilst it is undoubtedly a good table bird the colour of the meat renders it unacceptable to eating. The commonest colour is white but there are also black and coloured varieties.

Our Silkies originated from a casual conversation with a local wood-cutter who remarked that he knew a farmer who wanted to get rid of about fifty of these birds. I said we'd have a trio and the next day this man delivered two white hens and a coloured cockerel of doubtful origin. In due course the latter disappeared; Reynard was blamed but, as it turned out, unjustifiably so on this occasion. This bird had taken to roosting in our neighbour's hay barn and some months later its remains were discovered behind a stack of bales. It had fallen down, become trapped and died.

We replaced it with a genuine Silky cock who soon fathered a sizeable flock. These birds breed prolifically, the hens choosing a well-concealed nesting site, usually in an inaccessible corner of the hayshed, and a few weeks later mother and chirping chicks will turn up at the back door. They are hardy, seem to survive the worst of weather conditions and are happy to free-range with our guineafowl.

We lost a number of birds to a marauding polecat but apart from that one occasion they seem to survive the attention of predators.

I have known Silkies offered by specialist breeders at around fifteen pounds a pair but in the country they are often to be bought for a fiver as smallholders are usually keen to reduce their surplus. The advantage of having a flock of fifteen to twenty is that throughout the summer months you are rarely without a broody and although they will not cover more than half-a-dozen hen eggs you can usually rely on a hatch. If you find one sitting a clutch of eggs, remove the Silky eggs *after dark* and replace them with whatever you want hatching, hens, ducks, etc. Just leave the Silky to her own devices, don't try to move her. If you do, the chances are she will desert the eggs. I had experience of this once, the bird leaving her eggs and returning to her former nesting site. Once the chicks hatch you can move them to wherever you want them and the mother will be quite happy to stay with them.

Undoubtedly you will have a surplus of cock birds, it is always the way with any species you hatch. And with Silkies nobody wants the

Silky hens free-ranging in the garden

males. One year we had seven that were surplus to requirements so rather than kill them we took them to a large poultry market and hoped for the best. We fully expected to have to bring them home unsold, but much to our surprise when we returned to the market after lunch they had all been sold – at twenty pence each! We had got rid of them, it was, indeed, a cause for celebration. We have no idea what the purchaser wanted them for and we weren't going to ask any questions!

There is something soothing and relaxing about having a flock of Silkies around the place. And apart from a few handfuls of corn each day during the winter months they will look after themselves for the rest of the time.

Araucanas

One Christmas I was persuaded to go on television with my American Bronze turkeys. I agreed, somewhat reluctantly, fearing that the publicity might lead to a raid by thieves.

Television appearances follow a pattern; usually it's a three-minute clip on the regional news, and unless the TV centre remembers to give you a call and let you know which night you're being screened you are tied to nightly viewing, usually at a most inconvenient time, just in case. Unless of course you have a video! And then just when you've popped through to the kitchen to make a quick cup of tea there's an excited yell from the children 'Dad, you're on the telly!' When the children were very young they had great difficulty in understanding how I could be on the screen and sitting watching in the armchair at one and the same time!

You make a mad dash back through to the lounge and then the phone starts ringing. Often it's a distant friend who blurts out breathlessly 'hey, you're on the box!' So you learn to leave the receiver off; there's always a spate of calls afterwards anyway.

On this particular occasion one of the callers was a fancy bird breeder who lived locally. He wondered if I might be interested in a pair of birds he'd bred (he had been trying unsuccessfully for several weeks to find out what species they were!) and if I cared to call round he would give them to me.

I paid him a visit the next day and I confess I was as puzzled as he was. In appearance they resembled a cross between a parrot and a pigeon, greyish-blue plumage with an arrogance about them. Apparently my friend had swapped a bird out of his colourful aviary for four greenish-blue eggs and he had hatched all four. 'There's two cocks and two hens' he assured me.

As it turned out the following spring, when my two birds began to spar up to each other, he was wrong; he had bred three males and a female and I had ended up with two cocks!

I also discovered that they were *Araucanas*, a South American species originating from Brazil and in many ways not unlike our own Silkies. My friend was apologetic and said I could have a sitting of eggs from his birds. One of our Silky hens sat these eggs for five weeks and nothing happened. Apparently, I am told, Araucanas often have a fertility problem.

So I let my two birds free-range with the Silkies and the guineafowl. During the course of the summer we produced some Araucana x Marans from some eggs which I passed on to friends. Then in the autumn one of the Araucana cocks was amongst the victims of that marauding polecat so we were reduced to one. I thought about getting him a mate from somewhere but he seems more than content with the Silkies so for the time being I shall leave him to his hybrid pleasures.

Golden pheasants

I would never keep golden pheasants by choice. As it happened in this instance I didn't have any choice.

One February my brother presented Jean with a pair on her birthday.

104

They arrived in a parrot cage and I wondered where on earth we were going to keep them. Then I remembered that we had an empty poultry ark in the field; that would do temporarily.

The only redeeming feature with goldies is their magnificent plumage. Apart from that they are the most nervous, vicious birds we have ever kept. There is no way they can be free-ranged; ideally one needs a spacious aviary and a suit of armour with a visor for whenever they need catching!

One morning we discovered that the cock was missing. He had never gone to roost in the small attached house with his mate, preferring to sleep in the open up against the side of the run. A fox had burrowed under and pulled him out. Which I find strange because whenever we went near the pen, daytime or night-time, both birds panicked and fluttered up at the mesh roof.

Well, there was no point in keeping a hen on her own so I found another cock. The friend who provided it told me that it was a young bird and would not be fertile until the following year. I heaved a sigh of relief at that piece of news.

With no small amount of difficulty we moved the birds and ark down to the lawn by the house. I fed and watered them, ignored their screechings and periods of panic. Then in April the hen began to lay,

Golden pheasants are beautiful birds but can be extremely nervous and vicious

made a nest in the small house and sat a clutch of eggs. I let her sit, they would not hatch but at least she was occupied and would learn what sitting eggs was all about.

Imagine our surprise when one morning we discovered that she had hatched six chicks! I left them to their own devices, maybe we'd sell the poults later if we could find anybody to buy them. But goldies are only saleable when they are in full plumage and that means waiting until the following year.

Needless to say, the majority turned out to be males, our total golden pheasant population in that ark being six cocks and two hens. They should have been separated but we did not have the necessary accommodation. Consequently the cocks began to fight the next spring and killed their father. I was determined to get rid of them somehow.

Every summer we take the children to a holiday camp for a week, and at this particular camp the organisers were attempting to build up a mini nature-reserve and what better place to have colourful golden pheasants on show? I made a deal and they were willing to take the lot in November.

Fine, but there was just one problem – we had to catch and box the goldies to transport them to the camp. So one dark night Jean and I set about the task. I had made a net, a short handle so that it was manoeuverable within the confines of the ark, and Jean clad herself in thornproof clothing with heavy gauntlets, plus a motor-cyclist's helmet with a visor!

The golden pheasants flew at her viciously, scratched the visor. Somehow she managed to catch them, put them individually in cartons and I tied the flaps securely. We had cartons leaping several inches off the ground, rolling across the lawn as the occupants went crazy inside them! Some of the boxes had to be re-inforced with additional cardboard as a precaution. Battle-weary, we stacked them in the boot of the car; we had no regrets about getting rid of these beautiful but fierce birds.

Peafowl

I had always fancied having a peacock strutting about the lawn and I decided to use the money from the sale of the goldies to buy a pair.

It was our postman who located a pair for us. A retired local farmer and his wife had hatched a pair (guaranteed!) and we purchased the birds for forty-five pounds. Some breeders ask as much as sixty pounds so I was convinced that we had a bargain.

With winter already upon us I was unwilling to free-range our new

A pair of Peafowl add an exotic touch to the smallholding

arrivals so they went into the ark recently vacated by the pheasants. There was ample room for them although I would have loved to have given them their freedom but I wanted to hatch a few before I took any risks.

At least peafowl are *manageable*; they tame easily, are cheap to feed, two or three handfuls of corn a day and a bit of greenstuff. Such splendour, even in the mundane confines of a poultry pen, giving voice from time to time with that distinctive cry of '*ee-gor, ee-gor*'.

We learned from their previous owners that a mirror in the pen serves to make the cock bird spread his tail, possibly believing that he has a rival. I know of another pair who reside in a wire-netting enclosure and although the gate is left open during the daytime, the cock bird never ventures outside. The hen may range all day but he remains inside; possibly he feels secure there.

The owner of these birds has hatched peafowl eggs over the years with considerable ease. 'No different to hatching chickens' she says.

The peahen lays about mid-April, earlier or later if there are extremes of temperatures. Although she will sit a clutch, the safest method is to take the eggs away and put them under a broody. The chicks are hardy and will run with poultry, roosting in trees at night if allowed to do so as soon as they are able to fly. Ideally this is the best way to keep your peafowl for sheds and pens are restrictive and, like guineafowl, they learn to look after themselves.

I am told they are superb table birds; the lady who rears them accidently backed over one in her car and, rather than waste the bird, she plucked and dressed it. However, it does seem rather a waste to raise such noble birds for eating. Such a delicasy should be reserved only for accidents.

Our peafowl were christened 'the boys' before they came to us. Shropshire folk often use the male term to incorporate both sexes, even in the case of children. Our family re-named them 'Terry and June' but they are now called Igor and Maw, the cock so-called because of his call (it was also the name of Baron Frankenstein's assistant) and the hen from Rudyard Kipling's famous poem about this species.

Ornamental fowl add a touch of colour to the everyday holding with its usual domestic birds, they are there to remind one that life in the country is not merely a means of eeking a living off the land but rather a splendid lifestyle. You have your freedom and your livestock have theirs, and they are a constant reminder to you not to take life for granted.

Incubation periods for eggs

Duck	28 days
Goose	28 days
Chickens	21 days
Peafowl	26 days
Pheasant	23 days
Quail	18 days
Turkey	28 days

Eggs may not always hatch on the exact date, they could well be a few days over. We always leave ours at least a week over the due hatching date before removing them to check for infertility, dead chicks, etc.

CHAPTER TWELVE

Donkeys

I have never liked horses and a request for one from the children was turned down flat. Horses, it seems, have always gone out of their way to annoy me. They do their utmost to nibble the shrubs in our garden through the sheep-mesh boundary fence, and soon after we came to live here we had to erect another roll of netting above the existing one to stop our neighbours' horses from leaning over and pulling up newly planted bushes. The animals then proceeded to try to demolish the fence altogether, even to the extent of gnawing the posts and trying to push them over.

If a horse escapes he makes a bee-line for our back gate, thunders in at full speed, leaves a trail of holes across the lawn which would rival any post-hole digger, then finishes up with a lap of honour round the vegetable garden! Seemingly satisfied, he then stands and waits patiently for his owner to come and fetch him home.

One can argue that goats are equally destructive. The only difference, as far as I am concerned, is that goats are manageable, I can grab hold of them and take them where I want them to go. A horse, however, has the beating of me. Also horses are costly to keep, they eat expensive food, require loads of hay in winter, graze acres of grass in the summer, need the farrier's attention regularly and any vet's bills are frightening. So, as far as I was concerned, horses were definitely out for us.

However, I compromised. A donkey was a different proposition and if the children lost interest in it then it would be just another free-ranging pet in the field.

Consequently we found Jenny-Jane. Her owners had a number of donkeys, mostly ex-seasiders which they wanted to dispose of. Sometimes they called the three year-old grey jenny 'Jenny', other times she was 'Jane'. We split the difference and named her Jenny-Jane which in due course was shortened to 'J-J'.

J-J cost fifty pounds delivered and arrived one blustery October evening. We had ready-made accommodation for her in the sizeable

Donkeys are lovable pets

shed which had been the home of our loss-making cattle. She could come and go in the field as she wished, had ample grazing and water. Donkeys are also fond of eating gorse and thistles. Our annual crop of thistles in the field had always been a problem but a year on, one had difficulty in finding any. So in that respect J-J earned her keep.

Care of donkeys

Donkeys are not waterproofed like horses and cattle; they need shelter of some kind. Yet I have known J-J to stand out in the pouring rain when her hayrack is full and be none the worse for it.

Their feet need trimming regularly even if they do walk on a hard surface such as a road. This is important because if the feet are neglected then they can become malformed.

Foot maintenance can be quite a problem. J-J's needed attention when we had her but with myself straining to hold her and Jean working with foot-shears and a surform, we could not get them as we wanted them. A friend very kindly offered to have a go and made a very respectable job of them. After that whenever the farrier called to attend to the horses next door we persuaded him to trim J-J's feet. She doesn't like these occasions and usually it takes two of us to hold her.

Donkeys also need worming regularly. The best and easiest method is to ask the vet for a sachet of powder to put in the food. Spooning paste on to the tongue or shooting a pellet down the throat has its problems! Be sure that the treatment is also for lung-worm as this is something which donkeys are prone to. They also need frequent dusting for lice and regular grooming adds to their appearance. If you care for your donkey then you want it looking spruce, if you don't then you shouldn't own one.

During the summer months donkeys need nothing other than vegetation and water. On real pouring wet days I usually fill the hayrack; she will generally go outside to graze anyway but at least it eases my conscience.

By October the goodness is going out of the grass and your donkey will need supplementary feeding. At the beginning of November I buy a forty kilogram bag of shredded sugar beet pulp (nuts will do just as well) and J-J has half-a-dozen handfuls of this, soaked in a bucket over-night, together with a handful of pony nuts for protein. *You must soak sugar beet*; it swells to double its quantity and you don't want this happening inside your animal's stomach. I have a routine; each morning I take J-J her bucket of soaked beet and after lunch I collect the empty bucket, use it to put the eggs out of the henhouse in, and upon returning to the house I refill it and pour a kettle of boiling water on it. This way it has ample time to finish swelling before the next morning's feed.

Hay is imperative as donkeys need bulk feeding. Always buy good quality hay, dusty or mouldy hay is not conductive to good health. Eight pounds of hay per day per donkey is necessary.

The shed needs to be dry and well ventilated. During the winter months ensure that there is always plenty of dry straw on the floor. Re-litter it once or twice a week. A donkey in our free-ranging situation will be constantly coming and going with wet and muddy feet and an untended floor can soon become a quagmire.

Ample fresh water is a must at all times. A stagnant pool in the field is not good enough. And in winter don't forget to break the ice on the water bucket every morning and again at mid-day if the weather is exceptionally severe.

Donkeys over the age of ten should have their teeth checked regularly. Sometimes it is necessary for their teeth to be 'rasped'. A sign that this needs doing is if the animal appears to have trouble chewing and drops food on the floor, or has food impacted in the cheeks.

Donkeys are all the better for being ridden but nobody over eight stones in weight should climb on to them. The more they are ridden, the better they get used to people and donkeys love company. They get on well with most animals. During nine months of the year J-J has our goats for company but for December, January and February she only sees them on days when it is suitable for them to go up to the field to graze. The winter of 1986 was exceptionally severe; snow fell in the latter half of January and was followed by a freeze-up which continued until early March. During this time my three visits a day were our donkey's only company.

One bitterly cold Sunday afternoon when I went to thaw out her drinking water and take her some more hay, I made up my mind that I would get her a companion. And as Fate would have it when I returned to the house and settled down in front of the fire with the newspaper my eye caught a small classified advertisement which read 'Donkeys, phone . . .'.

I phoned straight away and that was how I found out about the Donkey Sanctuary.

Donkeys integrate well with other farm livestock

The Donkey Sanctuary was started by Mrs E. D. Svendsen M.B.E. at Ottery St Mary in 1969. In 1976 the International Donkey Protection Trust became a registered charity. The charity raised enough money to purchase Slade House Farm, near Sidmouth, Devon with fifty-four acres of grazing.

The aim of the Sanctuary is to provide homes for unwanted donkeys. Obviously they cannot accommodate them all at Slade Farm so they have a rehabilitation scheme whereby animals are 'farmed out' on a permanent loan basis.

In due course we applied for such an animal and filled in the relevant application form. The requirements are as follows:

1. Suitable grazing and stabling.
2. Good fencing.
3. Water facilities.
4. Time and patience.
5. A local farrier who will accept the donkeys on his list, as they are not his most favourite animals, and it is very important that they have their hooves trimmed every eight weeks.
6. A current household insurance policy that includes pets.

You are not allowed to breed from Sanctuary donkeys. Obviously the charity does not wish to rehabilitate a donkey and then find that they are requested to take it back together with a foal. They only supply females and geldings, and should any jenny come into foal then it is automatically returned to the Sanctuary.

Following our application for a donkey we had a visit from one of the Sanctuary's Field Inspectors who was pleased with what he saw and in due course we received confirmation that a gelding companion for J-J would be delivered within the next few weeks.

There is no charge for the donkey and the delivery is free. About a fortnight after its arrival the Inspector will call again to ensure that there are no problems and from then onwards his visits will be at three-monthly intervals. Any vet's bills incurred during the donkey's lifetime will be paid by the Sanctuary and they will take the animal back at any time if requested to do so.

It is a thoroughly worthwhile scheme for those interested in acquiring donkeys as pets. Donkeys are lovely companions and have a lengthy lifespan, sometimes in excess of forty years.

Anybody wishing to take a donkey on this rehabilitation permanent loan scheme should contact the Sanctuary. The Donkey Sanctuary, Sidmouth, Devon, EX10 ONU. Telephone: 03955-6391/6592.

No donkey is ever sold by the Sanctuary. Once they have been accepted they have security for life. In the Geriatric Units the old-timers may peacefully end their days with warmth and food, some of the animals having outlived their owners.

Benjamin III

Benjamin arrived at our smallholding from the Donkey Sanctuary late one summer's evening. There had been two other Benjamins at the Sanctuary so he was labelled 'III'. He had been kept in a small garden in the West Midlands and his owner was finding it difficult to keep him in such a small area, plus the fact she had two small children and was expecting twins. So she signed him over to the Donkey Sanctuary.

On arrival at the Sanctuary Benjamin was put in isolation for six weeks, during which time he was castrated. After his isolation period was finished he was moved to the Sanctuary's fifth farm, Town Barton Farm. Three years later it seemed that a suitable home had been found for him and he was put into a special rehabilitation group where donkeys are given extra individual attention, such as grooming, to get them used to being in a private home again rather than a herd situation.

However, on Benjamin's medical, prior to his despatch to his intended new home, a kind of wart was discovered on his hind quarters which the vet thought was better removed. So Benjamin underwent a small operation and another donkey was sent to the new private home instead.

So Benjamin came to Black Hill, and at once took to J-J. Within an hour they were inseparable companions. He is dark brown in colour and has a lovable disposition. The file on him, given to me by the Donkey Sanctuary, states that he is number 1481. He was the 1,481 donkey to be taken into care and I am informed that in May 1986 the Sanctuary's current number is 2,669.

Cats will reduce the vermin population around the smallholding

CHAPTER THIRTEEN

Cats and Dogs

For Snowy, Chloe, Smudge and Flo who died unnecessarily; and for Simon, the yellow labrador, who lived to seventeen and gave us many years of faithful companionship in spite of his blindness.

Cats

My original intention was that all cats on our smallholding should be 'farm cats', that they should live outdoors, the outbuildings should be their home and they would keep the rats and mice down by hunting for their food. That resolution lasted about a month!

When you have children it is virtually impossible to keep cats out of the house. Cats will be smuggled indoors, hidden upstairs in bedrooms and in the end you either have to give in or live a frenetic lifestyle.

Sadly, several of our cats have perished beneath the wheels of inconsiderate passing motorists, some of whom would not have passed a breathalyser test, the victims being callously left in the road for the children to find. Which was why I began keeping our cats indoors overnight.

Care of cats

If you are attempting a compromise between household pets and farm cats then you must pay more attention to your animals than does the farmer who is merely content to have them about the place. And in order to keep them in good condition you must feed them, they will not remain healthy with glossy coats just on what they catch. They will hunt because it is their instinct even though they may not eat all their prey.

More than once they have brought live rats and mice into the house. Once we had an inaccessible mouse in the piano! They will also kill

117

moles which is very useful, but will not devour them, leaving the corpses proudly on display on the patio.

Cats need worming regularly, particularly when children take them upstairs and often have them on the bed.

A tom cat will travel miles to find a mate. No matter how remote you are, you can be sure that one will show up at some time. Our first cat, Snowy, gave no sign of being pregnant although she was spending lengthy spells away somewhere. Then one morning she turned up in the hayshed with a sizeable litter!

We have had little problem disposing of kittens. An advertisment card in the local petshop will eventually bring a few telephone calls but most of ours were found homes by word of mouth. All the same, once a cat has had a litter I think it is preferable to have her spayed. The last one we had spayed, a few weeks after having given birth, was found to be pregnant again. There is a limit to the number of kittens one can accommodate or dispose of. Birth control is preferable to euthanasia.

Cats and chicks

We have never been troubled with our cats killing chicks. The only time we had a chick taken was by our neighbours' cat and this was deposited unharmed at the top of the stairs and soon returned to the mother hen.

One of our cats will sit on top of the hamster's cage playfully poking at the smaller creature but usually it is the latter who is the more aggressive. On more than one occasion the hamster has bitten the cat's feet.

House cats

When you keep a cat in the house, particularly at night, you must provide some kind of box for it to mess in. We have found that the cheapest and most effective are made from *square* plastic five gallon drums, cut in half lengthways with a hacksaw. Thus one drum makes two boxes, one to use and one to sterilise. Don't waste your money on expensive cat-litter; clean sawdust is just as good and costs nothing. Peat can also be used and afterwards put on the garden to good effect.

Cats are the cleanest of all animals and will rarely mess anywhere except in the necessary box unless in absolute desperation. If they are shut in a bedroom accidentally, for instance, then it is your fault, not theirs.

They are amazingly sure-footed but must be discouraged from climbing on furniture amongst ornaments. Likewise they will develop a habit of sharpening their claws on table legs.

Too many car drivers have no consideration for cats on the road. To them it is 'only a cat'. Little do they realise the heartbreak they cause by their selfishness.

Feral cats

Feral cats, however, are a different proposition. Mostly these are animals that have been dumped by unsympathetic owners and pussy soon learns how to look after itself to the detriment of poultry and game in the countryside. The cat is a survivor, its instincts revert to the wild, and its depredations are soon evident. Its coat becomes matted and filthy, it lives in the woods and there is no way it will ever be tamed again.

It must be destroyed as humanely as possible. By so doing you are showing kindness towards it.

Smoky, our latest feline acquisition, would surely have become feral had we not rescued her. She turned up at my mother's one day, having fallen into a disused ex-wartime underground air-raid shelter, and but for her plaintive mews she might have perished there. As it was, she was rescued and for some weeks made the garage at my mother's her home. She was nervous and wary but I managed to catch her and brought her home with me.

Whenever cats are taken to a new home they must be kept shut in for a few days otherwise they are inclined to stray and become lost in a strange environment. Smoky settled in well with us but did not care for the other cats. Even after a year she barely tolerated them. Nevertheless she was a very lucky cat.

Pets' cemetery

We have our own pets' graveyard in a corner of the field. Whenever we lose an animal it is buried and a marker erected on its grave. I think one owes it to a creature which has served one faithfully; its grave is a lasting reminder, far more fitting than having it incinerated.

Likewise it teaches children to accept death. Country children are much more resilient in this respect than their urban counterparts. The sadness and loss is no less but they learn to accept the inevitable. And a neat little cemetery is a fitting place to shed a discreet tear now and then, even for adults.

No smallholding should be without a dog. The dog is Man's best friend, whatever breed, but some thought should be given to the type depending upon the purpose it will serve.

If you keep sheep then you will need a good sheepdog, one that knows its business for an unruly animal will be worse than no dog at all. A well-trained Collie will halve the work of shepherding.

Good sheepdogs have the working instinct bred into them over generations but they will still require some rudimentary training. It is not intended to go into the intricasies of dog-training in this book for it is too complex a subject to be given even sketchy treatment, but those wishing to train their own dogs should purchase a reliable book on the subject as well as attending training classes in order to blend practice with theory.

However, if the smallholder is keen on shooting for the pot then he will need a dog just as surely as the shepherd will for his sheep. There are many choices available but I would underline the difference between labradors and spaniels for the two are in almost total contrast.

The labrador is a firm favourite both in and out of the sporting field. I cannot stress too highly its good temperament where children are concerned. I had yellow labradors for years, my best working one, Remus, living until fifteen. His replacement, Simon, reached seventeen although his working life was short because he went blind at seven from distemper. A strange dog, we acquired him when he was six, his previous owner having died and he had been sent to a kennels until his fate could be decided.

Quite obviously he had never been innoculated; we discovered this too late. It was touch and go when he contracted distemper and when he began to pull through the vet warned me that he was going to lose his eyesight. 'If you don't have him put down now, you never will', the kindly vet advised me.

I didn't because Simon's companionship meant more to me than his working capabilities. He became a pet, an excellent watchdog, and was marvellous with the young children. After we moved to Black Hill he always went on his daily walks on his own; the present scourge of lunatic motorists were still in their romper suits in those days and the lane adjacent to our house was relatively quiet. Simon had acute hearing and good road sense; if he heard an approaching vehicle he would crouch in the hedgebottom until it was gone. He enjoyed his daily constitutionals up and down the road, would sniff about contentedly for hours in fine weather. And strangely, in spite of his affliction, he loved moonlit nights. Often I would let him out of the house at around eleven

Springer Spaniel;
ideal for shooting

o'clock and suddenly realise about midnight that he had not returned. A search would reveal him in his favourite place, a wide verge by a farm gate, examining every blade of grass.

One morning we had a fright when he disappeared completely. After his feed he always went out on his accustomed route. I saw him by the back gate as I changed the water in the goats' buckets, a chore that took maybe two minutes, and when I had finished Simon was nowhere in sight. I searched the lane in both directions without result, then Jean and I went to look for him in the car. Still there was no sign of the greying yellow labrador. It was impossible, his doddering moochings could not possibly have taken him the length of our lane in the time. Then, quite by chance, we discovered his whereabouts, barely five yards from where we had been standing by the back gate. Our neighbour had dug a five foot deep drainage ditch round the rear of his house to try and cure a damp problem, and there was Simon standing patiently in this ditch, not in the least harmed nor worried by his fall!

121

Sadly, even the longest-lived dogs must die sometime. Simon is buried in our pets' cemetery.

As a working dog, a labrador is strong and methodical, yet for sheer speed and work-rate it cannot compete with the English Springer spaniel. The latter makes one feel tired just watching it about its business, an incessant eagerness, every patch of cover investigated not once but thrice. So fast and nimble.

After we lost Simon I decided to try a spaniel and through a friend of a friend I bought Muffin at twelve months old, untrained. Training her did not present too many problems, basically because my requirements were simple. I merely wanted her to be able to find and flush game in cover and to retrieve it when shot. Anything else was an incidental and I thought that as the majority of our land was steep hillsides she would be more suited to the inclines than a labrador.

Whatever breed of dog you have on a smallholding the essential part of its training is that it must not chase livestock. Muffin chased a sheep the first time she saw one; I dived on her as she brought the terrified ewe back past me and she had the most fearsome scolding she has ever had. She never looked at a sheep again; spaniels learn fast.

Once she caught and killed a hen in a wood where I was shooting. She had already been taught not to touch poultry around the henhouses but out in the coverts it was different. It was very difficult, I dared not scold

Guy and Muffin

122

her too severely in case she thought that she was barred from picking up pheasants too. And in any case, that hen should not have been in the wood, it belonged to somebody who lived half a mile away and was in the habit of letting his birds roam where they liked. Whether or not Muffin learned a lesson I am sure that the poultry keeper did! And graciously I paid him for the dead hen!

Breeding

My own experiences in breeding dogs may serve to help those experiencing difficulties with their own bitches.

All my good intentions were thwarted the first time Muffin came into season when a lustful straying sheepdog gnawed his way into the kennel and served her. I learned my first lesson then; we replaced the existing wire-mesh with weldmesh and called the vet to give Muffin an abortive injection.

The next time round I took her to a good stud dog. Two months later she showed every sign of having pups but nothing materialised; her 'bulge' deflated a few days before the expected date of birth and although she had milk she certainly was not in pup. That was *phantom* pregnancy number one. She had two more phantoms after that and I was already beginning to abandon the idea of breeding from her at all.

Then, in desperation, I put her to a neighbour's collie. It's an old trick, frowned on by some breeders, but if a bitch is capable of breeding then the odds are she'll have pups by a dog of a different variety. At least that way you will know, one way or the other.

We could not make up our minds whether or not Muffin was in pup. The vet called a few days beforehand, examined her and shook his head. Well, she obviously could not give birth and we would have to accept it. It was a bitter disappointment.

A week over the date Muffin gave birth to a dead pup on the settee! Just one, and a big one. Well, we now knew that she was fertile so we would try a pedigree stud next time and hope for the best.

This time there was no doubt about Muffin's condition. Jean and I began sleeping downstairs with her on the Monday night before she was due on the Wednesday. We checked her every two hours through the nights but there was no sign of anything happening. By the Sunday morning we knew there was only one solution – Muffin must undergo a Caesarean! I drove her to the vet's and returned an hour later with a comatose Muffin and seven lively Springer pups in a cardboard box.

Winter had set in with a vengeance so there was no question of mother and pups going outside in the kennel. I constructed a cardboard surround in a corner of my study, littered it with newspapers, and this was to be the home of mother and puppies for the next few weeks.

One of the greatest fears with a Caesarean birth is that the mother on coming round might reject the pups, not having cleaned them off herself. If that happens then you are going to have to feed those pups yourself every two hours for the next month! Fortunately, Muffin took to them, made a marvellous mother and reared the lot.

Selling pups

I don't like to sell pups under ten weeks old. Pups are a lot of work and you have to outlay some cash, just in case anybody thinks it's money for old rope. Below are some of the expenses incurred in rearing a litter of seven Springers up to ten weeks:

Vet's fees, Caesarean operation	£70.00
Kennel Club registration fee: litter	£5.00
7 pups each at £5	£35.00
Stud fee	£70.00
Food, approximately	£40.00
Advertising	£20.00
	£240.00

Income (assuming that you manage to sell *all* the pups at ten weeks old)

Seven Springer Spaniel pups at £75.00 each   £525.00

In which case you will have made a profit of £285.00

But you don't do it for money, at least if you do then you are being unfair to your bitch and there are much easier ways of making that amount of money. You are tied once the pups are partly weaned because you will have to feed them four times a day for the first three months and three times daily after that. The kennel will need daily cleaning and fresh bedding adding. I discovered that hay was a better litter than straw; the pups did not strew it out into the run and it gave more warmth. They must be kept warm and dry at all costs and any born outside during the winter should have the additional heat from an infra-red lamp.

Of course, if you have not sold them all at three months then you will have to incur the added expense of innoculations at around fourteen pounds per pup. Food costs will rise as they grow and eat more. I always use a complete puppy food, preferably one that has dried milk in it, such as Febo. You know then that you are feeding them a balanced diet.

Bitches sell more easily than dogs. Possibly because a bitch is easier to train and control and the breeder can establish his own bloodline. One argument is that dogs are inclined to roam more than bitches. True, but if you have a bitch then every stray dog in the neighbourhood will be visiting *you*! It's as broad as it is long but nevertheless we sold all our bitches and were left with the dogs.

We decided to keep one bitch, a sweet liver and white that was a carbon copy of Muffin. We called her Hobbit.

If your pedigree is good enough then advertise in the best journals. It amazes me how much money some advertisers waste with unnecessary wording. As a guide: E.S.S. (anybody in the know is aware that that stands for English Springer Spaniels and you pay for one word instead of three). For example, my initial advert read, 'ESS pups, excellent pedigree, KC registered. £75 each.' Add your telephone number and *county* (some people will only buy accessible pups) and at forty-three pence per word that costs around five pounds.

We sold two bitches at the first attempt, tried an ad in the local paper which brought no results, sold another by word of mouth and then, a month later, had a phone call from our first advertisement. You can never tell, there's no guide to the best time to sell. Except that when the time comes to breed from Hobbit I shall ensure that she's put to the dog at such time that she has her pups in the summer months!

A bitch is all the better for having a litter of pups. It is rumoured that it prevents cancer but I have no proof to substantiate this. Your animal is far more likely to develop cancerous growths from shooting over laid corn that has been sprayed. I have heard of two deaths resulting from poisoned ears of barley sticking in the skin.

Straying dogs

Straying dogs are of no use either to the farmer or their owner. If either of our dogs were missing then I should not rest until they were found. Certainly I could not retire to bed knowing that they were loose somewhere. Unfortunately, a number of dog-owners lack responsibility.

We were plagued for over a year by a collie dog which used to turn up in the night and sit and howl outside the bedroom window. He was not in the slightest bit interested in Muffin in her kennel, his prime objective, it seemed, being to keep us awake and then tip the dustbin out.

In all I made eight phone calls of complaint to the dog's owner. Once I caught the offending animal, brought Muffin into the house and shut it up in her kennel. It ripped the mesh off the inside and chewed the woodwork. Its master was summoned to collect it, which he did, but it was back the next night! And whilst we were away on holiday it continued its nocturnal howling in an endeavour to keep our good friends Barry and Alice awake.

Finally we could stand it no longer. I do not agree with shooting dogs, the fault lies with the owners. So one night I caught this creature, put him in the back of the car and drove eighteen miles to a police station with kennelling facilities where I handed him in. The farmer concerned had to leave his farmwork and go to collect his dog the following day – I know this for a fact because the collie was back howling beneath the bedroom window a few nights later!

In the end the police had to call and administer a stern warning, which in turn drew wails of dissent from the offending owner! But at least after that the dog was kept under control.

It is an offence to have a dog out of your control. The owner has a responsibility to look after his dog(s) and under the Wildlife and Countryside Act, 1981, those whose dogs are loose in sheepfields can be fined heavily and have their animals destroyed.

Insurance

If you have a valuable dog then insure it. It is bad enough losing any dog and money is scant consolation at the time – until you come to replace your dog. In additon you should have a third party insurance on all your smallholding animals. I recall the time once when one of our young billy goats dashed across the road and was run over by a passing car. The lady driver was terribly distressed, particularly as I had to shoot the injured goatling to put it out of its misery. Fortunately there was no damage to the vehicle or else I would have been liable.

A careless driver can run over a dog and the owner is to blame. On the other hand, according to the highway code, motorists are required to give way to livestock (which means driving cautiously past them or else stopping). The criteria appears to be whether or not the animals are under control (i.e. somebody is with them, herding sheep, cattle or goats) but there is no knowing how a court's decision may go. So be on the safe side and take out an insurance.

126

PART THREE: ORGANIC GROWING

CHAPTER FOURTEEN

Organic Growing

Why organic?

Few people today are unaware of the perils of chemical farming however much the agrochemical companies attempt to reassure us. The environment, wildlife and mankind has suffered terribly as a result.

I have already quoted the case of hares being killed by paraquat spraying and the dogs which developed cancer as a result of retrieving woodpigeons from laid barley. Those are but two instances amongst thousands. The decline of our partridge population was brought about by insecticides which destroyed their food. Possibly the most horrific of all was the introduction of myxomatosis, almost the entire coney population suffering an agonising death.

More and more ghastly chemicals were introduced, including the infamous DDT which, incidentally, is *not* banned in this country; only its *manufacture* is prohibited, it can still be imported from abroad and used.

Farmers were indoctrinated into using chemical herbicides and insecticides. We are familiar with the expression 'acceptable levels' in relation to toxic content but in reality no poisonous substance is acceptable.

Worse was to come. The farming community developed an obsession with weeds, the term 'weed' simply meaning a plant that grows somewhere where it should not! Labour could be reduced if chemicals prevented weed growth, apparently it was preferable for a farm worker to be made redundant and draw social security than to have him hoeing the fields. The fact that the crops were contaminated as a result was incidental; so long as they *looked* right, were the correct shape and size and colour, never mind if they were flavourless and harmful to the consumer.

Livestock, too, could be reared on chemicals, confined indoors and deprived of their freedom, but the criteria was the appearance and bulk of meat.

Lone voices in the wilderness protested but their cries went unheard or unheeded. Until a few years ago when everybody woke up to what was happening. I remember in my home town when mothers with babies under six months old were being supplied with bottled water because excess nitrates had infiltrated the natural supply. Only public opinion could stem this agrochemical mania. A few, like ourselves, made their personal protests in a practical and positive way. They found themselves a patch of land and began growing their food in the natural way, used good old fashioned muck and compost to feed it, avoided all artificial methods. It wasn't easy, no man can become an island. We have a friend who runs a demonstration vegetable garden in the heart of London; crops are produced but they are inedible because of the lead content from traffic. Even we, remote as we are, cannot altogether escape 'spray drift', that poisonous invisible chemical cloud which floats on the wind when a neighbouring farmer persists with chemical spraying and proclaims that 'you can't farm without it', a rhetoric that is as worn and tired as it is false.

Nevertheless, such as ourselves have made a valuable contribution towards organic farming's return, however small, and now the swing away from chemicals has begun. Is it too late? Only time will tell. Our wildlife has suffered, our domestic stock sicken because the valuable herbs have been sprayed out of the pasture, the minerals and trace elements reduced. Cancer-causing sprays which are already banned in the United States of America and other foreign countries are still permitted here. Why? For the same reason that tobacco has not been banned as a harmful drug. *Money*

However, organic growing is not simply an avoidance of all chemicals on the land, there is a great deal more to it if we are to produce crops of equal quantity and quality to the commercial sham. We are also interested in healthy eating and that stems right from basic farming. Let us look at the various methods by which we can attain a high standard of vegetables, rich in vitamins and flavour, a reminder of the days when Man still respected the land which provided him with life.

The no-digging/no-rotovating system

Why does the average grower dig, rotovate or plough? Basically it is a means of clearing the ground in preparation for planting or sowing, nothing else. It does not improve the soil, just the reverse, in fact. Even the dreaded commercial farmer does not plough his chemical fertilizer in, he spreads it on the top and leaves the rest to the rain.

The real gardeners of the soil are the *worms*. They tunnel through the ground, aerate it, and then along comes the digger and destroys all their valuable work. So by working the soil we are harming it, doing something which is not beneficial to good crop growing.

What then is the answer?

The answer is to mulch and to grow all our crops in that mulch, adding fresh manure and compost each season until we have a build-up of the finest propogation material available. Now let us look at a few ways in which we can successfully mulch.

1. *grass-cuttings and shredded newspapers* make one of the finest mulches for the gardener. Grass cuttings alone are fine and can be used straight out of the grass box on the mower and should be spread amongst *growing* crops, onions, carrots whatever. Not only do they feed the plants but they prevent weed growth and save an awful lot of hoeing. For longer term use, i.e. a bed in which to sow directly into, they should be mixed with shredded newspapers in a compost bin and left to rot, watered regularly to speed up the process. Use newspapers in preference to glossy magazines, the latter are very slow to decompose.

2. *thin* layers of newspapers, three sheets at the most, spread over the ground and then covered with grass cuttings. The paper will soon rot and you can plant straight through it and leave it to assist in restricting weed growth.

3. black polythene. This is possibly the finest material for restricting weeds; the ground beneath it will be completely weed-free. However, you need a liberal layer of compost, six inches at the most, beneath it, and in order to plant your crops you need to cut holes in the polythene. It is a favourite for growing potatoes in.

4. cardboard. I prefer this to polythene; there is an abundance of it available and, unlike the latter, you do not need to remove it after harvesting. Simply lay sheets of cardboard on the ground, weight them down with either stones or soil, and when you come to plant you do not need to cut holes for the rain will have softened it enough for you to push a dibber or a trowel straight through it. Also you can mulch in the same way around fruit trees; this helps to retain the moisture during dry weather.

5. leaf-mould. My own experiences in making leaf-mould have been arrived at by trial and error. I use the leaf sweepings off the lawn in the autumn but have found that it is essential to bag them in *black* plastic bags, fastened securely with a wire tie. Coloured plastic does not work, when you come to use the contents they are virtually in the same state as when you bagged them. Wet leaves

131

are essential, if the autumn is a dry one then you need to water them.

6. green manure. The seed can be purchased from most seed merchants but I do not use this method as the resulting growth needs to be dug into the soil.

7. manure. Every organic gardener needs manure and the small-holder should have enough from his livestock. It needs to be well rotted before use. I rot it in a bin made from four pallets which enables it to ventilate and decompose quickly. In addition I cover the top with old carpets which promotes heat and consequently aids rotting. Any manure will suffice, we use both poultry and goat and donkey.

8. hay. Hay is fine to mulch such crops as potatoes which need protecting from late frosts once they come through because when you have mulched with either polythene or cardboard you cannot ridge them.

9. comfrey. We shall deal in greater detail in the herbs section on comfrey but suffice to say it is one of the finest manures/mulches there is. No garden, allotment or smallholding should be without a crop of comfrey. You can cut it, spread it on the ground green and let it rot in, or else compost it in a plastic bin half-filled with water and use it as a liquid manure. The results have to be seen to be believed.

10. seaweed fertilisers: calcified seaweed and seaweed meal. Although this is expensive in relation to the other home-made mulches and fertilisers, I consider it well worth the money where a new garden is concerned. Applied at the rate of one ounce per square yard it revitalises tired soil, possibly where there has only been pasture before, such as ours was. Also I have noticed a considerable decline in the slug population when I have used it.

Making your own insecticides

For some years now I have successfully prepared our own insecticides. Garlic is my favourite: cut up two or three corms of garlic and steep them in boiling water, leave them there until the water cools. Then transfer the liquid into bottles for future use. Apply with a hand-sprayer on a windless day, soak the vegetation thoroughly. I have treated carrot-fly, blackfly and greenfly with this pungent-smelling mixture. Of course, a shower of rain will wash it away which is why you need to consult a weather forecast before applying (I detest the word 'spraying'!). A good dose of this on your crops will deter most pests.

Another alternative is Quassia Chips, the pungent bark of a South American tree, I believe. Prepare it and use it in the same way as your garlic insecticide. It can be purchased from the Henry Doubleday Research Association at Ryton-on-Dunsmore, Coventry CV8 3LG. More about this indispensable organisation later.

From the same source you can buy Fertosan, an organic slug killer. It is very effective but a shower of rain will wash it into the soil and render it useless. I prefer to use soot; when you sweep your chimney store the soot somewhere for later use and when you are troubled by marauding slugs sprinkle some around your plants. It acts as a very effective protective barrier.

Raised beds

When we first moved to Black Hill we had no garden, the unkempt grass straggled right up to the front door. Our first task was to persuade a farmer to plough up the ground so that we could cultivate it. After that we embarked upon reasonably conventional gardening with extreme difficulty for the land was very stony. Each spring a retired farmer used to call with his rotovator and cultivate the sizeable vegetable patch for us, an annual tradition that only terminated with his death.

Without appearing ungracious this was somewhat of a nuisance because this friendly man would never rotovate until the ground was 'right'. Always having been an early gardener this meant that I often could not commence sowing and planting until the middle of April.

Even though we are 1,200 feet above sea-level I have proved that early sowing is an advantage; many of our neighbours do not begin until the end of April. My theory is that a plant in the wild will go to seed, drop its seeds and the rain will wash them into the soil where they will germinate when they are ready. The same applies to sowing vegetables.

Once a passing gentleman called and asked if I minded if he had a look at our garden because he only lived a mile or so away and our crops were so much more advanced than his. He complimented me upon a superb garden, asked my 'secret' and I told him. He stared in amazement and said 'but you *can't* plant up here before May, nobody does!'

The growing season is short and at a high altitude you must make the most of every week from March to October. One way of forcing early crops, apart from the cold-frame and the greenhouse, is to sow under clear polythene. If some item of furniture comes by carrier it will inevitably be wrapped in a large sheet of clear polythene. Roll this sheet up tightly, heat the poker in the fire, and make a line of closely spaced holes the length of the roll. On unravelling it your sheet will be suitably perforated, enough to allow the rain to water your seeds.

However, after the death of our rotovating friend I decided to go on to the raised-bed system and to make a further growing area in the field. To make your beds simply shovel the soil from where your paths will be onto areas roughly two metres long by one metre wide. Keep the rectangle as neat as possible and build it up about a foot high. Then on this you must mulch with a foot or so of well-rotted compost or manure.

Theoretically beds should face from north to south in order to obtain the maximum sunshine. I number each one with a peg (we have forty-two in all) and keep a plan of them in my 'Growing Book'. This ensures that I know what is planted in each one and it also facilitates crop rotation.

What is the point of raised beds and don't they waste good growing land where the paths are? I am frequently asked this question. The answer is that you plant your seedlings *equidistant* from one another and

The raised-bed system of cultivation

134

Raised beds increase the crop yield and reduce the work

this way you will get a heavier yield. In any case on conventional garden lay-outs you have numerous spaces between rows. Added to the fact that by mulching you have eliminated hoeing and hand-weeding.

As you harvest, pile more mulch onto the beds for it is surprising how they sink. Deposit the ash from your wood-burner on them throughout the winter months and this will also help to improve their quality.

I estimate that I have reduced the organic growing work by two-thirds since the introduction of raised beds. And I can add, with absolute confidence, that there is virtually no physical hard work involved in this method of growing. If there is, then you are doing something wrong!

Organic farming on a commercial basis

The entire farming scene is undergoing drastic changes at the time of writing. We have already discussed how a vast surplus of grain, milk and meat has caused a slump in land prices and has subsequently put many farmers in dire financial straits, forcing them to sell off farmland

135

at low prices. The complete answer is, I have no doubt, a complex one but I am certain that part of the solution lies in a change to organic farming on a commercial scale.

I can already hear wails of dismay from the die-hard chemical farmers. Let us consider first *their* arguments. How can we farm without chemicals when there is a limit on the beef and milk which we can produce, and if we can't keep the cattle how can we provide enough manure to fertilise the fields and grow crops?

Organic farming is not totally manure; there are numerous other fertilisers available. Calcified seaweed and seaweed meal, for instance, and an acre or two of comfrey would provide excellent nutrition for the soil.

But organically our yield will be that much lower.

Agreed, but the price per ton will be higher, and with the removal of subsidies farmers will be producing the required tonnage for a better return. If the subsidy was removed on nitrates then surely this situation would come about naturally.

Where would we market our organically grown grain?

There are plenty of readily available markets. Many of the leading wholefood manufacturers, those producing muesli, muesli bars, whole-wheat bread, would eagerly snap up any organically grown oats and wheat. I know of one farmer who decided to experiment with an acreage recently purchased, some fields which had not seen chemicals for a decade or more. He secured a contract to grow organic oats for a wholefood manufacturer and was assured of selling his entire crop. Additionally he found a market for organic vegetables, a firm who would take the produce direct from the fields.

How can we change to organic farming when our fields have been chemically fertilised for years?

You cannot change overnight, it is a gradual process, but in the meantime these specialist suppliers of organic crops are prepared to accept produce under 'controlled' growing. This means that crops will be grown on that same land with organic fertilisers, but that no chemicals will be used in future and within three years the land will be classified as organic.

There is a natural resistance from many chemical farmers, born of convention, to change. They stubbornly persevere with harmful spraying but the winds of change are blowing. The public are increasingly demanding pesticide-free food and at all levels of commerce it is the demand which dictates the supply. Perhaps the continentals are more aware of this than we British, for we are importing a wide variety of organically-grown produce; fruit, figs and dates, even convenience foods are now being prepared with chemical-free produce.

Let us now consider a few varieties of organic foods available on a commercial basis:

Wheat is in demand from bakers for the making of wholemeal bread. Commercially-packed brands of sliced bread state that 'there's nothing taken out' which is a start but they then go one better and assure us that there are 'no artificial preservatives'. They will certainly be looking to a plentiful supply of organic wheat to be able to offer the discerning customer what he wants. In the meantime smaller bakeries are doing just this. The market is ready and waiting.

Oats is in even greater demand for those who breakfast on muesli and brose, and the many who have forsaken the harmful mid-morning confectionery snack for a muesli bar. It is a growing business; all that is in short supply is organically-grown oats.

Real Meat has been discussed elsewhere in this book and the market is growing. The pioneers have proved that it can be done, and with a reduction in the flesh-eating public, farmers should concentrate on cornering another contracting output and give those customers who still eat meat what they are demanding. There might be a mountain of beef but it isn't organic beef!

Potatoes are our staple diet but the Potato Marketing Board restrict farmers to how many acres they can grow. They are guarding against another 'mountain' but they are also keeping prices up! There would be no necessity for any limit if potatoes were grown organically and the crop would hold its price, due to demand. Everybody would benefit.

The potato crisp manufacturers have long enjoyed a regular demand for their products but now they, like the farmers, are having to make changes. I first became aware of this some years ago when I purchased a packet of instant potato powder, the potatoes having been grown organically in the United States of America. I wondered how long it would be then before crisps 'went organic'. Not very long, and within twenty-five miles of my home a company began producing top quality potato crisps, their potatoes having been grown with 'organically based fertilisers'. Then we saw 'wholewheat crisps' made from wholewheat, corn oil and with 'added sea salt'. Not organically grown wheat (yet!) but at least this company had realised the potential of a market geared towards more healthy eating. Low-fat crisps are being produced on a mass scale and the latest I have seen are jacket potato crisps made from organic potatoes.

137

Surely only the foolish potato grower would ignore such potential. *Vegetables* are not a buoyant market these days as any market-gardener will tell you. The main competitors are the firms selling processed and frozen vegetables. The average housewife limits her kitchen duties to a minimum, and a packet of frozen veg can be taken out of the freezer and be steaming on the plate in a very short time. She cannot be bothered to prepare the fresh variety.

Likewise, the average urban shopper has his or her own idea of how vegetables should look. They must be the right shape and size, and washed! Not for her the near-fresh product with soil clinging to it which actually serves to prolong its life. Much of the vitamin content is destroyed in washing, some of it already having disappeared during the time-lag between harvesting, distributing and retailing. So, in effect, these conventional vegetables have lost most of their goodness long before they are eaten.

So if the housewife demands processed vegetables at least let them be chemical-free! The demand from the large commercial suppliers would be that much greater, and instead of 'fresh' veg withering on the greengrocers' stalls, a large percentage would find their way into pre-packed bags and cold stores. The market-gardener would see an upsurge in his sales and the customers would be getting what they want.

But there is still a market for real fresh organic produce. I have already mentioned the farmer contracted to grow vegetables which the wholesaler bought direct from the fields but in addition to this there are several organic produce warehouses in the large cities which can barely cope with demand.

The change from chemical to organic farming on a large scale will be a slow process but in the meantime the conventional farmer would be prudent to explore the possibilities. Far better to make the change before it is forced upon one, and the stubborn few then find themselves at the rear of the queue.

But essentially this is a book for the smallholder, the small grower, and we must look carefully at his share of the market now, what he must grow and how he can sell it.

CHAPTER FIFTEEN

Which Crops?

Below are listed the varieties which we grow and have found to be successful. As our land is at 1,200 feet then the test has surely been proved.

Asparagus Grow from seed rather than roots, these are expensive to buy. Transplant the seedlings after the first year; it will take three years to establish a mature bed. Use the stems for eating, there is a demand for the ferns for decoration.

Beans:
Runner (Kelvedon Wonder) Early heavy cropper. Sow seeds in cold-frame or greenhouse and plant in position after frosts have finished.
French (Tendergreen) Do.
Daffa. Not seen much these days, a field bean that is generally used for animal fodder but also makes delicious eating. We use them as a vegetable, freezing our entire crop. Very hardy, will withstand the winter.
Broad (Aquadulce) Sown in autumn it will stand a hard winter and this way avoids blackfly. Very prolific cropper.

Beetroot (Crimson Globe) This variety is suitable for early sowing and rarely bolts. A good keeper, it clamps well. Needs watering in dry conditions.

Brassicas:
Cabbage (Greyhound) Sowed outside April–May it is a good autumn cropper.
Cabbage (Savoy) Sow outside April–May for winter use.
Cabbage (January King) Sow May–June, transplant in August for December onwards harvesting.
Cabbage (Red Drumhead) Ideal for winter salads. Sow outdoors

139

February–April, plant out in August for cutting autumn onwards.

Cauliflower (All the Year Round) Sow outdoors in early spring onwards for a succession of cutting from July to October.

Broccoli (Purple Sprouting) Sow outdoors in March, transplant June–July for use the following spring. A good standby when greens are in short supply after the winter.

Brussels Sprouts (Darkmar 21) Sow outdoors in March for transplanting in June for November onwards picking.

Kale (Tall/Dwarf Green Curled) Use the Dwarf variety in windy areas. Sow outdoors March/April for autumn onwards use. Can also be grown for animal fodder. Not a popular seller except in Scotland.

Spring Cabbage Sow in July and plant out in September for cutting the following spring. Eat it young as your first fresh greens of the season.

Carrots

(Early Nantes) April sowing for September harvest or January sowing under polythene for July digging.

(Autumn King) Sow in May for autumn digging.

Carrots should be sown thinly and not thinned out for this lets the carrot-fly into the crop. We leave ours in the ground over winter, they withstand the frost well, better than in clamps. Digging them and storing them in peat or sand is, in my opinion, unnecessary work. If however, a severe spell of weather is imminent, dig enough for a few weeks' supply and layer them between newspapers in a box. They store perfectly this way and when there is a thaw you can begin digging fresh carrots again.

Celery Sow the seed in a pot indoors from February-March and prick out the seedlings. Plant outside in June in trenches fifteen inches wide and nine inches deep, and earth the plants up when they are about nine inches – one foot high when the soil is dry. A paper collar will make blanching easier and prevent the soil from getting between the stalks. The secret of growing good celery is plenty of water and manure.

Cucumber (Pepinex 69 F1) Sow indoors in March, prick the plants out into individual pots and then put in a cold-frame in late May or early June after the frosts are over. Grow the main stems up to three feet, the laterals from fifteen inches. Remove laterals at the first leaf after the fruits are formed. If growing conditions are not ideal it is best to remove some of the embryo fruits to allow about two to each joint. Water well.

Chinese Cabbage (Kasumi F1 Hybrid)   Sow in July for late autumn harvesting. One of the main problems with Chinese Cabbage is that it is inclined to bolt. This is mainly due to either sowing too early or not watering it enough. If you can produce a good crop it will generally sell well.

Courgettes will need to be sown in April indoors and transplanted outside about June after the dangers of frost are past. Give them plenty of manure, see that they are well watered and you should have a little soot around each plant.

Jerusalem Artichokes   These will grow virtually anywhere and can be planted either in the autumn or in February. Once you have established a crop you will never be rid of it! A few tubers will multiply tenfold and are best harvested about November. Use the stalks as fodder for your goats. An acquired taste, Jerusalem Artichokes are an uncertain seller. One year we grew a lot and sent them to market where they fetched twenty pence per pound but it was an awful lot of work washing and netting them for a small reward. A smoky-earthy flavour, they make excellent soup and we sometimes use them as a substitute potato. Our favourite method of cooking is to roast them with pheasant or wild duck. The crop itself is an attraction to pheasants which like to scratch down for the tubers, so even if you can't sell them and don't like eating them, a patch could still be an investment.

Köhl Rabi   Mostly grown as animal fodder, it is also delicious cooked like swede or eaten raw in salads. There is not much demand commercially for this turnip x swede. Sow thinly in the open and do not transplant. Although seed packets may advise sowing as early as March if you wait until May you will probably overcome the bolting problem.

Leeks
  (Goliath)   Sow in March or April for September harvest.
  (Musselburgh)   Sow in April for havesting through the winter. I find that the most successful method of growing is to sow the seeds in boxes in the cold-frame and transplant when they are about three inches high. The secret of 'prize' leeks is to mulch them deeply in order to avoid wastage by leaf and grow thick stems. An

141

invaluable winter vegetable that sells well. Beware – hens will eat the tops if you don't net them!

Lettuce
(Webb's Wonderful) is the most popular variety. Sow early indoors and plant out under cloches. Upturned clear ice-cream cartons make effective and cheap cloches. A good seller if you can grow them early enough but by June most people have their own.
(Winter Density) Begin sowings in June for this more solid kos-type lettuce which will withstand a certain amount of frost and we often cut them right up to Christmas. I have tried planting them in the cold-frame after we have cleared the cucumbers but they never seem to heart well. Not a good seller, my own experience is that the housewife's idea of lettuce is solely the Webb's.

Marrow (Green Bush) I always grow the bush variety in preference to the trailing one because they take up so much less room in the garden. Sow indoors in pots in March and harden off in the cold-frame for a week or so in June before planting outside. Don't be in a hurry – I once lost our entire crop in the cold-frame to frosts in mid-May. A newspaper beneath the lying fruit will prevent them going rotten on wet ground. Plenty of manure and water are essential, also pick off the flowers which do not have a fruit beneath them. Marrows hung up individually in vegetable nets will keep perfectly, right up until the following spring. They sell reasonably well and can mean a small winter income to the grower.

Onions
(Sturon) sets, planted in late February.
(James Long Keeping) seed, sown in February to March in well-manured ground or in the autumn for pulling green. Thin out the seedlings, don't transplant. The secret of keeping onions – harvest when the tops start to bend over, or if they don't in a wet season then don't leave them in the ground after September or they will not keep. Twist the stems off and dry quickly for three days at a temperature of 90°F. Ideally, empty your airing-cupboard and place them on the slats. They will dry very quickly after which time they can be hung up in a frost-free place in nets.

Parsnips (Tender and True) Sow early in March. Parsnips are notoriously slow germinators so sow two seeds together and remove one if both sprout. Ideal under perforated clear polythene. Like carrots, leave them in the ground throughout the winter, digging

142

them as you want them. They are inclined to go wizened if harvested in advance. A fairly good seller.

Peas (Kelvedon Wonder) Sow in early March. We prefer to grow one large crop, harvest and freeze in July, rather than have a succession. They are our staple frozen vegetable. This variety only grows to one and a half feet so is ideal in windswept situations. My method of supporting them is to stick a cane at both ends of the rows and run a length of binder twine from the hay bales across them. It does the trick! Unless you grow peas in large quantities you will have difficulty supplying your own household *and* selling the surplus. If you want to sell peas then perhaps Pick-Your-Own is the best labour-saving way.

Perpetual Spinach Sow thinly outdoors in April. In order to have a continual supply we sow one row each year and leave the previous year's in the ground for pulling until it goes to seed, when it is dug up. A marvellous source of iron yet not popular commercially on a small scale.

Potatoes
(Ninetyfold) Early Plant at the beginning of April under cardboard or black polythene. I always grew this superb variety in my youth but it went off the market in 1960. Then, twenty years later, I found a specialist grower who supplied me with four tubers from which I developed my own Ninetyfold crop.
Captain D. MacLean of Dornock Farm, Crieff, Perthshire grows over three hundred varieties of potatoes on his farm from which he supplies specialist growers who remember what potatoes used to taste like! If there is a variety which you remember from years ago and can't find in the shops then in all probability he will be able to help you.
(Doctor McIntosh) Maincrop Plant towards the end of April for autumn harvesting.
(Pink Fir Apple) Maincrop A beautiful 'waxy' potato, often used in salads but superb for conventional use, it is knobbly in shape, rather resembling a Jerusalem Artichoke. Plant at the end of April.

Watch out for frosts once your potatoes are showing above ground. If you have grown them in the open ground then ridge them up; on raised-beds cover them with either straw or hay, or newspapers weighted down with stones.

Taking your own seed potatoes: keep enough seed back for the following year when you harvest. In the case of old varieties no longer easily obtainable this is essential. You should be able to do this for three years providing no disease afflicts them. If there are signs of blight then cut the tops off and harvest as soon as possible. Lay your seed out in trays in a frost-free place – we keep ours under the bed!

Potatoes for eating should be stored in paper or hessian sacks, *not* plastic as they sweat and go rotten. Check the bags frequently and throw out any bad ones or the rest will soon follow suit. Make sure also that you keep the bags closed because daylight turns potatoes green when they are then unfit for human consumption; eating them in this state can be dangerous.

Pumpkin (Mammoth) Grow as you would marrows except that when planting out they need more room. They will keep perfectly hung up in nets. Delicious to eat, they are not a good seller except around Guy Fawkes' Night when people will buy large ones to make lanterns from.

Radishes (French Breakfast) Easy to grow from March onwards in open ground. Sow thinly and in succession for a continual salad supply. They can also be sown in drills along with slow-maturing seeds, such as parsnips, to mark the rows for the convenience of those who hoe between their vegetables.

Rhubarb Once established all you need to do is to separate the roots every two years so that it does not grow too dense. Plenty of manure, water in dry weather, and if you want an early feed then place an upended bucket over some to force it. It is easily grown from seed, in fact often it seeds itself down. Never put the leaves on a compost heap – lay them to rot amongst their own crop. Ideal for freezing but not a good seller as almost everybody seems to have a clump in their own garden.

Shallots Plant in March along with the rest of the onion crop. Harvest about September. Strangely, my own experience is that it sells better as seed than for eating. Very useful for stews when you have used up all your onions.

Swedes (Acme) For some reason the best swedes are almost always grown in the field as opposed to the garden, even under the same conditions and spacing. There is no hurry to sow; I generally sow about late May, some people leave it another month. Early sowing results in bolting and going to seed. A useful crop both for your animals and the household.

Generally swedes will keep well in the ground. If you find that they are going rotten in the middle then your soil may well have a boron deficiency. I once had this problem and solved it with an application of calcified seaweed. Swedes can be dug up, the tops cut off and stored in bags from December onwards. They are a good seller but only in small quantities. If you keep goats or sheep and cattle then it will pay you better to use swedes for fodder. Cut up a few fresh ones daily for your animals.

Tomato (Amateur) Unless you have a greenhouse you have to make up your mind whether it is worthwhile to grow tomatoes. This variety is, in my opinion, the best outdoor one. Sow indoors in February and as soon as two leaves are showing on the seedlings prick them out into individual pots. Plant outdoors about the middle of June; I usually plant them on the end of raised beds growing other crops and stake them and leave them to it, apart from watering in dry weather. I have found that those planted outside always do better than the ones on the windowsill. You cannot do better than to use your own liquid comfrey manure for feeding them. Those that are still green by the end of September will ripen if you pick them and lay them out on newspapers. If you want to go in for tomatoes commercially then you will definitely need to invest in a greenhouse.

One recurring problem I have had with tomatoes is what I term 'horticultural thrombosis'! Everything seems to be going fine, the seedlings look strong and healthy and are growing fast when suddenly, for no apparent reason, they furl like a coiling spring from the top downwards, wither and die. I have consulted local tomato growers but nobody seems to know the cause nor the cure. Sometimes I lose as many as fifty per cent of my young plants in this way.

Turnip (Snowball) These small turnips are delicious if eaten young; old, they are stringy. So you need to sow a few seeds every three weeks from March onwards. They will not keep. Neither does anybody seem interested in buying them, from my experience.

The importance of keeping records

It is important to keep records of all your smallholding activities, most important of all your growing. Without it you will not be able to keep a check on crop-rotation nor to rectify last year's mistakes, such as sowing or planting out at the wrong time. I have always kept a 'Growing Book', meticulously recording each crop, a numbered plan of raised beds, and a sowing and harvesting schedule. This has been my 'bible' over the seasons, adding information to it year by year.

I feel that it would be a help to the reader, particularly the novice, if I reproduce the parts relevant to crop growing. The exact dates, of course, are flexible to within a week or two, depending upon weather conditions, time available, sickness or health, but I give the dates as a guide; I try and keep to them as far as possible for I am a firm believer in a calendar and not putting off until tomorrow what you could well have done today.

When to grow – Sowing and harvesting schedule

January
20. Begin re-mulching all raised beds that have been cleared of growing crops.
25. Prepare clear polythene for early growing, perforate any new sheets needed.

February
 3. Re-mulch paths round raised beds with newspapers in preparation for commencing work.
 6. Sow Broad Beans in cold-frame.
23. Muck out poultry and spread manure on raised beds.
24. First lawn mowing, use grass-cuttings to mulch garlic which should be showing well by now.
25. Plant onions and shallotts.
27. Sow tomato seed indoors.

March
 2. Muck out goatsheds and fill-up compost bins.
 4. Sow parsnips and spring onions.
 5. Sow peas, parsely, out of doors. Indoors, in pots, sow marrows, pumpkins and cucumbers.
28. First tomato seedlings should be ready for pricking out.
    Sow in boxes in cold-frame:
        Leeks (Musselburgh)
        Cauliflower (All the Year Round)
        Brussels Sprouts
        Cabbage (Savoy)

146

Cabbage (Greyhound)
Cauliflower (Winter-heading)
Lettuce (Webb's Wonderful)
Broccoli (Purple Sprouting)
Sow indoors – Celery seed
Out of doors:
Early potatoes
Kale (Tall/Dwarf)
Carrots
Radishes (first sowing)

April
11. Sow (out of doors):
Beetroot
Turnip (Snowball) first sowing
Runner Beans in boxes in cold-frame
Sow Courgette seeds indoors
14. Plant out Broad Beans from cold-frame
16. Plant maincrop potatoes
24. Sow carrots (second sowing)
Lettuce (first outdoor sowing)
Radish (second sowing)

May
22. Plant out Runner Bean plants
Transfer cucumber, pumpkin, marrow plants to cold-frame to harden off, put out of doors in a few days
23. Sow swedes and kohl rabi
Begin making liquid comfrey fertiliser
Plant out tomato plants
Sow turnip (Snowball) second sowing
Sow January King Cabbage seed in seed-bed
24. Begin mulching extensively with grass-cuttings around seedlings planted out
Plant out leeks

June
1. Pull first rhubarb
2. Sow carrots (third sowing)
5. Plant out: Cauliflower (All the Year Round)
Cabbage (Greyhound)
Cabbage (Savoy)
Purple Sprouting Broccoli

147

Tall/Dwarf Curled Kale
Brussels Sprouts
6. Plant out pumpkins, marrows, courgettes
Top up comfrey compost
Spread last autumn's leafmould
10. Plant out lettuce plants and celery
Turnips (Snowball) third sowing
13. Carrots (final sowing)
Make hay from road verges for goats
16. Dig up last year's perpetual spinach
26. Thin swedes and kohl rabi
27. Sow: Chinese Cabbage
Lettuce (Winter Density)

July
6. Pinch tops off Broad Beans and Daffa Beans
De-frost the freezer in preparation for the coming harvest
Sow radishes (third sowing)
10. Cut any garden hawthorn hedges. By trimming now you will not
have to touch them again for the rest of the year
12. Plant out Cabbages (January King)
Buy in hay for winter now if you don't have enough of your own
13. Broad Bean harvest
18. Sow: Spring Cabbage
Lettuce (Winter Density)
Top-up liquid comfrey fertiliser again
20. Dig first boiling of new potatoes
22. Pick first lot of raspberries

August
5. Harvest Daffa Beans
Begin picking Redcurrants and Blackcurrants
Raspberry picking should be in full swing now
Soft fruit needs to be picked daily from now onwards as it ripens
7. Kohl Rabi should be ready for harvesting now
8. Begin picking gooseberries
9. Trim conifers/garlic trees where they are used as a windbreak
round vegetable growing areas (not spruce trees)
Harvest garlic and hang in an airy place to dry before taking indoors
Dig first lot of carrots
17. Prick out Winter Density lettuce
20. Take early potato seed and store in open trays
23. Begin feeding pond to encourage wild duck

26. Harvest beetroot for pickling and freezing
26. Loosen onions gently with fork to speed up ripening
29. Plant out Spring Cabbage
    Sow Daffa Beans for following year
    Cauliflowers should be ready by now
30. Prune raspberry canes, remove old wood

September
 1. Bring garlic indoors to dry before early autumnal mists begin
 4. Lift onions and shallotts. Dry off onions for three days at 90°F
 6. Harvest maincrop potatoes if tops have died down, leave them to
    dry out in the sunshine
 7. Bag up potatoes and store them indoors
    Cut down Jerusalem Artichoke tops and give to goats
    Take maincrop potato seed and lay them out in trays
 8. Runner bean harvest should be at its peak now
    Watch marrows and pumpkins carefully for signs of over-ripening.
    If in doubt, pick and store by hanging up in vegetable nets

October
 1. Pick apples *providing the pips are brown*. Pick plums
    Apply fruit-tree grease to fruit trees
 4. Apply dressing of calcified seaweed to raised beds that are clear
 8. Pick last of Chinese leaves
15. Plant next year's garlic crop
18. Make blackberry wine and pick sloes for sloe gin
20. Pick elderberries for wine-making

November
 8. Leaf-sweeping, make bags of leaf-mould
14. Cut down last of fennel and give to goats
19. Send next year's seed-order off
24. Plant comfrey
    General tidying-up of garden

December
 6. Get up swedes and store in bags in cool, dry place
24. Pick sprouts for Christmas, kill and dress turkey

This is by no means a complete list of jobs but rather a guide to the
basics. Whatever branch of farming you are in then a *routine* is the secret
of success; not a boring routine but rather a systematic approach. Don't
trust your memory, write out a list until you become used to the round
of annual jobs.

All our seeds are purchased from Chase Organics, Coombelands House, Addlestone, Weybridge KT15 1HY. As we are an organic smallholding we feel that we might as well begin with organic seed, not that I honestly think that it makes much difference prior to germination. Nevertheless they are good seeds, we have had excellent results and have been able to buy a few of the good old varieties which other firms have discarded in favour of more prolific yet less flavourful hybrid varieties.

Annual growing report

As well as just keeping records it is well worthwhile going to the trouble of writing up an annual report on individual crops, how they fared in relation to the climatic conditions etc. This, combined with a plan of your growing area, will often show up mistakes, you will see where you went wrong last year and ensure that it does not happen again. And, in any case, it is nice to have something to look back upon rather than just hazy memories in years to come.

CHAPTER SIXTEEN

Herbs for Health

Herbs are the oldest medicine known to Man. For centuries innumerable ailments have been successfully treated with plants from the wild but the advent of modern medicine over-shadowed them, reduced them to the remedy of the 'quack'. Yet many of our drugs today have been derived from simple herbs but scientists have learned how to produce them synthetically.

In recent years there has been a revival in natural medicines. Long-forgotten herbs were resurrected, offered for sale in a variety of forms by health-food shops; tablets, powders, liquids, booklets listing ailments and their herbal treatment. Our family has always supported natural medicines. This does not mean that we dismiss modern drugs altogether, rather that we regard the old remedies as *complimentary* to that which doctors prescribe. We have had success on more than one occasion, the most notable being the time when we were being urged to have Gavin's tonsils removed but instead opted for homeopathic treatment, and in a matter of a few weeks the problem resolved itself and the need for surgery no longer existed.

I make no extraordinary claims, except perhaps in the case of garlic and comfrey, only to state that herbs have worked for us and many of our friends. Whatever the extent of your land you should never be without a small herb garden. Unlike other growing areas it needs a minimum of attention, mostly prefers poor soil and will reward you tenfold both in culinary and medicinal plants.

Setting up a herb garden

My advice to the reader is to peruse a good herb book and to find out about the various plants. Some smallholdings specialise in herbs but this is a full-time occupation and will take up a lot of land. You must determine which herbs you need and concentrate on those.

151

Innumerable packets of seeds will result in a huge surplus of plants, more than you will need, and unless you are skilled in herb-growing, and have the necessary knowledge, they will be wasted. Also it will entail an awful lot of work, some will not germinate due to your inexperience and your enthusiasm will wane. Far better to compile a list of those varieties which you would like to grow and then visit a good herb nursery and purchase the plants. You can then set out your garden accordingly; some herbs prefer shade, others sunlight, and it is important to site them according to their needs to obtain the best results. The last thing you want is a tangled undergrowth, most of which when they reach maturity you are unable to identify.

When I started our herb garden I designated a particular patch of ground, designed it much in the same way as a raised bed except that I did not mulch it for, as already stated, most herbs prefer poor soil. I bought something in the region of fifty plants and marked each variety, recording them in the 'Growing Book' so that there would be no identification problems. Keep the area weed-free, you can mulch it with cardboard if you so wish for this purpose but otherwise there should be a minimum of compost and manure.

Preferably the herb garden should be in close proximity to the house for those plants needed for flavouring can then be snipped at a moment's notice when the lady of the house is in the course of preparing dishes. Believe me, most foods are enhanced in flavour by the addition of a small amount of herbs; even if the herbs themselves go virtually unnoticed, the taste of the food will be improved.

Selling herbs

I know more than one grower who considerably subsidises his small-holding income from herbs. Indeed, we ourselves sell quite a lot of surplus, but if you are intending to grow herbs for selling then, like the tomato-grower, you need a greenhouse and a number of cold-frames for hardening off.

Next time you go into town take stock of those shops who sell potted herbs. It may be a health or wholefood shop which has a rack of them in the doorway or out on the street, even a petrol station with a sideline in plants. Mostly these traders have a friend who grows them and they take a few plants to oblige him. So look for your own market. Perhaps the village shop might care to give them a try on a sale-or-return basis. Put a few on the produce stall at your local garden fête and even if you derive no income from them your pots have your name on them and you are starting to establish a reputation. *But send your best stock*, a few straggling plants that ought to be thrown on the compost heap will not give you the reputation you are seeking.

Packaging is very important. Margarine tubs with holes bored in the bottom for drainage with a red hot poker are handy for your own use, but they do not look *professional*. Black polythene containers are best, are cheap to buy and come folded flat. Use a plastic marker to identify the species and put your name on as well. You can use your own soil, fine by riddling or molesoil and produce a product which will tempt the casual browser. With a revival in natural gardening many housewives who enjoy pottering in their small patch will buy herbs rather than bedding-out plants, preferring an unusual perennial rather than a conventional annual which requires taking out again in the autumn.

Make a list of your herbs, type up a 'catalogue' and have a few photocopied; it gives that added professional touch. With each variety give a brief guide to their uses, whether culinary or medicinal *but don't make any outrageous claims*. Today there are a few practising medicinal herbalists who rely solely on herbal remedies for ailments so leave that to them.

Herb 'teas' are also very popular. Health food shops sell innumerable varieties and these specially prepared and packeted beverages provide endless delightful flavours. We drink herb teas mostly during the summer months, they are delightfully refreshing and contain neither caffein nor tannin.

You could try an advertisment or two, either in your local paper or a card in a shop window. A sign at the gate might bring in the odd passer-by but really the best method is to persuade a shop to take them. Sales will be slow at the outset, you need to be patient. Once again, you must not take account of your labour when costing your enterprise. You will spend hours pricking out, potting, watering but apart from your time there is a good profit margin. A packet of seeds will cost on average around fifty pence and may produce up to a hundred plants. Plants sell at anything from thirty pence to ninety pence but don't be greedy. Don't price yourself out of the market, neither undersell. Rather go for a middle price; better to sell a dozen herb plants at forty pence rather than three at seventy-five pence. Your production costs will have been the same and you don't want to be left with waste.

Herbs are invaluable to the organic smallholder with livestock. Modern farming has destroyed many of the medicinal plants so vital to good health from pastureland. Now is your chance to rectify that balance with your own animals. Most days I pick a few handfuls of comfrey, marjoram, borage, lavender, etc., to add to the goats' buckets of concentrates. A corm of garlic cut up is a prevention against worms. The benefits are many.

In recent years Tara has become our herb specialist. It is her chosen field on the smallholding and consequently we have been only too happy for her to take over this section of our growing. The following list of herbs has been compiled with her knowledge and expertise, both for our own use and for supplying our customers. It is by no means complete but we have endeavoured to grow those herbs which are most beneficial to the organic farmer as well as a commercial enterprise. The choice of varieties covers *our* needs and should suit the reader who is attempting to build-up a smallholding on the same basis as our own.

Bergamot Makes a delicious beverage, either using the leaves fresh or dried but if drying then do so in a dark place for it preserves the colour and gives a better appearance. The fresh leaves can also be chopped up and used in salads.

Borage Is one of the most colourful of all herbs with its sky-blue flowers and dark centre. The flowers are beneficial in salads as they contain mineral salts and vitamins. If you keep bees then Borage is a must for they love it. It grows up to three feet tall and spreads so that it has to be kept in check otherwise it will take over the herb garden. It also makes delicious tea and if you have a surplus your goats will eat it ravenously. The dried flowers are often used in pot-pourris. When gathered it takes a long time to dry.

Basil Loves a sheltered, sunny site. Once it begins to flower cut it back and dry the foliage. It adds flavouring to soups, meat, eggs, fish and cheese. It contains valuable mineral salts which sharpen the appetite. A few leaves chopped and used with vegetable oil will often relieve constipation.

Caraway We are all familiar with caraway cake, that delicious bake loaded with flavoured seeds. The plant should be pruned in the autumn and allowed to seed itself down. For taking the seed out cut off the plant and hang up in a dry place. Once dried, shake the seeds off and store in airtight containers. As the plant grows tall it may need support. The roots can be used as a vegetable and the seeds made into a beverage to aid digestion.

Chamomile Needs a dry, sunny place. The flowers can be used as a tea to aid digestion, soothes sore gums and mouth ulcers and can also be used as a rinse for *fair* hair. Make an infusion and inhale to relieve a heavy cold.

Chervil   Chervil can resemble chickweed in appearance and it spreads with an equally prolific growth as we found out the first season we grew it! It is rich in minerals, salts and vitamins A and C, iron and magnesium. For use in salads, soups and sauces. It is an annual yet seeds itself down so that it has to be kept in check otherwise, like borage, it will overgrow everything else in the herb garden and spread into the vegetable patch and borders as well. It can also be made into tea where it has blood-cleansing qualities.

Chives   Need a richer soil so spread a little compost around them. Another herb that needs some nourishment otherwise the tips of the leaves turn brown. A partly-shaded position is best; the clumps need to be divided in the autumn. Complimentary to onions, chives are superb in salads or soups as well as having other culinary uses. They contain vitamins A, B and C. They are of benefit to anybody with high blood pressure.

Comfrey   Next to garlic, I rate comfrey the most important plant in the garden. Its uses are numerous; it can be used in composting, as a liquid fertiliser or as fodder for goats. Known as 'knit-bone' it can be made into a poultice and used for bone or muscle injuries; Rowan once had a sprained wrist which was cured overnight in this way. It is also a good salad herb and can be made into comfrey tea. We dry the leaves in the autumn, shred them and store them for this purrpose. If drunk with a little milk it is sometimes difficult to tell the difference between this beneficial beverage and conventional tea.

Once comfrey becomes established you have got it for ever! It puts down roots up to three feet long and separating them entails a major excavation job! Regarding its many medicinal properties, I would add that when our ageing labrador, Simon, got to fifteen he began to be troubled with arthritis. I started giving him four comfrey tablets a day and within a matter of weeks his limbs were restored to reasonable flexibility, a condition which continued up until his death at seventeen.

For detailed information on comfrey, readers should contact the Henry Doubleday Research Association at Ryton-on-Dunsmore, Coventry, CV8 3LG. Henry Doubleday, whom the association was named after, was the pioneer in comfrey in this country.

If you have any spare ground then plant some Russian comfrey on it and use the surplus as either animal fodder or compost.

Dill   Likes a sunny position but needs watering in dry weather or else it will bolt. An aromatic ferny plant, it is a relative of fennel, and may even cross-pollinate with the latter if grown too close to it. The leaves

155

are best picked just before the plant flowers and then hung up to dry. The seeds are ideal with fish or in soups, and have a similar flavour to caraway.

Endives This small plant with rich green curly leaves contains valuable mineral salts and has small amounts of vitamins A, B1, B6, C and E. We sometimes use it as a substitute for lettuce in salads or together with it. The seed should be sown in drills each spring and thinned out to six inches apart; it does not transplant well. Sow again in mid-summer for successive pickings.

Fennel An aromatic tall herb which is decorative as well as having many culinary uses. It is exceedingly rich in minerals and vitamins. Dry the leaves and make into tea in order to benefit from its blood-cleansing properties; it also aids digestion. It makes a soothing eyebath; allow the brew to cool and bathe an inflammatory eye with it.

We use it regularly in salads and flavour fish with it. It can also be added to egg and meat dishes. We always seem to have self-set fennel plants appearing in the garden during the summer months and rather than waste these we dig them up and supply them to various friends and neighbours. Goats are exceedingly fond of fennel.

Feverfew Feverfew is often to be found growing on old stone walls or in some shady corner of the garden where the soil is poor. Its leaves are bitter to the taste but are reputed to be a cure for migraine. As it is not particularly palatable, put a leaf or two in a sandwich to mask its flavour and take daily. Like most herbs, one needs a build-up of them in one's system in order to benefit from them. I know a man who claims that feverfew eases his arthritis.

Garlic *The most important crop grown on our smallholding.* I eat a clove raw every day, usually for supper in a sandwich of peanut butter. I can state quite caterogically that I seldom have a bad cold, the viruses I pick up usually affect me only mildly. Garlic was used during the Plague of London to ward off disease, and long before that when the Roman legions went on their lengthy marches they never went without their garlic. Use it liberally in salads and cooking, make your own insecticides from it as I have already explained, and if you believe in vampires then hang some garlic over the doorway! A powerful panacea, it has a remarkable range of nutritional and medicinal properties.

Garlic likes a long growing season and does not mind the cold and wet. We usually plant about November for harvesting the following August. The bulbs should be hung up to dry in a well-ventilated place and will keep through until the next year's crop is ready. Always keep a few back for seed. I repeat, garlic is the most beneficial plant grown on our holding.

Lavender This aromatic herb is used in pot-pourris and almost everybody is familiar with its scent. Unless it is cut back each autumn it is inclined to become too overgrown. Goats adore it and if anything it improves the flavour of the milk, giving a delicate, almost indiscernible tang which possibly only the connoisseur will recognise. Lavender grows better from cuttings than seed but is better in poor soil.

Lemon Balm If you want your garden pleasantly scented then grow a clump of lemon balm. This hardy perennial makes a delicious drink, just put a few fresh leaves in the teapot, top up with boiling water and allow to infuse for a few minutes. If you prefer it cold then put the infusion in the fridge and serve chilled. The leaves can be dried and stored and will add to the flavour of game birds and fish. I have heard of people using it in their baths as a deodorant, it is also beneficial to the skin, and supposedly induces relaxation if drunk in the manner already described.

Lovage This perennial can grow up to seven feet tall but needs plenty of moisture. The flowerheads need to be cut to encourage foliage growth. It can be used in salads and has many of the properties of lemon balm although its flavour is different, more like strong celery. The roots can be cooked as a vegetable and the seeds used in sauces and soups.

Marjoram (Golden) This herb has many uses, primarily as a tea which eases sore throats and stimulates the appetite. It is also used to flavour sauces and soups. I generally give the goats a handful every so often as they love it and will often sort it out first from a mixture of herbs.

Mint There are three main mint flavours in our herb garden, Ginger, Apple and the common variety. Peppermint I will deal with separately. Almost everybody is familiar with the common mint used primarily in mint sauce and to flavour new potatoes. Ginger mint has the flavour implied in its name and Apple is also distinctive. All three make ideal teas, either fresh or dried for out-of-season use. They aid digestion and leave a pleasant tang on the palate. However, they need separating in the autumn or else they will spread across the garden.

Nasturtium Few people realise how palatable nasturtium leaves are. We use them in salads and sometimes on their own in sandwiches. The seeds can be used as a substitute for capers. The dried flowers are sometimes used in pot-pourris.

Parsley Who would be without parsley in their garden either to make parsley sauce or to flavour new potatoes? A garnish for many dishes it can also be infused and drunk. It contains iron and for this reason I feed a handful periodically to the goats. Surprisingly it can withstand severe weather although it is primarily an annual but one winter I dug down through a foot of snow to pick some leaves.

Peppermint My favourite herb tea, preferably fresh, two or three leaves picked seconds before infusion, but it also dries very well and can be stored. Don't let it grow straggly, cut it back frequently and it will bush.

Rosemary Basically used as a flavouring for both savoury and sweet dishes. It also makes excellent jelly which is delicious with lamb. Sweet-scented, it can also be used in pot-pourris. It can be grown in containers indoors as well as outdoors but needs cutting back.

Sage Traditionally used with onion stuffing so why not save money and make your own instead of buying the packeted variety? This herb has a multitude of uses, as a hair tonic, for flavouring fruit drinks or in sachets in the bath. It requires digging up and dividing about every three years.

Sorrel (French) This herb is related to the dock and has larger leaves than the wild sheep sorrel. The young leaves should be used only in spring before they become bitter when they have a lemon flavour and are refreshing in salads at a time of the year when few salad crops are available. It is rich in oxalic acid, and if it grows in abundance from its own seed then it is a sign that the soil needs lime. So if it is found growing wild anywhere other than the herb garden add a sprinkling of lime to the soil.

Stonecrop A green creeping plant with round squelchy leaves, it is usually found covering old stone walls. It likes sour ground. Years ago I dug up some which was growing in my mother's garden and planted it here; we now have an abundance. Although it is reputedly used for cancers and tumours I grow it primarily as ground-cover in the flower borders. It spreads, has a pleasant appearance, and saves an awful lot of weeding!

Tarragon Useful for flavouring savoury foods, particularly Jerusalem Artichokes which on their own may be too 'earthy' for those still to acquire the taste. Tarragon can also be used in egg dishes, and in herb butter.

Welsh Onions This herb is invaluable, the tubers growing on top of the leaves and are ideal for stews and soups. A crop close to the kitchen is handy for a last-minute decision to add onion flavouring. Much milder than onion in taste and more acceptable to some people. They can also be grown in containers indoors.

Woodruff This herb really likes the shade, in fact it will do no good at all if exposed to hot sunshine. In a flower border it has all its requirements and is excellent ground-cover. Some people like it in ice-cream and desserts, it has a smell like new-mown hay when dried, and is occasionally used in pot-pourris. Ours is in the herb garden because a few years ago a friend gave me a plant; I would not recommend it for anything other than a pleasant scent indoors.

Wormwood Another very useful herb, one which we grow on the edges of many of our raised beds. It is reputedly a garden pest repellant with its strong and bitter scent. I regard it as yet another 'insecticide', one more reason why chemicals should not be used on the land. How effective wormwood is I would not be prepared to say, but certainly its sharp odour is discernible on a balmy summer's evening and that is good enough for me. Grow a plant or two, every little helps in the organic cause.

These are the herbs we grow; there are many, many more but merely to research their use would be to defeat the object of this book. Unless it is the reader's intention to specialise then those which I have listed should be more than adequate for his requirements. A few well-chosen varieties that are used regularly are better than masses of untended ones that waste ground and are allowed to go to waste.

Certainly one's general health will benefit from the regular use of herbs.

159

CHAPTER SEVENTEEN

Fruit and Soft Fruit

Fruit is an important item on the organic smallholding. Like other crops, commercial fruit is heavily sprayed with chemicals. Again, it is the *appearance* which is of prime importance to the large fruit farms. An apple must look shiny as though it has been polished, it must also be preserved. Much of our fruit outside the season is imported and it is anybody's guess how many different kinds of insecticides and fungicides have been sprayed on it in foreign countries. So the grower is advised to produce as much of his own fruit as possible.

However exposed and windswept your land is there is sure to be a corner somewhere where you can grow a fruit tree or two. When we first came to Black Hill we had no cover whatsoever but I was determined to plant some fruit trees and bushes; the sooner they are established the better. You can always plant a few conifers as a windbreak around them even if it means waiting a few years until you reap your first harvest. The longer you leave it, the longer it will be before you have any of your own fruit.

Always buy good stock. Cheap trees or bushes will yield poorly and may develop all kinds of disease. I would always go for the bush varieties as opposed to standards or half-standards. They will not be so vulnerable to high winds, which can batter them and disturb the roots, and also harvesting will be that much easier. November is the best month for planting.

Space them liberally, they look small when you buy them but in a few years you could find them over-crowding and the yield will be less. When we lived in a suburban area with only a relatively small back garden I planted several bush trees which matured within three years and fruited superbly.

Ensure that the hole you dig is deep enough for the roots to spread out and stake the trees firmly. When staking, rather than tie a length of baler twine directly onto the trunk, use a length of old bicycle tyre to prevent the string from cutting into the bark for this will encourage disease. If any of the branches have had to be pruned to aid transportation (I had this problem once when I went to collect some trees and they would not fit in the back of the estate car) then dab a little bitumastic paint on the end of the cut branches to seal them.

Towards the end of September treat the trunks with a liberal application of fruit tree grease to prevent the grubs crawling up into the tree and lying there in readiness for spring. My method of pruning is to cut off any branches that straggle, to give the tree a *compact* appearance. Ours were barren for five years and then, even at a height of 1,200 feet they began to fruit well. It is important to cut off all suckers.

Apples

For preference I would choose Bramleys (cookers) and Cox's (eaters), two tried and proven varieties. Don't be in too much of a hurry to pick them even though they *look* ready. A good guideline, as already stated, is to test an apple and if the pips are still white then leave it and try another in a week or so. One year I overlooked two or three apples that were 'hiding'; only discovering them by accident a few days after Christmas. They were perfect!

Bramleys should be your stand-by for cooking right up until the end of the spring. The secret is to ensure that they are not bruised during picking and to lay them out carefully in trays in a cool but frost-free room. Some growers wrap their apples individually in tissue paper but I prefer just to lay them out, ensuring that none are touching. Check them weekly, throw out or use any which are starting to go brown. Don't be too fussy about the odd grub-hole – a grub will do you a lot less harm than an application of toxic spray!

Crab apples are fine for making jelly but apart from that they have little use except for the hens to peck at. I would not go to the trouble of planting any but if you have one or two on your land and they are not in the way then make a pot or two of jelly.

Japonicas are another sour apple suitable only for making jelly yet they have the added advantage of attractive flowers and many people grow them for ornamental reasons only. They like a sunny, sheltered position, preferably against a wall. Some years ago a friend gave me a fruit to try. It was decidedly bitter but I kept the pips, dried them and sowed them in a pot in the porch. Out of sixteen pips I successfully grew thirteen Japonica seedlings.

Pears

Again there are only two varieties I would consider; William and

Conference. The former is, in my opinion, the best eating pear of all whilst the latter is a superb keeper and if stored in the same way as your apples will keep until March or April.

I have experimented with growing fruit trees from seed. At the seedling stage this has been very successful with a high rate of germination but it will be many years before I am able to report on the trees themselves. The best fruit trees are obtained from cuttings and grafting.

Plums and Damsons

These are a 'must' if you are a jam or wine-maker. They grow fairly easily without a lot of attention. My choice for plums is Victoria; we have a yellow plum tree but it does not fruit nearly as well as the latter. Once these fruit start to ripen they need to be watched carefully and picked the moment they are ready. At this stage wasps are your worst enemy.

I remember in my boyhood we had a *Damseen* tree at home, growing on top of an old underground air-raid shelter. The fruit were a cross between a plum and a damson and were delicious eating. For some reason the tree died, I remember my father cutting it down one Saturday afternoon and a man called to saw it up into logs. Many years later I chanced to remark to one of our neighbours on Black Hill that I had never been able to find a damseen tree. 'There's a small one growing in our orchard,' he remarked, 'and if you care to dig it up you can have it.'

Eagerly I transplanted this three foot sapling into our own garden. It is now eight feet high but there has never been any fruit on it.

With regard to disease on fruit trees, and we have never had anything more than an odd patch of blight, I spray with Quassia Chips (obtainable from the H.D.R.A.). In all, I just let the fruit trees get on with it themselves and I can't complain about the results!

Blackberries (cultivated; Giant Himalayan)

These are a new introduction to our soft fruit garden. Over recent years we have been disappointed with the crop from the wild. Some years we seem to have so little sun that the blackberries are late ripening and the majority are still red on the briars when they start to go rotten. Or else you get a dry spell during July and August when there is not enough rain to swell the fruit, so that although they ripen they are so small that they are scarcely worth picking. I think that the cultivated variety is the answer to this problem, a luscious fruit which can be watered in dry weather and is close at hand for the harvest. Likewise, a bunch of blackberry-picking weekend tourists will not suddenly arrive and beat you to your favourite patch.

The bushes cost around two pounds each and you won't need many! Plant them in some corner of the garden where there is plenty of sunlight and well away from everything else because once they mature they take up an awful lot of room. They will also provide a good screen and deter all but the most persistent trespassers.

Blackcurrants

Our four blackcurrant bushes are more than sufficient for our needs. Usually we freeze the majority of the crop for use in pies but Jean also makes a very effective blackcurrant vinegar for treatment of coughs. Indeed, we have found it superior to many proprietary brands of cough mixture and for anybody interested in giving it a try the recipe is as follows:

one pound blackcurrants
one pint of white wine vinegar
half a pound honey
one pound raw sugar

Remove the stalks, wash and crush the fruit, cover it with vinegar and leave it in a sealed container for forty-eight hours, shaking it occasionally. Strain through a filter but do not press the blackcurrants. Add honey and sugar and stir slowly. Heat to 175°F. for a quarter of an hour, removing any scum. Warm some bottles, pour in the liquid and seal immediately.

Blackcurrants are a valuable source of vitamin C and should figure in your healthy lifestyle. They take an awful lot of picking but it is a good job for the children in the summer holidays. In the autumn I cut the bushes well back from the paths and this pruning seems adequate.

Gooseberries

We have far more gooseberries than we need. Just prior to our move to Black Hill I called at a garden centre to buy a stock of soft fruit bushes; gooseberry bushes were on sale at one pound each but if I bought a dozen then they would be reduced to seventy-five pence. So I had twelve, they looked so small that I wondered if they would be enough. After some years I had to dig up eight and replant them in the field; they scarcely seemed to notice the move and flourished well.

Nobody seems to want gooseberries. A gate-sign has been ignored for years and we end up filling half the freezer with bags of this fruit at the expense of valuable goats' milk space. We use a few for puddings at weekends and make gooseberry wine but apart from about ten pounds the remainder are surplus. I have even tried giving them away without success; friends either have their own bushes or else they don't like them. In order to use them up we boil them and have them on our muesli for breakfast.

The only problem we have had with our gooseberry bushes is an occasional attack of red spider; this pest, which strips the foliage, seems only to affect our gooseberries and redcurrants (the blackcurrants escape for some unknown reason) and the willow tree on the lawn. I give the affected bushes a liberal application of Quassia Chips and my own garlic insecticide and it seems to do the trick. The children claim that gooseberry picking is much easier when the red spider has cleared the foliage for them!

Raspberries

Raspberries are our favourite soft fruit. A dozen canes served us for eight years with only annual pruning and removing the old growth. Then we replaced them.

Raspberries need to be picked as they ripen, a daily chore especially in wet weather or else they will go to mulch and be wasted. Muck the bushes well in the autumn; we also mulch with newspapers to restrict weedgrowth. Nettles are fond of growing in amongst raspberry canes which can be decidedly unpleasant when picking the fruit.

Eat raspberries fresh and freeze your surplus. If you make jam then use the surplus up that way.

Redcurrants

Except that they have a different flavour, redcurrants are little different from blackcurrants. With one exception for us, Jean makes redcurrant jelly, using raw sugar, for use with poultry and game throughout the year. Watch carefully for the fruit ripening and pick them as soon as they are ready; picking might go on in stages for a fortnight. The birds seem more eager to plunder the red fruit than the black, perhaps it is the bright colour that attracts their attention, like raspberries.

Marketing soft fruit

For the small grower there is very little profit in soft fruit if you take your time into consideration. If anybody requests any redcurrants or blackcurrants then I tell them to come and pick their own. Time yourself and see how long it takes you to pick a pound of either fruit and you will see that it just is not worth it. If any of our friends want any then they are welcome, they come round and help themselves.

Without the children's help even gathering enough for our own needs would barely be possible. Now that they are an integral part of the set-up they are only too willing to assist but a few years ago it was hard work persuading them. Listed below are the stock excuses given for not gathering the small fruit:

1. Gooseberries: they're too prickly.
2. Blackcurrants and redcurrants: they take too long.
3. Raspberries: there are nettles growing in amongst them.

Parental answers to above:

1. Wear gloves, then.
2. Well, pick a few and see how you get on.
3. Hang on a minute and I'll cut the nettles down.

Or, to all three excuses 'you'll need some pocket money for your holiday, won't you?'

Bribery is preferable to forcing them to do an irksome task but more of this on the children's role in the running of a smallholding in a later chapter.

CHAPTER EIGHTEEN

Free Food From the Hedgerows

There is an abundance of free fruit to be gathered from the hedgerows every year, genuine organic produce except that bordering a field of growing crops where you can be sure that it has been well and truly soaked in spray-drift! Personally, I do not favour a roadside harvest; apart from the very real possibility of a farmer's toxic spray on the blackberries or whatever fruit, they have been subjected to petrol and diesel fumes, dust or mud thrown up by passing vehicles according to the weather, and in any case never pick low-growing berries for you never know how many motorists have pulled up at that spot and walked their dogs along the hedge in order to let him do what he has to do!

Always go for the hedges alongside a public footpath or bridle path. Do not trespass on to private land and be conversant with the relevant section of the Wildlife and Countryside Act, 1981. Not that it particularly concerns the genuine blackberry-picker, rather the amateur botanist who might be tempted to dig up a plant by the roots, for which one can be prosecuted. Do not deviate from the task in hand and get yourself into trouble.

At relevant times of the year we conduct a foray away from our own land in search of Nature's harvest, wild fruit that add an extra flavour to our chosen lifestyle. Let us look briefly at the fruits that are to be gathered and how they are best prepared.

I would add that we do not make jam, simply because it is our policy to reduce sugar to an absolute minimum in our diet. Consequently any jam we eat is in fact preserves with no added sugar. Jean has experimented with making preserves using fructose (fruit sugar) quite successfully, but from a cost angle it is as cheap to purchase a reliable brand of the product. We do not need added sugar, least of all refined sugar; there is ample natural sugar in the fruit itself. Likewise, today many varieties of canned fruits are being sweetened with natural juices instead of syrup and this is a move which we, as a family, wholeheartedly support.

Blackberries

There is an old country saying to the effect that one should never gather blackberries in October because 'they have the devil in them'. There is some truth in this because in October, particularly in a wet year, the fruit has begun to go mildewed and might cause stomach ache. However, one has to use one's commonsense, for in an Indian summer blackberries can be at their best in October. A combined family effort can result in enough being gathered in one session to supply their needs.

The fruit should be picked over, washed and used as soon as possible for the object of the exercise is to reap a *fresh* harvest. Blackberries make superb wine and jam and can be frozen whole for pies throughout the winter.

Bilberries ('whinberries' in Wales)

Possibly the most delightful of all wild fruits but very time-consuming to gather. The small bushes grow on heath and moorland often amongst the heather.

Some years ago I made a 'comb' for gathering this fruit in the quickest possible time. I used a tin mug on to which I fixed a dozen or so steel knitting needles about a quarter of an inch apart. By sweeping this comb through the bilberry bushes the fruit is dislodged and falls into the mug. Certainly it works but the snag is that you collect leaves as well. So when gathering bilberries you have a choice; you either gather larger quantities in a short time and then use the time you have saved picking your haul over when you arrive home, or else you carefully gather your bilberries by hand on the moor and take longer over it. So there is no real short cut. I have tried tipping fruit gathered in the comb into a bowl of water so that the foliage floats to the top but the bilberries are inclined to become soggy.

I know people who spend days, sometimes weeks, during July and August gathering this fruit to sell. That's fine if you enjoy picking but smallholders usually have other things to do.

We always enjoy the first bilberry pie of the season, perhaps the total family effort going into one meal. After that we mostly freeze the fruit in containers to use during the winter. On those short dark days the flavour of August bilberries brings a reminder of summer, a taste of fresh wild fruit in the dead of winter. Bilberries also make excellent preserves.

Danger from snakes

There is a very real danger to the bilberry-picker from adders. These reptiles will often lie curled up amongst the bilberry bushes, drowsy on a warm August afternoon. Generally they will only bite if trodden on; most of the time they will slither away to a place of safety at the approach of humans.

In the case of a snake-bite medical attention must be sought immediately. Death from this cause is very rare in this country but if you do get bitten then go straightway to the doctor. I have known one or two people bitten by snakes over the years on Black Hill, an unpleasant experience at the time but all was well that ended well.

Wild gooseberries and raspberries

Both these fruits have a slightly more delicate flavour than their cultivated counterparts yet are usually much smaller. Raspberry canes and gooseberry bushes are often to be found growing in the hedges and for anybody who has not had a good crop in the garden this is their chance to make up the loss.

July and August are the best times for picking although sometimes the fruit is still available in September.

Bullaces and Sloes

The bullace is to the plum as the sloe is to the damson. The bullace tree very much resembles the blackthorn, except that its branches are brown instead of black and it grows much taller than the blackthorn and has less spikey boughs. The Wild Plum itself is very similar but lacks all spines. It is all rather confusing to the amateur but he should have no difficulty in recognising the fruit. All three are of the *prunus* family.

Bullaces can be either black or greenish fruit, the latter much smaller than the former. They are virtually only of use for wine making and should be picked in the autumn.

I never miss gathering my annual two pounds of sloes and have a note in my working schedule to pick these around 23 October. Sloe gin is easily made, rather expensive I'm afraid, but nevertheless it makes a welcome fruity alcoholic drink amidst the customary Christmas booze. My recipe is as follows:

> Two pounds sloes
> Half a cupful of castor sugar
> Two full bottles of gin (vodka is also sometimes used in place of gin; it makes little difference to the flavour)

168

Prick the sloes with a fork after washing them and put them in a demijohn. Add the castor sugar and then pour on the gin. Shake it after corking it, and store in a dark place for this enhances the colour. Shake it once a week and by Christmas the liquid content should have doubled when it can be bottled and is ready for drinking.

Rosehips and rowanberries

Rosehips make a good wine, as do rowanberries, but the latter can also be used for making jelly to eat with meat. Both are the last of the hedgerow harvest, rosehips some years taking a very long time to ripen and sometimes we have gathered them as late as December when there have been few frosts.

Elderflowers and elderberries

Elderflowers should be gathered in the morning when the sun is on them to produce that subtle flavour so important for the delicate taste in a clear white table wine. Elderberries, on the other hand, are seldom ready before the end of October when they turn a ruby red-black. Pick them in bunches and then separate the fruit afterwards – another job for the children! The benefit of leaving those elders growing in your hedge when you come to cut it is that you will harvest two worthwhile wine crops from the bushes – the flowers in May, the fruit in the autumn.

Wine-making

This is not intended to be a guide to wine-making, there are innumerable books available on this subject, far more detailed than I could hope to give in the section designed to whet your palate for the rich harvest which the hedgerows have to offer. However, I offer the reader Jean's four best recipes, those which are firm annual favourites with us, wines which are a delight to drink rather than having to pretend that you like them simply because it is all part of your chosen lifestyle to make wine when, to be truthful, you would sooner sneak off to the local off-licence and buy a bottle of commercial 'plonk'!

These recipes provide us with most of our wine for very little outlay. Obviously ingredients such as yeast have to be bought, we know people who never add raisins as they think they are too expensive and they can get away with leaving them out, but as a result the wines they make will be less full-bodied. Even with bought ingredients, making your own wine gives you extremely cheap country beverages and an awful lot of satisfaction.

One word of warning – it is extremely difficult to keep the brew for the length of time advocated by the recipes – ours rarely last beyond the stated two years!

Blackberry wine

A sweet and full-bodied after-dinner drink.

Six pounds blackberries
Three-quarters pound raisins
One gallon of water
One teaspoonful pectin enzyme
Campden tablets
Two teaspoonfuls citric acid
Half teaspoonful tannin
Yeast and nutrient
Three pounds sugar

Sterilise all equipment.

Wash and crush berries; wash and chop raisins, put berries into large pan (a jam pan is ideal) with water and heat to 176°F/85°C, maintaining temperature for fifteen minutes.

Strain through a fine mesh bag or fine muslin and press dry. Add the raisins, pectin enzyme, one crushed campden tablet and citric acid to the resulting fruit juice. Cover well and leave for twenty-four hours.

If using a hydrometer now is the time to check the specific gravity, add the tannin, activated yeast and yeast nutrient. Ferment on the raisin pulp for five days, stir every day and try to keep the raisins submerged. Cover very closely during this period, a tea towel under the bin lid is one good way to prevent infection if your container lid is not a good fit. Strain out juice, press raisins dry and discard the pulp. Stir in a third of the sugar, pour the must into a fermentation jar and a spare bottle. Fit an airlock to the jar and a plug of cotton wool to the bottle.

Ferment for one week.

Then stir in another one pound of sugar and repeat the process with the remaining pound after a further week. Leave to ferment. Syphon the clearer wine into a sterilised jar, add one crushed campden tablet and top up from the wine in the bottle with the cotton wool plug; it is a good idea to check the wine in the bottle first. Ours has turned to vinegar before now!

If fermentation has completely stopped, bung the jar tight and store until the wine is bright. Syphon into another clean bottle and store for at least one year, two if you can manage it!

Filter if you wish, bottle and keep for a further six months. This wine should not need sweetening but if you wish to you can just before serving. For a drier wine reduce sugar to two pounds and citric acid to one teaspoonful and keep for one year.

Elderberry wine

Three pounds elderberries
One pound raisins
Three pounds sugar
Half ounce citric acid
Yeast and nutrient
Pectic enzyme

Pull the berries off the stalks taking care to remove all green branches and foliage.

Boil one gallon of water, put elderberries in a bowl and crush them and add the chopped or minced raisins.

Add elderberries and raisins to the water and maintain a temperature of 176°F/85°C for fifteen minutes.

Leave to cool.

Strain into a suitable bin, pressing the fruit dry.

Discard the pulp.

Measure specific gravity if using a hydrometer. Add citric acid, one crushed campden tablet and leave for twenty-four hours, covered closely.

The following day add the yeat nutrient, yeast and one third of the sugar.

One week later add another third of the sugar and the following week the remainder. Leave to ferment. Syphon the wine into a sterilised jar and add one crushed campden tablet. If wine has stopped fermenting, bung tight and store. When the wine is bright rack into a clean jar. Store in bulk for two years. This wine improves with age and can be very strong. Bottle and keep for six months before drinking.

Our elderberry wine always turns out dry but of course it can be sweetened before drinking. You can also use four and a half pounds of elderberries for a richer wine, or add bananas and use oranges and lemons instead of powdered citric acid.

Gooseberry wine

A dry white wine.

>Four pounds gooseberries
>One gallon of boiling water
>One teaspoonful of pectic enzyme
>Campden tablets
>Three pounds sugar
>Yeast
>Yeast nutrient

Sterilise all equipment.

Top and tail gooseberries, wash them and put them into a polythene bin. Pour on boiling water and leave to cool. Drain off and reserve the water.

Mash the softened gooseberries with a potato-masher or similar. Return to the water and add one teaspoonful of pectic enzyme and one crushed campden tablet. Cover very securely and leave for two days.

Strain and press the fruit dry.

Measure specific gravity if using a hydrometer. Add the activated yeast and yeast nutrient and stir the sugar into the must.

Pour into a fermentation jar and any excess into a bottle with a plug of cotton wool in the neck. Fit the jar with an airlock and ferment in a warm place. When fermentation is finished move the wine to a cool place for a few days and then syphon into a clean jar. Add one crushed campden tablet.

Bottle after about six months when wine is bright and leave for about one year.

If necessary, as always, wine can be sweetened to taste just before serving. A sweeter wine can also be made by using more gooseberries and slightly more sugar.

Rowanberry and wheat wine

A very strong wine.

One quart of rowanberries
One gallon of boiling water
Three pounds sugar
Half pound wheat
Two tablespoonfuls of raisins
Campden tablets
Yeast and yeast nutrient

Wash rowanberries, remove all stalks and leaves.

Pour the boiling water over the rowanberries in a suitable container and let them stand for five days, stirring every day and crushing the berries.

Strain the liquid onto the sugar, chopped raisins and wheat. Stir well until sugar is dissolved.

Add activated wine yeast and yeast nutrient and leave well covered in a warm place for seven days.

Strain into a fermentation jar and fit airlock, putting any spare liquid into a bottle with a cotton wool plug. Leave until wine is clearer, rack into a clean jar, adding wine from bottle to top up the fermentation jar.

Leave until the wine is bright, then add one crushed campden tablet and bottle after about three months.

This makes a very clear, straw-coloured wine which packs a punch. So beware!

CHAPTER NINETEEN

Healthy Eating

Having built up your smallholding on the lines indicated, produced your own toxic-free vegetables, additive-free meat and organic fruit, it would be pointless to spoil it all by eating a proportion of unhealthy commercial foodstuffs; for nobody can really be one hundred per cent self-sufficient, which is what this book is all about, and we have to rely on the shops for some of our supplies.

I regard bread as the most important food one eats; eat good wholesome bread and you will be healthy, eat the mass-produced white variety and you will not. That is my belief and I began making the family's bread a decade ago, before we moved to Black Hill, because I realised the importance of it.

Bread-making is simple; I have heard farmer's wives who spend most of their time baking cakes and pastries complain that they can never make bread. This baffles me because I never had any problems right from my first attempt. And for those who would like to try their hand then I will give them my recipe; it is neither complicated, nor fancy, but produces a wholesome bread for the family.

> Three pounds wholewheat flour (organically-grown if possible)
> Three teaspoonfuls of dried yeast (I have used fresh but I find the dried equally as good)
> One teaspoonful of honey
> One and a half pints of lukewarm water
> A pinch of sea salt

> Pour the water onto the yeast and honey, leave it for five to ten minutes until it bubbles and froths and then pour it onto your flour.
> Knead until the dough is supple, not too dry and not too sloppy.
> There is no need to 'prove' it twice, once is sufficient.
> Cut in half and put the dough into two loaf tins and leave until

they have risen; it usually takes about an hour, depending upon room temperature.

Bake at 250°C for forty-five minutes.

In order that we have a continual supply of bread I generally bake once a week, one loaf to eat and three to freeze. Then every other week I bake twice so that we have a stock of up to a dozen loaves in the freezer which we use in rotation. Sometimes I make a batch of rolls, using the same recipe but making into rolls instead of loaves.

Recently Tara has taken on the task of bread-making although I also bake to enable us to keep a reserve in the freezer. This is important because a busy smallholder has not always got the time to bake when bread is needed.

I make no stupendous claims about my bread, there are many more and doubtless better recipes, only that it is *real* bread. I cannot understand why somebody came up with the idea of taking the wheat-germ out of flour and manufacturing an inferior variety of bread, less-nourishing, less flavour and minus much of the fibre so necessary to Man's well-being. Fortunately, within these last few years the public has been made aware of the dangers of refined foodstuffs and the current trend is towards natural eating.

Vitamins

In theory, the grower of organic fruit and vegetables should obtain all the vitamins necessary for good health. Unfortunately this is not always the case due to no fault of the organic grower, the blame rests on chemical farming which has eroded many of the natural vitamins, minerals and trace elements in the soil. If these are not in the soil then plant life cannot absorb them to pass on to us, and therefore we must rectify this deficiency in our bodies by supplementing these missing vitamins etc.

In 1977 a Ministry of Agriculture report stated that there were not sufficient deposits of selenium in British soil to supply our needs. With the exception of one small area on the north Norfolk coast where the selenium level is adequate. This village boasts extraordinary longevity; it has several centenarians, there is a waiting list for the local Darby and Joan Club and for several generations life expectancy here has been high. This in itself is proof enough of the benefits of selenium.

In America selenium is the fastest-growing daily food supplement and the USA has a higher content of this trace element in its soil than

Britain! Natural selenium is found in such foods as wholewheat grain, liver, kidneys and fish but little or none in convenience or fast foods.

Nowadays it is possible to buy selenium in tablet form, plus the bonus of containing vitamins A, C and E. I have benefitted from taking one of these tablets daily for some time now.

In addition I have benefitted from a regular intake of Ginseng, the tonic that comes from the East. I also take lecithin tablets daily which is a guard against hardening of the arteries, raw garlic or garlic capsules, and two grams of vitamin C.

Low-fat diets

Man is not a carnivore in spite of propaganda put out by those engaged in the meat trade. They argue that our earliest ancestors lived on several pounds of raw meat a day. Certainly primitive Man ate meat but a large proportion of his diet consisted of nuts and berries. Anthropoids are not meat-eaters either. So we must compromise and call ourselves omnivores.

I do not suggest for one moment that we should become a race of vegetarians overnight; I am sure that a little meat, say once or twice a week, harms nobody but I do think we should pay attention to the type of meat which we eat. Meat should be lean, as low in fat as possible and killed in such a way that the adrenalin is not released into the bloodstream, i.e. slaughtered quickly and painlessly with an absence of *fear*.

Our meat supply comes from the wild in the form of rabbits, pigeons, pheasants etc., but I am not advocating that everybody takes up shooting, that is a matter for personal conscience.

I have already mentioned Philip Hockey of Fordingbridge in relation to organic poultry foods. Philip and Carole Hockey also breed livestock for slaughter free of hormones, implants, growth promoters etc. They supply beef, pork and lamb which have been fed on a chemical-free ration, grazing natural herbages and drinking clear spring water. Only a few beasts are slaughtered each week, this carried out in a private slaughter house in a calm and efficient manner.

Philip and Carole also make their own sausages, patés, faggots and burgers to their own special recipe, all free from chemicals, colourings and added fats. Bacon and gammon, however, must be preserved so brine is used but no colour is added.

This is how meat products should be, free-ranging, fed naturally and killed humanely. The trade will argue that it cannot be done commercially. Of course it can, the Hockeys and others are already proving that.

Wherever possible we use products containing vegetable fat as opposed to animal fat. We ensure that our margarine is polyunsaturated, mostly the sunflower variety and using sunflower oil for cooking.

Sugar

We eat as little sugar as possible and then only *raw* sugar. There used to be a common myth in my boyhood that you loaded sugar (white, of course) onto your breakfast cereal and you ate sticky puddings after every main course to give you energy. Thankfully, due to marvellous coverage by the media on healthy eating habits, this myth has now been exploded.

I have already mentioned the 'no sugar added' varieties of preserves (apparently it is illegal to refer to them as 'jams' unless there is added sugar). Concentrated fruit juices provide adequate healthy sweetners, and cakes and puddings can be sweetened with dried fruit. Neither our Christmas cake nor puddings ever contain sugar. None of our children take sugar in tea or coffee and I can add truthfully that we have not had to work hard on them to get them to do this. Certainly they eat sweets but not in any quantity. Like us, they have discovered the delights of fruit bars from the health food shop and carob instead of chocolate.

A couple of years ago Jean went even further to promote a healthy lifestyle when she took a 'Look After Yourself' course run by the Health Education Authority. She obtained her diploma and now runs courses locally which have been well attended. I joined her first session of courses and, as we expected, I was the only male present. The response from the women was encouraging; farmers' wives who traditionally had served up fatty, sugary meals showed a real willingness to change the diet of their families, albeit deviously. From our experiences it is the menfolk who are the stumbling blocks, who reject a change to healthier foods.

We feel that our own diet compliments our rewarding lifestyle. Wherever possible we eat uncooked foods, plenty of salads during the winter months to provide us with all the vitamins we need, supplemented where necessary, fish and meat that is low in cholesterol, an absence of salt, decaffeinated coffee and herb teas, no sugar or perhaps a little raw sugar sometimes.

177

We are often asked, particularly now that Jean is a registered Look After Yourself instructor with the Health Education Council, to recommend a healthy diet. So one evening we sat down and compiled a list of what we eat and what we avoid. One has to be rather open-minded about the subject unless one wishes to become anti-social or even a hermit, but certainly at home we adhere to the foregoing diet:

No red meat or pork, including sausages, bacon, etc.

Eat poultry, game any *wild* meat because it is low in fat.

Soya substitutes, such as Sosmix makes tasty non-meat sausages. Textured Vegetable Protein can be flavoured and used as a meat substitute, i.e. mince, etc. Or try a NUT ROAST.

No white bread. Eat wholewheat bread, wholewheat crackers and biscuits etc. For baking use eighty-one per cent or eighty-five per cent flour.

No white sugar. Eat *sparingly* raw cane or demerara sugar.

Cheese: avoid processed cheeses, eat cottage cheese, Edam or Quark.

Drink low calorie soft drinks.

Jam/Marmalade. Preserves made with *fruit* sugar. We eat the Whole Earth variety.

Brown rice, spaghetti, etc.

Decaffeinated coffee – we use HAG.

Tea. Herb teas, raspberry leaf, comfrey, etc.

Eggs. No more than three a week!

No butter. Substitute with a low chloresterol marg. Flora, etc.

No salt. Use either salt substitute (Ruthmol) or *Sea Salt*, sparingly.

Substitute CAROB for chocolate. Carob bars or carob flour.

FISH is important. Do not fry. Eat oily fish, herring, mackerel, tuna, etc. AND/OR Maxepa/Lanepa tablets containing fish oil.

GARLIC is probably the most beneficial of all herbs. Raw or in capsule form.

OATMEAL. Oatcakes, oat biscuits prevent fatty residues building up in the arteries. MUESLI is one of the most nourishing of all breakfast cereals.

LECITHIN. Lecigran contains only pure natural soya lecithin, turns fat into energy. One teaspoonful three times daily.

GINSENG. Probably the most beneficial tonic of all. In powder, tablet or elixir form.

VITAMINS. A daily multi-vitamin tablet is useful in preventing any vitamin deficiency. We use GEVETABS.

FRESH FRUIT AND VEGETABLES. Are essential. The latter should only be cooked lightly to retain the vitamins.

SALADS. Very important and can contain almost any raw vegetable. Winter salads are nourishing and beneficial.

Allergies

There is a price to pay, in some cases, for being healthy, a penalty for isolating yourself from mass-produced foodstuffs full of unnecessary additives – *allergies!*

I have had allergies since childhood, clear-cut ones which I can avoid. Strawberries, the doctor informed me the last time I had a nasty bout of stomach illness after inadvertently having had a trickle of the juice of this fruit in a trifle, would in all probability put me in hospital. Any meat from a pig gives me a headache. But as I do not particularly like these foods then I am quite happy to do without them. It is the insidious allergies, the unknown enemy, which catches you out. And all because you have been living on pure foods, additive-free, so that when you eat elsewhere those additives will hit you where it hurts because, without a build-up of them in your system, you are vulnerable. But far better to be so than to have these monstrosities lurking in your body the whole time.

We are a family fraught with allergies. Angus developed asthma and migraines at nine years of age. He dare not eat cheese nor any food that has E102 in it, which is tartrazine, an artificial colouring. Of course, he is allergic to hay as well. Jean shares my allergy to white flour; I also have problems with white sugar. So I just don't eat away from home and if I do I ensure that I go to a bona-fide wholefood restaurant or friends who understand the problem.

179

Dowsing food for additives is a good guide to whether or not a particular foodstuff is harmful to you. We learned dowsing with a pendulum a few years ago; it is easier to master than water-divining although we have had some success in that field as well.

I made my own pendulum from sealing-wax, a very sensitive agent, and the process is relatively simple. You hold the pendulum over the product (if the food is a commercial one then ensure that it is unwrapped or else the wrapping may confuse the pendulum), hold the string between forefinger and thumb and place your free hand on your stomach. Then ask the question – is this food good for me?

After a few seconds you should feel the pendulum begin to move. Relax, let it go its own way. If it moves in a clockwise direction then the answer is 'yes', anti-clockwise is in the negative. On occasions you may find that it swings half-heartedly in a straight line to and from you, which means that it is either unsure or else the food is neither good nor bad for you.

Of course this method is not infallible. The pendulum works on your body electrics, it is not magic! Consequently if you are convinced of what its answer is going to be then you are likely to influence its gyrations. I have met people who are unable to work the pendulum at all, possibly because they doubt it from the outset.

Bear in mind that the pendulum will only give you an answer to a situation which already exists, it cannot forecast future events. So don't think that you can win a fortune on the football pools with its help!

You can either divine water or you can't. You use the same approach, and if you are searching an area then divide that area up into squares and dowse each one. I have also managed, on occasions, to locate missing items in the same way.

It is a fascinating hobby but overall I regard it as a basic guide to discovering whether or not certain foods contain additives which are harmful to me. All the same, if one is invited out to dinner one cannot very well dowse each course at a host's table!

CHAPTER TWENTY

Tree Growing

I once read somewhere that it is the duty of every man to begat a son and to plant a tree. I consider that I have done more than my share on both counts!

Many years ago our steeply sloping smallholding was an oak wood. The trees were felled and the ground put down to pasture. This is but one minute example of what has happened throughout Britain this last half-century. Farmers have seen a way to increase their arable or pasture at the expense of the environment. Trees were only good for firewood in the opinion of many, and we had a 'boom' in wood and hedge clearance to the extent that much of the habitat of the creatures of the wild was destroyed. In reverse, the Forestry Commission were purchasing tracts of upland ground and planting millions of conifers, creating an artificial landscape that offered nothing except shelter to foxes and other vermin species because the undergrowth was stifled beneath the thickly growing branches. There was no compromise.

Thankfully, at last, a balance is in the process of being restored. The Commission are now planting broad-leaved trees on a scale that makes these vast forests less symmetrical and artificial, and many farmers have seen the errors of their ways. Where once they received grants for uprooting hedges and woodland and extending their farmland, they are now being offered grants to replant. It makes sense. I personally know of farmers who regret their tree destruction policy and are now attempting to make amends.

Trees are an integral part of any farm or smallholding, provided of course they are planted in the right place. In the wrong place they will feed on the nutrients in the soil and rob growing crops of sustenance, or else they will shade areas that are dependant upon sunlight for growth.

As described earlier, the gobbling flail-cutter has much to answer for with its destruction of foliage that not only provided birds and beasts of the wild with shelter but also served to provide livestock with cover from the elements. This hedgerow desecration left not only mile upon mile of unsightly hedges throughout Britain but also failed to contain sheep and cattle in fields which they were supposed to graze. So we have straying stock and another unnecessary task for the farmer in rounding them up.

Unfenced woodlands provide valuable sheltering places for cattle and sheep in the depths of winter. But the trees must be mature before this is allowed to happen otherwise saplings will be grazed off.

Wind-breaks

Thickly growing conifers provide the best windbreaks on a farm. They grow quickly and will shelter buildings and arable areas from the elements. Here the grower can obtain a bonus by planting spruce thickly, for within seven or eight years the trees can be thinned and the surplus ones sold as Christmas trees.

The Christmas tree market is an uncertain one. Some years they make good money, other years there is a glut and they are barely worth the labour and cost of transporting to market. The best way for the busy farmer is to sell them 'standing'; a contractor will offer an overall price and he will fell and transport. That way you are guaranteed a fixed sum.

On a smaller scale I would advocate a more ornamental fir tree. The Lelandei is ideal for protecting your garden but they will need trimming annually once they have reached four or five feet in height otherwise they will obstruct the sunlight from your crops.

Holly

Along with those Christmas trees plant a few holly bushes. They take an awful long time to reach maturity but the longer you leave it the longer it will be before you are cutting a few decorative boughs for the festive season. The secret of growing holly successfully lies in the initial planting, particularly where you dig up a self-set and transplant it. Always plant in the autumn and ensure that the tap-root is undamaged; lay this tap-root horizontally in the hole, don't squash it up and it will strike. In a dry spell water liberally.

If you need a fast-growing stockproof hedge then invest in a few quickthorns (they grow fast and are very thorny) and intersperse them with a few holly bushes.

Holly thieving is always a problem on roadside hedges in the fortnight prior to Christmas. Holly these days fetches a good price in the festive markets and roaming vandals with vans and pick-ups will do your bushes an immense amount of damage apart from the branches they steal. Sunday morning thefts seem to be the favourite time in our area. And on Sunday afternoons the local moochers are likely to follow. The latter are mostly ignorant of the ownership of holly trees; if one is growing in a hedge bordering a road or public footpath they seem to think that they have a right to cut it. Explain the position to them in no uncertain terms or else they will come with their secataurs every year!

Gorse is not the ogre it is made out to be. Keep it in check but always leave a sizeable patch for it provides good shelter for livestock in the winter months.

Planting self-set seedlings

We decided to plant an acre or so of our land with trees, not so much as a wind-break but as a habitat for wildlife. I approached the owners of a large woodland and requested permission to dig up a few self-set seedlings of which there were thousands. Permission was granted only too readily for this seeding-down can present problems to economic forestry. One word of warning, though; in order to take small trees, even seemingly useless self-sets from private land other than your own, you need permission. Otherwise it is theft under the Wildlife and Countryside Act, 1981 and you could be prosecuted.

Don't be tempted to take the larger saplings for they will almost certainly die. The wind will rock them and prevent them from re-rooting. Take trees about a foot high, dig them up with a spade even if they pull out fairly easily in soft ground for you will surely break some of the roots. Leave as much soil on them as possible, dig an ample hole where the roots can be spread out, and heel them in well. Autumn is the best time for this re-planting programme.

We used conifers on the outside of our wood to protect the trees from wind damage and allow them to establish. The interior needed to be mixed varieties and mostly we used silver birch. I have heard claims that these trees do not take very easily but the secret is in keeping the roots in darkness, during the period of transportation from wherever you obtain them, and not allowing them to dry out. Don't plant too many because there is no tree like the silver birch for re-seeding prolifically. Space them well, ten feet between each isn't too great a distance.

The mistake most laymen make when planting up a new wood is to plant the trees too close together. Small saplings are barely noticeable, there seems to be huge gaps all over the area. But they will grow and spread their boughs, and the last thing you want is a tangled jungle in which it is impossible to walk.

A few rhododendrons won't come amiss; woodcock favour a silver birch wood with rhododendrons. But you will be very lucky to find any of these latter as self-sets. What you must do is to take a few of the trailing branches on a mature shrub and heel them into the ground, leave them well covered with soil until the following year. Then you will find that most of the buried boughs have put down roots. Cut the branch off nearest to the central growth and replant the roots where you want them. They don't always take but a percentage will. You don't need too many anyhow.

If I was asked what my favourite food is I would unhesitatingly answer that it is nut-roast, a delicious roast made from hazel nuts. Consequently I planted a few hazels; they will take a long time to grow but nevertheless I have some on my land. Actually it is more convenient to buy shelled nuts; one appears to have gathered a basketful but when you have cracked them the quantity of kernels hardly seems worth the effort.

There is nothing so typically English as a horse-chestnut tree, its splendid autumnal foliage loaded with 'conkers', a reminder of those far-off schooldays when we used to bake them in the oven to harden them and challenge all-comers with zest and confidence.

One year Gavin and Angus came home from school and told us with great excitement that all the other children were collecting conkers and an economic forestry group were buying them for planting. Our boys sallied forth at the weekend with cartons and after several hours returned home with about twenty kilograms of horse-chestnuts between them; they weighed them out and worked out how much they would be paid for them on Monday.

On Monday afternoon, however, two very dejected sons came home carrying their heavy load. Apparently the forestry group had decided that their requirements in horse-chestnuts had been met. So the two cartons remained in a corner of the utility room over the winter and in the spring Jean asked me if I would throw them out as they were in the way.

It seemed such an awful waste to jettison them but I did not fancy planting them singly. They would choke our small wood if they grew and in the field the goats would surely graze them off. I was sure they would not germinate anyway, any excuse not to have to plant them!

Anyway, I cut out the turf on the edge of our wood, about one metre square and three or four inches deep, filled the area with the conkers and put the turf back. I completely forgot all about my 'conker grave' until some months later I happened to notice a mass of horse-chestnut seedlings, about two inches high, peeping up through the grass! One of these days I shall have to get round to dividing them up and re-planting them, it is all a matter of whether we want a horse-chestnut forest on our land.

Our 'Donate a Tree' scheme

I never waste a seedling tree if I find one growing around the garden. It only takes a minute or two to dig it up with a trowel and re-plant it somewhere else.

Then we hit upon our 'Donate a Tree' scheme. Even in suburban gardens you will always find a seedling or two coming up somewhere. Mostly these are pulled up and consigned to wherever the weeds are dumped, usually tied up in a plastic bag and put out for the refuse cart. Vast tracts of prospective forestry must be wasted in this way every year. And such a variety of trees, too.

So we told all our friends that if they cared to 'donate' a self-set tree from their garden we would plant it in our small wood, note its position and record it, together with their name, in our records book. Silly as the scheme sounds, it was greeted with enthusiasm. And so the project got under way.

It isn't just a means of obtaining free trees for our holding. It is a way in which we have a permanent reminder of our friends, we have given them a small stake in the place. And for their part, whenever they visit us they can go and check on how their tree is growing. It is a kind of 'companionship growing'.

Growing from seeds and cuttings

I have experimented with growing trees from seeds in pots in the porch. Of course it will be years before one sees any worthwhile result but it was an interesting trial. Apples, pears, etc., grow fairly easily, as do hazels, sycamores and silver birch. I tried hawthorn but never managed to germinate a single seed. As already mentioned, Japonicas were the most successful.

Cuttings, however, are a different proposition. I took several branches off a Lawson's cupressus in my mother's garden (a lovely tree, one of my favourites amongst the evergreens), and carried out a series of experiments with the small growths that make up the large branches. Peel one off right to where it joins the main wood and this is the end which will root. I also dip the ends in rooting powder.

1. Take a plastic bottle of at least one litre size and cut out three sides of a square about two inches from the base, i.e. make a small door in the side. Fill up the bottom of the bottle with two inches of soil or potting compost. Push the small cutting firmly into this soil, water it, close the 'door' and leave it until the following spring. You will note how the interior of the bottle runs with condensation as the cutting provides its own irrigation.

   Do not be in a hurry to transplant your rooted cutting. When you do, re-pot it into a larger pot and keep it well-watered. The reason why so many cuttings fail after the most difficult part has been achieved is because they are allowed to dry out.
2. Fill a plant pot with soil or potting compost and push your cutting firmly into this. Then water it, and cover the pot with a polythene freezer bag, securing it with an elastic band. This is another version of the above-mentioned method, in effect you are constructing a miniature greenhouse in which to grow you cutting.
3. Take a larger cutting, even a small main branch from the tree, and plant it straight out into the open. But first remove all foliage up to two-thirds of the way up the branch and push it into the ground up to this depth. Choose a fairly sheltered place where the wind cannot rock it. The success rate is not high but those cuttings which do strike will have a start on the smaller ones from the pots and bottles.

Your tree-nursery

Trees grown from cuttings are far more likely to survive if they are transplanted into a nursery before being put in their final position. It is a good idea to visit a commercial forestry nursery and pick up a few tips.

Cuttings planted in their permanent growing positions will not receive the attention they require. You will not have time to go round inspecting them regularly and consequently they will go unwatered in dry weather, weeds will choke them, rabbits might graze them off; a thousand and one accidents can befall them.

Choose a small, well-sheltered patch of land, it need be no more than a few metres square, and plant out all your well-rooted cuttings here. Keep it weed-free, water it regularly during a drought and don't be in a hurry to transplant the seedlings.

Trees grown by your own efforts will afford you an immense amount of satisfaction.

I have bought very few trees, I can obtain most of what I need for nothing. I did, however, buy a monkey-puzzle tree. One does not see many of these today but they were very fashionable in Victorian times on the spacious lawns of large houses. We had one at home, I remember going to fetch the three foot high tree with my father when I was a very small boy. Now it is some thirty feet high and very strong.

After we moved to our present home I decided I would like one of these trees. They are evergreen with needle-sharp leaves, deriving their name from the fact that a monkey would find it impossible to climb one! I have a rather worn out joke about my tree because almost everybody who has never seen or heard of one before asks me why it's called a monkey-puzzle tree. I reply to the effect that its purpose is to keep away monkeys.

'But there aren't any monkeys around here!' they reply with incredulity.

'No, there aren't,' I have perfected the art of keeping a straight face as I point to my prized tree, 'that's why!'

The monkey-puzzle tree grows about a foot each year and pushes out a new growth of branches each season. So it is a simple matter to calculate its age.

I also purchased fifty red cedars from a tree-nursery. These firs are fast growing and ideal as wind-breaks or for hedgeing. They were planted in mid-November within an hour or so of being dug up by the nurseryman.

The following summer the foliage began to turn brown so I rang the nurseryman and told him about this. He replied that red cedars often did this in the summer but they would green up again in the autumn. They didn't; forty-three of them died! I have no idea why and neither has anybody else I have spoken to.

Trees are part of our heritage. If we cut them down then we have a duty to future generations to re-plant. There are now grants available for planting up woodlands, a larger grant for broad-leaved trees than for conifers.

Trees are vital to life itself for they provide the oxygen which we breathe.

PART FOUR: MAKING IT WORK

Family help is essential on the smallholding

CHAPTER TWENTY-ONE

The Day's Routine

The family are the most important part of the smallholding set-up. Without them all your livestock and crops count for nothing, you would face a routine of drudgery day after day, with no purpose to it all. In fact, you could not manage, the chores would be either skimped or neglected altogether. You would eat unhealthy convenience junk foods because you had neither the time nor the inclination to cook, the house and garden would fall into disrepair because you had nobody to tend it for.

The lifestyle which we have examined throughout this book is *teamwork*. But for a family organisation to run smoothly then it has to be organised. Everybody has to have certain jobs of their own but they must also be able to take over when somebody is ill or absent. We are 'departmentalised' yet at the same time we are a complete unit; we all work with and for one another.

Let us look first at the role which is the focal point of our smallholding, the housewife's job which has to incorporate that of wife, mother, cook, housekeeper and farmer.

The wife

Jean's day begins at 6.45 am during schooltime. Rowan's W.R.V.S. car arrives at 7.30 to collect her, and Tara and Gavin have to be taken down to catch the school bus at 7.50. Then there are breakfast crocks to be washed (fortunately in this household we do not have a traditional English breakfast otherwise the washing up would be phenomenal!). Jean usually milks the goats in the mornings on weekdays. After that there is the usual drudgery of routine housework. The postman arrives around 10.30 so that will entail some bookshop work, books to be invoiced out and packaged ready to take down to the post office before lunch.

For three years Jean was president of the local Women's Institute

191

which meant a lot of extra work which in turn meant that I helped out with many of the chores. The afternoon usually takes care of itself but whatever Jean is doing she has to break off at 4.30 to go and fetch Tara and Gavin back. Angus has school transport from door to door which saves an additional journey.

In between all these interruptions Jean has to cook, make wine and innumerable other jobs related to our lifestyle. And, these past few months, she has taken a part-time job with a friend as well!

The husband

My day begins at 8.00 am. I don't start before then because my routine lasts until around eleven o'clock at night. On rising, my first job is to empty the ashes out of the stove, feed the free-ranging guineafowl, silkies, etc., take Muffin and Hobbit with me for their morning run whilst I feed the donkeys and the birds in the enclosure in the field. After that I lay the fire in the lounge in readiness for the evening, snatch a quick cup of coffee and a plate of muesli, and try and get some writing done before the postman arrives. The rest of the morning is taken up with completing the bookshop work and taking the mail to the post office.

After lunch I take the dogs out. In the winter months this means an expedition with the gun for an hour or two and on my return there are birds to be shut up, hayracks to be filled, etc. Jean and I split the farm chores so that she does the milking Mondays to Friday in the mornings and I do it in the evenings. At weekends I milk morning and evening and allow her to have a bit of a rest. Then if I have not managed to complete my quota of writing during the day I generally work until about ten o'clock or after at night. Then there are the final routine tasks to be done, dogs to be taken out, stove stoked up in the winter and fuel to be brought in.

The children

If the children do not play an active part in this lifestyle then life can be very hard for the adults. Young children can be very demanding and one has to learn to encourage them to help; forcing them to do so is no good, it will only result in a rebellious attitude as they grow up.

Begin by encouraging them to have pets of their own which they must look after. Angus has his hamster; unfortunately these lovable small creatures have a very short lifespan, about a year, so soon there will be a

192

Hamster; children should be encouraged to keep pets, an ideal one to begin with

sad occasion. But it is all part of a child's upbringing, particularly on a farm they must realise that where there is life there is inevitably death. The departed pet is buried in the pets' cemetery with due reverence and a new one purchased as soon as possible in order to maintain the continuity.

Gavin has his guinea pigs. These are not without their problems either and we seem to have had more than our fair share of these. We lost three adult hamsters and a whole litter of guinea pig young with some mystery virus, but all credit to Gavin he persevered. It is all good training for when they move on to bigger animals.

The girls look after the cats and are only too eager to feed them. But already Rowan has learned to milk the goats and in order to instil a sense of responsibility into her as soon as she was sixteen we began leaving her at home on occasions when we went out for the day. She did not mind this and with a list of duties to be performed she soon became competent.

The next stage was to teach the children to manage overnight without us otherwise we should be tied to the smallholding for life. So we booked in at an hotel thirty miles away for dinner on Saturday night and breakfast on Sunday morning, and left the family to it. And what a pleasant surprise we had when we returned around 11.30 the following morning! Everything was done just as we would have done it ourselves and in addition the boys had vacuumed the house and tidied up. But that wasn't all – Tara had prepared a three-course lunch for us as well as baking for tea! We were over a major hurdle.

This training takes time and needs to be started when the children are young. You cannot expect youngsters who have never been encouraged to suddenly start when they are in their teens.

Gardening can be an irksome task for children if they have not been brought up with it. Each of our four have a raised-bed of their own. They are allowed to choose what they want to grow on their allocated plot; the boys prefer to raise vegetables which they can sell to some of our customers and thereby earn a little bit of money on top of their

Guinea pig; not always easy to breed

194

pocket money. Tara and Rowan grow flowers, mostly wallflowers which my mother buys off them rather than purchasing bedding-out plants from a nursery.

But any gardening jobs in addition to their own small plots they are paid for. Gavin sometimes mows the lawn, the others will help with the borders. But we have a system which gives them an incentive to work throughout the year.

'Work Books'

The children each have an exercise book of their own which is known as a 'work book' and is kept on a shelf in my study. The purpose of these books is to record jobs performed; they are responsible for the entries which might read:

21 April. Lawn mowing.

I fill in the end column with the amount they are to be paid according to the nature of the job. Lawn mowing, I consider, is worth fifty pence as we use a hand mower, the advantage being that you obtain a good cut with an old-fashioned cylinder mower and also the grass does not have to be completely dry, as it does with an electric device.

There-are two 'pay days' in the year. The first is just prior to our annual holiday in August. This works out nicely for the children because, hopefully, the pea and soft-fruit harvest will just have been completed which will have boosted their earnings. The second pay-out is in Christmas week which enables them to buy their presents. Any worthwhile job goes into the books and if we happen to be up to-date then they can wash the car or the Land Rover. There is little in the way of weeding to do as our mulching system takes care of all this.

Tara is allowed to book her baking which is only fair as it relieves Jean of yet another job.

Self-reliance

Our children have always been encouraged to do things for themselves. Jean and I much prefer a home-made birthday or Christmas present to one bought in the shops. It may be something quite simple like a container to hold pens and pencils constructed from lollipop sticks and varnished, or an oven-glove. We have had a variety of ingenious presents over the years and it stands the children in good stead for the future when they will need to be independent. And making your own

195

entertainment is a pastime that many of the current generation seem to have ignored. Television has bred a laziness into today's youth.

Yet television does have its benefits. I would hate to be without it. BBC2 shows some excellent wildlife programmes which are educational and I wish that I had had the opportunity to view these in my boyhood. Likewise there are some excellent gardening programmes from which even the experienced grower can learn; one point I would mention in relation to these, though, and that is that it seems perfectly in order for gardeners to use chemicals but not the farmer! Our national gardening experts are repeatedly prescribing the cure for some plant disease, or the control of weeds with some diabolical new chemical which has just come onto the market, the long term effects of which have still to be discovered. Let's keep the record straight; the gardener who uses weedkillers and plant sprays is as guilty as the commercial farmer for there are many more gardeners than farmers and the environment will be polluted the length and breadth of the country.

Is there a future in smallholding?

It would be exceedingly difficult for anybody to make a full-time living off a smallholding the size of ours. I know a family with ten times our acreage and they all go out to work and run the farming as a profitable hobby. Certainly conventional farming, even organic, could not bring in a living wage. However, there are other ways in which this can be done.

We must be realistic and admit that there is very little chance of our children finding work, except in agriculture, in our remote area. With the exception of Rowan who will probably go on to university to take art.

Tara's ambition is to run a vegetarian-wholefood restaurant so we need to incorporate this into our future plans. Gavin will run the farming side whilst Angus has a desire to be an ornithologist (not the most well-paid of jobs!). How can we amalgamate all these ambitions into an organic smallholding?

To do this we must open to the public and to do that we need to have sufficient of interest to persuade them to part with their one pound at the gate for a look around. At the moment we are short in a few departments.

We have raised beds that are as good as any you will find in any alternative lifestyle demonstration centre. We have a variety of methods of mulching and composting, records to prove our results.

We have ornamental free-ranging fowl, including guineafowl and peafowl which are in evidence at most wildlife parks and show centres. Wildlife on the pool; American Bronze turkeys and pure-bred old-fashioned poultry. Donkeys, and of course, our miniature nature reserve which has scope for expansion.

The 'Nature Walk' would lead down the small valley from the pool, along the trickling brook beneath the spreading oaks and through a mass of wildflowers; we have taken steps to preserve plantlife as well as wildlife, scattering broadcast handfuls of mixed wildflower seeds and letting Nature do the rest.

Up to the spinney and the tree-nursery where most species of native trees are in evidence. The visitor is virtually guaranteed a glimpse of a soaring buzzard or a raven cronking overhead. Then back to the wholefood café for a variety of herb teas and healthy snacks. The postal bookshop has been incorporated with a bookshop specialising in books on everything from vegetarian cooking to alternative lifestyles, including our own booklets on organic growing. Postcards and souvenirs, herbs for sale, grown and potted by Tara. A supply of freshly-dug organic vegetables for sale, and a few machine-knitted garments by Jean.

Gavin, as well as organising the growing, will in effect be our gamekeeper, rearing pheasants for the shoot along with turkeys and old breeds of poultry so that we may offer a few days' shooting to selective paying guests during the winter months when the 'centre' will be relatively quiet.

Angus, too, will play his part for ornithology and conservation, as already stated, go hand-in-hand with shooting. The wild birds will be an integral part of our venture. Only recently he compiled a list of all the species to be found on and around our land and this provides an interesting study for those whose hobby is wildlife:

Game birds
Pheasant
Partridge
Woodcock

Wildfowl and waders
Mallard
Teal
Canada Geese
Snipe
Curlew (summer visitor)

Birds of Prey
Buzzard
Sparrowhawk
Kestrel
Goshawk
Red Kite (I first saw one in the
    mid-1960s here but they
    have been spotted here since
    then)
Owls, Barn and Tawny

Others
Woodpigeon
Raven
Carrion Crow
Rook
Jackdaw
Jay
Magpie
Green Woodpecker
Water-wagtail
Cuckoo
Swift
Swallow
Fieldfare
Heron
Starling
Sparrow
Blue-tit
Coal-tit
Great-tit
Thrush
Robin
Bullfinch
Yellow-hammer
Blackbird
Chaffinch
Dipper

Stock Dove
Goldfinch
Linnet
Skylark
Greenfinch
Kingfisher
Lapwing
House Martin
Redwing
Tern (Common)
Wren

Animals
Rabbit
Hare
Fox
Polecat
Stoat
Weasel
Roe Deer
Grey Squirrel
Rat
Mouse
Shrew
Field Vole
Mole

We have the ingredients for a wildlife/alternative lifestyle centre together with the most important factor, our own family workforce. The build-up is a gradual process, in fact it began when we moved here and started to shape a windswept smallholding into something a little more interesting than just the conventional sheep and cattle farm.

This book has been about our successes and our failures but I have attempted to show the reader wherever we went wrong. In spite of many set-backs we have achieved a worthwhile way of life but there always has to be another goal, a further ambition.

It is the *quality* of life that matters, not the monetary reward.

CHAPTER TWENTY-TWO

Subsidiary Incomes

It is most unlikely that your smallholding will provide you with a living. In fact, during the early days you will spend more than you earn from it. Stocking it is costly, you need to do some repairs, erect some out-buildings. So where does your money come from?

Usually on established holdings the husband goes out to work whilst the wife sees to the routine farming and then he helps in the evenings and at weekends. Farming is more of a paying hobby than a job on this scale. However, times have changed; there are very few jobs available in rural areas apart from farming and forestry, and if you have come straight from the town you stand little chance of finding employment in either of these.

I have a firm belief that if one has a particular skill then one should reap the full benefit of that talent rather than sell it to somebody else in return for a wage. Somehow you must find an income; possibly the wife would be better equipped to get a secretarial job and leave the husband to cope with the farm. This is something which a couple have to work out between themselves. Today it is quite acceptable for a man to remain at home whilst his wife works. But overall I think it is better if either or both of you can do something for yourselves which earns money rather than find a job. Let us look at a few possibilities outside regular employment.

School transport

As mentioned in the previous chapter, in rural areas children have to be delivered and returned home from school and this is usually done by a member of the community who is paid by the county council for his or her services. It is by no means a lucrative job but at least there is a regular wage, in all probability it takes no more than a couple of hours per day, and you are paid on mileage and the number of pupils carried.

In most cases the driver will need to be on the road by eight am in time to connect with a school bus from a village or to deliver the children direct, so he or she will be back home by 9.30. The rest of the day is free until around 2.30 in the afternoon; the children will be collected, dropped at their respective homes and by 4.30 at the latest you should be finished for the day.

The only snag is that your day is broken up. Whatever chore you are working on you will have to break off in the middle of the afternoon. And, of course, the winter months can be quite hazardous on these steep, narrow lanes.

But in any case it is well worth approaching the transport department of your local education authority to see if there is a vacancy for such a driver. If there is then check carefully with your car insurance firm to make sure that you are fully covered; if extra cover is necessary then weigh the additional premium against your remuneration to see if the job is really worth it.

Jobbing gardening

Unfortunately gardeners are more in demand in towns than in the country. However, there are always retired people in rural areas who are finding that they can no longer cope with their garden. There certainly is a market for the 'jobber' but it needs exploring carefully. The odd half-day could turn out to be a nuisance and scarcely worthwhile in monetary terms; what you want is to build up a regular round throughout the spring and summer so that you are suitably rewarded for your time spent away from your smallholding.

Work out how many days each week you can devote to gardening for somebody else. If you can manage four then plan your week accordingly; perhaps two of your customers only want you for half a day, so arrange to go to one in a morning, the other in an afternoon, which leaves you with three uninterrupted days elsewhere. Also bear in mind that the weather will not always be suitable so be prepared to re-arrange your schedule accordingly. Sometimes you may have to leave one garden until the following week if the weather is exceptionally bad; preferably be prepared to work weekends to catch up. You must establish a reputation for reliability; there are far too many casual gardeners about who tend to turn up when they feel like it. You must capitalise on their laziness! Likewise during May and June lawns and borders grow at an alarming rate and you must keep on top of them.

Most village shops allow customers to put advertisments in their windows for a few pence a week. Give it a try, it may well bring you those extra couple of gardens which will make your round worthwhile. Don't expect instant results, though. Country folk never do anything in a hurry. In all probability they will make a few discreet enquiries about you before contacting you.

It is a good idea to have your own garden neat and tidy. If somebody calls to engage you it is hardly a good advertisment if your own patch is an untidy jungle of weeds.

You must work out beforehand how much you are going to charge and fix a standard rate. If you have different hourly rates for different people word will soon get around and you will find yourself having to reduce your labour charge. It is no good thinking that Mr So-and-So up at the big house can afford to pay more than the retired couple at the other end of the village; your labour is for sale, there must be no cut-price offers. The going-rate for gardening varies from place to place. In towns it is sometimes as high as five pounds an hour whilst in my own area it averages at two pounds fifty pence to three pounds. Don't be greedy and price yourself out of a job.

Once you have got started your aim must be to become established. If you do a good job then people will recommend you to friends and neighbours. It is preferable to be in a position where you have to turn jobs down rather than to have to go looking for work. *And give value for money*.

There are too many gardeners about who try to do as little as possible in the time. A quick break mid-morning, half an hour for your lunch, and a cup of tea in the afternoon. You deserve a rest but don't overdo it. Don't try and pinch ten minutes by leaving early when your employer is away for the day. It will not go unnoticed in the countryside, neighbours notice things and they also gossip.

If there are holiday cottages in your area then approach the owners with a view to tending their gardens for them. People who only come to stay for weekends don't usually want to spend their breaks gardening and they might well be glad of a regular dependable workman. Again, be honest with them; they are not there to watch over you but skipping a lawn cut might well land you in trouble if they turn up unexpectedly. Honesty is the best policy by far.

Remember also that the customer is the boss. If he wants a job doing in a particular way then carry out his wishes. Right or wrong, everybody has their own views on gardening and you cannot afford to be dogmatic. Your aim is to please the customer so that you will have a regular job.

During the latter part of my schooldays I found that jobbing-gardening was a fairly lucrative business. I charged half-a-crown an hour, and on a fine summer's evening I could often earn ten shillings which bought quite a lot in those days.

I always liked to carry my own tools with me. You can waste a lot of time searching in somebody's shed for the right implement but if you have your own tools with you there is no problem. It is far better than finding that the spade has a broken handle or else the shears are blunt. You need a van or a pick-up truck, a kind of mobile workshop so that you always have the tools you need with you.

A lot of gardeners cart their rubbish away with them when they have finished. Often there is no means of disposing of it at the places where you work; gardens too small or too close to the house to light bonfires, or maybe even a smokeless zone if you are close to a town. Some of that rubbish can be useful on the smallholding; some is suitable for composting, ash is certainly useful, and it might pay you to stick some of your hedge-cuttings in the ground to see if you can strike a few privet. Surplus leaves can be made into leafmould.

You may be asked to do a number of jobs outside gardening, depending upon how much of a handyman you are. You can't afford to be choosy because when winter comes, and there is no gardening to do, the opportunity of a few chores under cover will mean that you are still earning.

Always leave a tidy finished job behind you. Sweep up all your hedge-trimmings carefully, rake over any borders which you have walked on. And if you are carting rubbish away in a wheelbarrow check that you have picked up anything that has fallen off en route. At the end of the day your work should be pleasing to the eye of the employer; it could mean the difference between keeping or losing work.

Working from home

Ideally you should aim at working from home wherever possible. If you can build up some kind of craft that fits in with your smallholding jobs then you will have the best of both worlds. Let us examine one or two possibilities:

Machine-knitting

A few years ago I bought Jean a knitting-machine and it has certainly proved its worth. For an outlay of around two hundred pounds she began by knitting garments for the family which in itself was a big saving. We were the advertisers, wearing these clothes, and before long friends and neighbours were asking her to make them jumpers, jackets,

A knitting machine: a useful source of income

socks, etc. One of her best-selling lines last winter was ankle-warmers.

With a machine items are made quickly, a sweater in a day to sell at around twenty pounds. Not a fortune but some useful money; even twenty to thirty pounds is useful when the telephone or electric bill arrives. Of course it is not all profit, wool is far from cheap, but you have to disregard your labour. In many aspects of a self-sufficiency lifestyle if you counted your labour the job just would not be worth doing. *The secret is to find something which you enjoy doing and combine work and pleasure. Fortunate, indeed, is the person who gets paid for doing something which he or she likes.*

Selling

It will be some time before you have built up enough produce to start a Farm Sales shop. You will not require planning permission to do this provided that everything you sell is produced on your own holding, but permission is needed if you are going to buy in from outside. Sales at the door are fine; eggs, vegetables, goats' milk, there are no restrictions on these, but there is always the possibility that an inspector might call to view your milking parlour. Needless to say, cleanliness is paramount at all times.

Selling somebody else's product always requires a cash outlay unless you can persuade them to let you have produce on a sale or return basis. Honey is a fast-selling product, particularly if it is labelled '*local* honey'. The weekend tourist is always tempted by home-produced goods to take back with him. Unfortunately they always seem to expect gate sales to be considerably cheaper than in shops or markets. Their argument is that the smallholder does not have the retailer's overheads; which is nonsense, they overlook the cost of feedstuffs, the work. My advice is not to sell cheaply, I base my prices on those at local markets.

Selling other than farm produce can be a chancey business. Don't be tempted by any advertisment offering 'fast selling products'; you could find yourself out of pocket with a load of unsaleable items left on your hands. I have been wary of all get-rich-quick schemes since the days of pyramid-selling when a friend of mine lost a considerable sum of money. However, only a year or two ago we did become distributors for Heatlogs and Peatheat (see page 17) which are compressed fuel for both open fires and closed stoves. We stocked these simply because we found it economical to use them ourselves and each bag we sold reduced our own heating costs. Unfortunately trade was small, which was probably only to be expected in a country area where people were suspicious of anything other than conventional fuels. However, the product was a raging success elsewhere, for by Christmas we were unable to replenish our own stock because demand had exceeded supply nationwide and there was a waiting list for heatlogs and peatheat.

Postal bookselling

By far our most successful subsidiary income has been derived from selling second-hand books by post. We were fortunate, however, that when we decided to break with a conventional existence I was already an established writer, having had some fifty books, both fiction and non-fiction, published. Without that cushion we might not have taken the plunge but our bookselling venture goes back long before I ever turned to earning my living from writing. Indeed, it began in our early married years, working from a city centre flat, and there I established a small business in selling old boys' papers and books and science fiction, horror and fantasy material.

The guideline is to buy the right material at the right prices; anybody can fill a room with cheap rubbish accumulated from jumble and car-boot sales. Selling it again is a different proposition!

You need to have a 'feel' for books and some knowledge of the field in which you intend to deal. Always go for first editions and scour other second-hand bookshops, Oxfam shops, and jumble sales. Buy discerningly, do not try to rush it, and wait until you have sufficient stock before compiling your first catalogue.

Your first catalogue is probably the most important one you will ever compile. Pick up other dealers' lists in order to give yourself a general idea of how to describe items, list the books in author alphabetical order, and number each book because that is a great help to both buyer and seller, especially in the case of telephoned orders where the caller wishes to keep the call to a minimum.

Your list is typed, duplicated or photocopied, and now all you need are customers. You will have to outlay some money in advertising; try the trade journals and any other publication which carries a 'Books for Sale' column. State the type of books you are selling and request

A postal second-hand bookshop can provide a valuable subsidiary income

205

stamped-addressed envelopes for lists. If you don't ask for a pre-paid envelope you will be inundated with replies from a seemingly large section of the public whom, it appears, merely collect other people's booklists!

You will experience a thrill when a pile of letters drop through your letterbox, perhaps a dozen or twenty requests for lists. You can't wait to mail them; within a few days half your stock of catalogues has gone out.

Sometimes orders come thick and fast; I have been fetched out of bed at seven am on more than one occasion by a hopeful buyer who is determined to beat all other contenders to the book or magazine he wants. Another regular buyer will phone around eleven o'clock at night. Some rely on the postal service.

If your books are priced right you can expect an early rush of orders; the most sought after items go first. Once I had sixty phone calls in one morning, everybody after a particular book which I had underpriced. One learns by one's mistakes!

Keep a note of all your buyers because you must ensure that they receive a copy of your next list. You will not need to advertise regularly after a time because you will have compiled a mailing list of your own. Like any other business, though, you need to become established, win the trust of your customers. Below are a few 'golden' rules to help you build up a bookselling business:

1. Always despatch books promptly; some dealers wait a week or more and then parcel up their orders, but this is annoying to customers who are eager to receive the book they ordered.
2. Wrap books securely, using corrugated paper beneath a layer of thick brown paper and always tie with string. As an additional precaution I slip each book into a polythene bag. An added saving is the use of clean paper feedbags for wrapping and used baler-twine for string.
3. Enclose a typed invoice; always charge for postage and in order that the invoice can accompany the goods add to the final amount 'postage as per parcel'.
4. Pencil the price lightly inside the cover of the book; it saves you having to consult your catalogue with each order.
5. Ask for payment within seven days; if you have not received it within a fortnight write politely but firmly. In the case of a bad payer, send a recorded delivery letter accompanied by a stamped-addressed envelope.
6. Always keep detailed records of sales and purchases. You will be able to tell at a glance then how your business is going.
7. Never reduce prices of unsold items. If a person wants a book he

will, for argument's sake, pay a fiver for it. If he doesn't want it he won't be tempted to buy it for a couple of pounds less.

With regard to general pricing of books you need at least a fifty per cent mark-up in order to cover you for unsold items, postages, advertising and printing of lists. For a time you must be prepared to plough your profits back into the business. You need to have as large a selection of *good* stock as you can afford to carry and to turn it over frequently.

If bookselling is operated methodically and sensibly it can be a sound secondary business for the smallholder; it could earn him more than taking a job somewhere. Above all, he can work from home, fit it in with his farming chores. Which is exactly what Jean and I do.

Let us now look at a few more possibilities for subsidiary incomes:

Furniture restoring

A neighbouring friend of ours has successfully built up a cottage industry over the past decade in restoring old furniture and re-upholstery. Her trademark has been the quality of her work; she recovered a settee for use in a local doctor's waiting-room and what could have been a better advertisement for her work! Patients sat on it at morning and evening surgery, admired it, and word got round. Gradually her workload increased until she was operating at full stretch which was when she asked Jean if she would care to go and help her for one day a week.

Jean was thrilled at the prospect. One day led to two, and currently she is working three days most weeks and thoroughly enjoying it. And all the time my wife is learning a new craft which may come in very handy one day.

Craft shops and cafés

Craft shops and cafés are widespread throughout Britain. Virtually every village has at least one and they are very prolific in Wales where people like ourselves, and possibly the reader of this book, has branched out to find a new and better lifestyle.

With the slump in the farming industry, the government are now considering grants to farmers who wish to create subsidiary light industries on their farms, and craft centres and cafés fall within this sphere. But before one invests in such an enterprise it has to be thought out carefully.

Many farmers' wives already provide bed and breakfast facilities for tourists and some of them do very well at it. The occasional bed and breakfast is fine, fifteen pounds or so for the trouble of providing an extra meal at family mealtimes and changing the sheets in the spare bedroom. But in order to make this a worthwhile business it is necessary to advertise in nationwide magazines in an effort to have a regular flow of guests. Countryside publications, especially hikers', cyclists' and bird watchers' journals are a lucrative source of finding custom.

However, you must do more than just put an extra helping out at family mealtimes if you wish to be renowned for your culinary skills. Bed and breakfast is much more sophisticated in this modern age; certainly urban dwellers wish to sample rural fare but they look for a choice of menu, some prefer to have their meals served in a separate room rather than with the farmer's family, and during the evenings they do not wish to feel obliged to visit the local pub simply because the farmer's wife wants them out of the way.

Try and provide accommodation which is a little more than just a room to sleep in. There will be wet days and cold evenings and in all probability your guests will appreciate watching some television without being compelled to view *your* favourite programmes.

Like any other business, you need to invest before you can reap the rewards of your labours. Many households do not use their lounge regularly so set this aside for paying guests during the holiday season; a separate television (colour is a must, an old black and white set isn't good enough and only serves to show a miserliness which isn't good for repeat custom) and ensure that the room is comfortable. A real fire is much more homely than an electric heater.

A variable menu is not as formidable as it sounds. For starters you can offer fruit juices as well as the conventional soup, and the alternative to the family's main course can be either salad with various cooked meats or egg dishes. You can offer cheese and biscuits, tinned fruit, ice-cream and a host of other acceptable sweets which can be conveniently kept in stock.

Mostly your guests will be looking for home-made fare so don't dish up convenience foods. If you haven't time to make your own jams and chutneys then there are always plenty on offer at bring-and-buy sales and coffee evenings.

In order to be really enterprising you can offer vegetarian fare, possibly specialise in it. Nowadays many visitors to the countryside are opposed to the eating of meat and most farmhouse accommodations presume that their guests are automatically seeking a bacon and egg breakfast. Many would-be visitors are dissuaded by this and seek hotel accommodation where there is a choice of food and, at the worst, just a cheese salad.

If you state in your advertisement that vegetarian fare is always available, in addition to conventional farmhouse meals, then you will almost certainly tempt those who are seeking meatless sustanance.

Serving bed and breakfast is a good insight into what running a café entails. An initiation into providing food for others, and if you don't like it then you can close it down overnight whereas with a café you will have gone to considerable outlay in both time and money.

There are several types of cafés; a coffee and teashop, snacks, or full meals. Having had a twelve-month spell of bed and breakfast you should know which of these you are able to cope with.

First, you must consult your local planning department to ascertain whether you need full planning permission, change of use, or if you can simply go ahead and dish up meals in your own farmhouse for consumption by passing tourists. At the same time have a word with your local Ministry of Agriculture office and see if you can qualify for a grant in respect of an auxiliary farm industry. Of course, this will only apply if you are a bona-fide farmer or smallholder but it is worth investigating.

The purpose of these grants is to assist farmers in 'less-favoured' areas (i.e. hill farms unsuitable for anything apart from grazing) and are granted to support 'tourism and crafts'. They cover a wide field from caravan sites and camping areas to craft shops.

The applicant must invest at least one thousand five hundred pounds in his enterprise and may receive grants of twenty-five per cent up to twenty-four thousand pounds. Prospective applicants should ask at their local Ministry of Agriculture office for leaflet A1 S6 which will explain in detail the requirements for obtaining a grant.

A café is a different proposition from serving bed and breakfast on a casual scale. You will be inspected by officials from the department of health and your kitchen and eating areas must be scrupulously clean – which they should be anyway! If you don't comply with the required standards then you are likely to be prosecuted and even closed down. Even if you escape the latter then your bad reputation will travel fast and you may end up closing down anyway, because you have no customers.

Again, home-made fare will be expected from a country café and all your spare time will be devoted to building up a stock of cakes and pastries. Again, go for the discerning eater who is looking for wholefoods and always have wholemeal bread available. And if you can manage to grow your own organic vegetables, and rear poultry which is free-range for both eggs and meat, then you will soon establish a reputation.

Before you start up, enjoy a few car rides out in the countryside and call in at some cafés – not to copy what they are doing but possibly to try and find a niche for yourself in what they are *not* providing.

Serve conventional foods as well as wholefoods and vegetarian meals. In other words, provide a full service to suit everybody. If you decide to go into the catering business then do it properly.

In addition to your café you may decide to run a craft shop. You must aim at the tourist market, and remember that visitors from other parts of the country are more interested in buying locally-made items than souvenirs purchased from a national wholesaler.

If you have a talent for making something, then use it whether it is corn-dollies or embroidery or whatever. Perhaps one of the family is a budding artist and a painting of a local view, nicely framed, will sell if it is not too highly priced. Once you become established you can have postcards made from photographs of your own premises if it is sufficiently attractive.

It is better to have a few local craft products than a room full of bought-in items. Except in the case of other local craftspeople; perhaps some of your neighbours specialise in a particular product but do not have their own outlets and would be willing to supply you.

The possibilities are endless but first and foremost you must look after your café. Hungry and thirsty passers-by have called in for some kind of sustenance and they won't be interested in your trinkets and paintings if the meals are sub-standard. Get your priorities right!

In the early stages you will have to do everything yourself because an auxiliary business can rarely afford hired labour. But should you be more than moderately successful then you will have to employ help. Which means that your café and craftshop has virtually become a full-time occupation. Usually casual labour isn't hard to find in rural areas because of a shortage of work outside agriculture and forestry. But you will need to take on somebody suitable; a scruffy or rude employee will soon lose you the custom which you have strived to build up.

If you employ somebody to help with the cooking ensure that they are capable of producing well-cooked meals speedily. A waitress should be smart, clean and obliging, showing a willingness to please the customer. But, of course, once you have progressed to this stage you must have a fair idea of general business principles or else all your previous hard work will be undermined by bad management.

General business principles

From the outset you must keep records of income and expenditure, for without it you don't really know whether you are making a profit or a loss. I have already illustrated the necessity for keeping concise records on the smallholding and so you must with your subsidiary business.

The cost of setting up your craft shop and/or café is your capital outlay. You will hope to recover this over a period of time but in the meantime you must ensure that you are really making a profit on the food or goods you sell. Consequently, you will need to have a set of accounts prepared each year, taking into account capital depreciation (your vehicle, your fixtures and fittings). Accountants are expensive but if you have no knowledge of book-keeping then it will pay you to engage one; his fees are offset against tax.

Even if you do not borrow money from the bank to set up your business, at least go and have a chat with your bank manager and he will advise you accordingly. It is important to get off to an organised start otherwise you may fail through muddling and not because of your own talents, which will be wasted as a result.

It is important to pay your bills promptly; unless you do this you could be lulled into a false sense of financial security and then suddenly find that you are unable to meet the monetary demands made on you. In any case, if you become known as a slow payer, your suppliers will be unwilling to deal with you.

You will be liable for income tax on your profits. As a self-employed person you will pay your tax bills a year in arrears, in two half-yearly instalments in January and July. It is important to keep this money on one side, preferably in a building society where it will earn interest; if you spend it, and have a poor financial year following, you will be in serious trouble with the Inland Revenue because you are unable to pay them.

In the beginning you will have to plough most of your profits back into the business. Obviously you will want some reward for your work so after you have studied your first year's accounts, estimate a reasonable weekly wage which you can pay yourself without draining the resources of your enterprise. You must be patient, you are working for yourself and even putting money back into the business is an investment which you should benefit from once you are firmly established.

My advice to the beginner is to be honest, work hard and don't be greedy when allocating remuneration from the takings to your own pocket. That is my own recipe for success. It is better to have a small self-supporting business of your own than not to have one at all.

CHAPTER TWENTY THREE

Wild Meat for the Pot

We have already discussed the need for eating lean meat, low in cholesterol, and the duty we owe to those birds and animals which provide us with food to kill them quickly and cleanly. They must not even suspect that death is imminent, for humane reasons and also because in that way the adrenalin does not pump into their blood-stream. Man is a hunter by nature, and sport with the gun in the hands of a true marksman is a kindness to the birds and beasts of the chase; without culling a true balance could not be maintained in the country-side. Vermin species would predominate and not just gamebirds but

A pheasant just out of the oven; wholesome wild meat low in cholesterol

212

Meat from the wild is all part of the smallholder's harvest

songbirds, too, would decline as a result.

Nevertheless, it is a matter for personal conscience whether or not one hunts for the pot. If not, then those who do should be allowed to pursue their legitimate sport unmolested, for in this age of protests and demonstrations the 'anti-everything' brigade are very often ignorant of the true facts, mostly because they are ill-informed by the media who repeatedly add fuel to the flames of misrepresentations. If you do not shoot, nor wish to do so, then perhaps this chapter on the basics of shooting wild meat for the table will portray the mode and ethics of a sport which goes hand-in-hand with conservation. For the shooting man is a conservationist first and foremost.

I can do no more than give a brief introduction to the sport in these pages but those interested in learning more about it might care to read my two books on the subject *The Rough Shooter's Handbook* (Boydell and Brewer) and *Gamekeeping and Shooting for Amateurs* (Nimrod).

Before you buy, borrow, or use a shotgun you must obtain a shotgun certificate, obtaining an application form from your local police station. Failure to do this will almost certainly result in prosecution. And if you shoot game then you must acquire a game licence, available over the counter at most post offices at a cost of six pounds.

Gun and cartridges

I would recommend a good sound double-barrelled 12-bore. You don't need to pay an extortionate price for it but do buy it from a reliable source and have it checked over by a gunsmith. Remember, a gun is a lethal weapon, it must not be pointed at anybody, whether loaded or unloaded, and a faulty weapon could result in serious injury to yourself or somebody else.

With regard to cartridges the standard load of 1 1/8 oz, number 6 shot is adequate for most quarry; you should never shoot at anything beyond forty yards. Keep a few heavier loads, Nos 3, 1 or BB, handy in case the occasion arises, as it usually does at some time or other on a small-holding, when you will take a shot at a prowling fox.

Learning to shoot

Some people have the erroneous idea that just because you are firing 'scattershot' you are bound to hit anything you shoot at. Nothing could be further from the truth! Your shot charge will form into a close pattern, widening the further it gets from the barrels, and although this results in a greater spread the density of the shot will be less, and consequently you will not hit your target with the full charge. This means that long range shots will result in pricked and wounded birds. On the other hand, if you fire at a pigeon or rabbit at close range you will undoubtedly blast it to pieces and render it inedible.

So you need to learn to judge *range* effectively. The best way to do this is to pin a sheet of newspaper out at thirty-five yards and shoot at it. Examine it afterwards so that you get some idea of how your gun patterns. Ideally you need a gun which has its right barrel choked for half-choke and the left full. This means that the spread from your right barrel will not be so dense and will be more suitable for shots of twenty-five to thirty yards, but your left barrel pattern will be much denser with more pellets in it. So the first quarry will be shot nearer and the second, which will have gained distance, will be killed with the denser pattern.

Don't involve yourself too much in the subject of ballistics for it is very complicated and will only serve to confuse you. Learn at what distance you can kill *cleanly* for that is the whole objective of shooting.

In order to kill a moving target you must swing your gun with your quarry, and this must become a natural process each time you shoot without having to think consciously about it. Keep both eyes open, firmly fixed on the bird or beast, and do not take them off it for a

214

second; watch it all the way. And in conjunction with this your barrels will be swinging. Fire whilst you are still watching your quarry and once you have developed this knack you will begin to kill consistently.

You need years of practice to become an accomplished shot and in the initial stages you would benefit from visiting a shooting school and trying your hand at clay pigeons. You will have the bonus of a qualified instructor at your side to advise you where you are going wrong. If you do not have this expert coaching then you will not be aware of your mistakes and will make them time after time without realising it.

Safety is paramount at all times. All the game in the countryside is not worth the risk of one man killed or maimed. So never take a loaded gun indoors, and when walking in places where there is no chance of a shot, carry your gun 'broken', i.e. open at the breech. Always have the safety catch on except when you are about to shoot.

Never shoot against a background where you cannot see what lies beyond; the countryside is fraught with danger for the sportsman, picnickers or courting couples in the undergrowth, livestock seeking shelter under the hedge on the opposite side from you. Be alert to your surroundings, particularly where you are close to a road or public footpath. It is against the law to discharge a gun within fifty *feet* of the centre of a carriageway. That is about seventeen yards and is effective killing range for a 12-bore so don't shoot towards the road.

If you have companions shooting with you, where possible walk abreast of each other and *keep in line*; where this is not possible, along a woodland track for instance, then those bringing up the rear must carry their guns broken.

Your aim is to kill as sportingly and as humanely as possible; your quarry will fall into two sections:

1. edible species
2. vermin species

Let us now look at the birds and beasts which you are entitled to kill and the times of the year when you may do so:

Game

Pheasant   1 October – 1 February
Partridge   1 September – 1 February
Grouse   12 August – 10 December
Blackgame   20 August – 10 December
Ptarmigan   12 August – 10 December (Scotland only)
Capercaillie   1 October – 31 January
Hare   There is no close season but hares may only be shot by the

occupier of land and those authorised by him, and may not be offered for sale from 1 March to 31 July. Hares may only be shot by those holding a game licence.

Snipe   12 August – 31 January

Woodcock   1 October – 31 January in England and Wales
                    1 September – 31 January in Scotland

Moorhen, Coot and Golden Plover   1 September – 31 January

Vermin species

Rabbits, pigeons and vermin species may be shot at any time. It should be noted that whilst corvines can be killed all the year round, ravens are protected by law and it is the duty of the sportsman to learn to identify this bird by its larger size and deep-throated 'cronk'.

All birds of prey (hawks) are protected.

Wildfowl

The under-mentioned birds may be killed between 1 September – 31 January but the season is extended until 20 February in areas below high water mark on the coast.

Coot	Mallard
Tufted Duck	Moorhen
Gadwall	Pintail
Goldeneye	Golden Plover
Canada Goose	Pochard
Greyalg Goose	Shoveler
Pinkfooted Goose	Common Snipe
White-fronted Goose (in	Teal
England and Wales only)	Wigeon

Rearing pheasants

If you shoot regularly throughout the winter months then you have a moral duty to re-stock. Pheasants do not breed well in the wild these days, primarily due to the modern farming methods which have destroyed much of their habitat and the abundance of corvines. So in order to continue enjoying your sport you must put something back into it. Otherwise your land will be barren of game.

Pheasants are not easy to rear, I would compare them with turkeys in this respect. They are prone to disease, will die of pneumonia if they get wet at an early age, and once released they are in danger from vermin, particularly foxes.

Some brushwood in the enclosure provides birds with both shelter and shade

Begin in a small way with a few pheasant eggs under a broody hen. Let the hen do all the work for you rather than encumber yourself with incubators and brooders at this stage.

When the poults are six weeks old they will need to be confined in a release-pen in the woods which are to be their home, the purpose of this being to acclimatise them, for to let them straight out into the wild would be to pronounce the death sentence on them. They must learn about the dangers of the woods, go up to roost in the trees where they are safe.

Your release-pen should encompass a sizeable area and be constructed of strong mesh, six inches buried in the ground to prevent foxes from digging beneath it. In effect it will be on the lines of the fox-proof enclosure described in the chapter on poultry and ducks and geese, except that you will need to construct small mesh funnels through which the pheasant poults can come and go, small enough to prevent entry by foxes.

The top should be roofed with nylon netting if possible, otherwise ample brushwood put inside for the birds to hide beneath when there is a winged predator in the vicinity. There should be undergrowth inside, anyway, for they will need to shelter from storms.

The process of release must be a gradual one, the birds regarding the

217

Releasing pheasant poults into the wild (from carrying boxes)

area as their home and you must feed them here twice daily. If you do not then they will wander in search of food and perhaps find another place more to their liking and not return.

Even when they begin going up to roost in the wood itself your worries will not be over for there is always the threat of poachers, particularly at night in this day and age, and you will need to be vigilant.

Shooting

If you shoot on your own then a couple of forays once a week with dog and gun should not unduly disturb your pheasants providing you do not make a habit of shooting close to the feeding area. You will need a dog (see chapter on dogs) for a wounded pheasant will elude you otherwise and will die a lingering death, not to mention the waste of a bird which has cost you money to rear.

If, however, you invite a couple of friends to shoot with you then the day has to be organised. Always try and drive your birds back in the direction of their roost wood rather than towards a neighbour's boundary. Work the boundaries first, paying particular attention to any worthwhile hedgerows which you might be lucky enough to have! Root crops will generally only hold birds on drier days, on pouring wet days they will skulk in hedges or woods.

Begin shooting about ten o'clock in the morning after the pheasants have had time to feed. If a full day is planned then do not shoot after mid-afternoon in the winter months for the birds need to be allowed to return to roost in peace.

Partridges are generally not the quarry of the smallholder or small farmer for he has not the expanse of land necessary to hold them. However, if you have an acreage of old pasturland, seeded thick grass, then this is where you are likely to find a covey. The partridge population in this country has declined considerably since the war and as a result don't harrass your birds. Take a brace for the pot and then leave them in peace.

Rabbits

You are required to control your rabbit population anyhow so you might as well have a few for the larder.

Snaring is an effective way of taking rabbits once you have become accomplished at setting rabbit wires. You need to learn to recognise well used runs from hedgerows and woods to the fields where they feed, night and morning. A rabbit's mode of travel is to run and hop and you must set wires in between these 'hops'. My book *Ratting and Rabbiting* (Nimrod) explains this in greater detail but basically you must secure your snares with stout pegs and inspect them night and morning, not only for humanitarian reasons but also because foxes and buzzards will soon learn where there is an easy meal to be had if you don't beat them to it.

Alternatively you can ferret and net your rabbits (see my book *Ferreting and Trapping for Amateur Gamekeepers*); the advantages of snared and netted rabbits over shot ones is that you will obtain a higher price for rabbits that have not got lead shot in them.

You need to learn all about ferret management first, for unless you have good working ferrets all that will happen is that your animals will lie up underground with their kill and you will have an arduous time-wasting job digging them out. Ferrets are clean, friendly creatures; if they are not then it is the fault of the owner.

When netting rabbits in this way you must move about quietly placing your nets over the holes or else the rabbits below ground will

219

An old quarry; a likely place to find a rabbit

Setting a snare for a rabbit

hear you and will be reluctant to bolt. You cannot always guarantee that you have covered every hole, there could well be an unseen one in a thick clump of briars, so it will be necessary to be on the alert with the gun for the elusive coney which bolts into the open. Ideally you need a companion in this sport, one of you to shoot and the other to pounce and despatch a rabbit the moment it hits the net. Safety must not be overlooked; ensure that you both know where the other is because a snap-shot in thick cover could have disastrous results otherwise.

Some farmers shoot their rabbits at night in the headlights of a vehicle, usually a pick-up truck, one man driving, the other shooting from the back. Certainly large bags of rabbits can be made in this way providing you do not shoot too often.

Rabbits soon learn that approaching headlights mean death and whereas on the first occasion you find them hopping away in the lights, the next time they will have dived for cover at the first sound of an approaching vehicle. Shoots of this nature should not be conducted more frequently than once a month.

Vehicles and guns are not a good marriage and driver and shooter need to have a firm understanding before setting out. Don't push your safety-catch forward until the truck has stopped; thump on the roof of the cab to signal to your companion to pull up and only shoot then. Do not, under any circumstances, fire from a moving vehicle; you will almost certainly miss as you are bumped up and down over uneven ground, but if you are thrown over with a loaded and cocked gun in your hands the consequences are unthinkable.

Rabbits provide a cheap and nutritious meal and can be cooked in a variety of ways so that if you shoot them regularly the fare does not become monotonous. They can be roasted, fried, made into a pie, curried, etc., and the flavour bears a resemblance to chicken. Most important, the meat will be tender, lean and low in cholesterol.

Pigeons

You won't find much better sport than the humble woodpigeon offers. Its numbers need to be controlled for it is a rapacious eater and can decimate large tracts of crops which will cost you money. Again, there is a worthwhile harvest to be reaped and you can do this in the most humane way possible with your gun.

Pigeons are a worthy quarry but you need to know something about their habits to enable you to come to terms with them. These birds fly out from their roosting wood to feed at daybreak in the fields, return towards mid-day to rest and digest their food, and then feed again until

The best way to make a bag of pigeons is with decoys

late afternoon when they will go back to roost. You can either:

1. shoot them on their feeding grounds
2. shoot them as they return to the woods

For the former you will need decoys to have any real chance of making a bag. Decoys are only of use in areas where the birds are actually feeding. Just by putting out decoys on a field previously unfrequented by woodies you won't succeed in encouraging pigeons to show an interest.

First, find out where the birds are feeding. Don't delay; for no apparent reason they change feeding grounds from day to day so act swiftly. Go to that place, build yourself a hide which needs to blend in with its surroundings. On a stubble field a few bales will suffice. Or use a hedgerow and cut some foliage to shield you. Camouflage netting is handy and can be easily carried in your game-bag. The essence of a hide is to break up the human outline.

The secret of pigeon-shooting from a hide is to have the hide *above* head height so that oncoming birds do not see you mount your gun. Use any shot birds as additional decoys, propped up with a forked twig under their heads. Dead pigeons, placed properly, are more effective than artificial decoys.

You need to be comfortable in your hide, an oil-drum or something similar to sit on and room to move. Cramped conditions are not conducive to good shooting.

If you decide to shoot the birds coming back to roost then ascertain the geography of the wood, find out which are the best flight-lines in relation to the favourite roosts. You will not make such a large bag as when decoying on the fields but if you are in the right place you will enjoy some good shooting.

The woodpigeon is vastly under-rated as a table bird. In effect the only worthwhile part of its anatomy from an edible point of view is the breast, and if you are shooting a lot of birds then 'breasting' them will save you time and freezer-space. Simply pluck the breast feathers and peel the skin back, lift the breast upwards from the bottom and snip through the joints with a strong pair of kitchen scissors. You then have a neat 'steak' which is ideal for use in casseroles. More convenient, in fact, than rabbit which has innumerable bones.

A hide constructed out of four pallets

Wild duck

If you have a small pool on your land and if duck are not already using it they can be encouraged to do so fairly easily. The mallard's downfall is its greed; scatter some barley in the shallows and once the duck have found it they will keep on coming. But don't overshoot or the duck won't come for long. Once a fortnight is ample, and then don't keep on shooting until darkness; allow the late-comers to feed in peace for they will return and bring others with them.

Wild duck feed by night and rest by day, hence you will obtain your sport at dusk.

If you don't have a pool on your land then you can always make one, as described in chapter eight.

In addition to mallard you will occasionally find that teal are flighting in to feed. In spite of their small size (they are Britain's smallest duck) teal are delicious eating and offer superb sport.

Wild duck, in my opinion, are superior eating to the fattier farmyard variety. But the enterprising smallholder can enjoy the best of both worlds; he can keep domestic duck on his flight pond as well, and as an additional bonus these will act as decoys to draw the wild birds in.

You may be fortunate in having a stretch of river flowing through your land. In this case you can flight duck more regularly than on a pool for they will be birds of passage, following the waterway rather than using a specific place to feed.

Snipe

Snipe offer a testing shot, possibly the most difficult of all, and are a delicasy on the table. They frequent boggy ground, so that waterlogged stretch at the far end of your holding might not be so useless after all. Snipe feed by night, often flighting in when it is too dark to see them but usually they are to be found there next morning. Walk them up, flush them and learn how to kill them in flight. There are two schools of thought on snipe shooting:

1. take them immediately they rise
2. wait until their early jinking has finished and their flight is not so erratic

Only *you* can decide which method you prefer. Personally, I prefer to shoot them immediately they jump.

Roast your snipe and eat them either on toast or with croutons. The traditional way is to eat them un-gutted and to leave the head on, using the long beak for a skewer. We always clean ours and remove the head.

Woodcock

The woodcock is a winter visitor to the British Isles, arriving at the beginning of November although there are some resident breeding pairs in this country. Of all the sporting birds none engender such excitement amongst sportsmen than the woodcock as it rises unexpectedly from a clump of bracken or beneath a rhododendron where it has been resting up. It takes a cool head and a steady hand to kill one; often the beaters have already flung themselves prone at the dreaded cry of 'cock for'ard!'

In many ways woodcock shooting is similar to snipe shooting except that the former is to be found in woodlands. Its delicate gamey flavour is quite different from that of other game birds and I would recommend cooking it in the same way as snipe.

Hares

I have already described how paraquat sprays are decimating the hare population and for that reason I shoot very few.

Never take a long shot at a hare for it is a large animal and will carry on after being hit if not struck in a vital place. A larger shot size, such as No. 4, is advisable.

Hare meat is dark and full-flavoured. The traditionalist advocates hanging them for a week or even a fortnight but we prefer ours reasonably fresh, eaten or frozen within twenty-four hours of shooting, as we do with all our game. Hanging dates back to pre-refrigeration days when a surplus of game had to be kept and consequently meat was deemed to be more acceptable when 'high'. In effect you are eating decomposing flesh.

The B.A.S.C.

The sport of shooting has been under threat for many years now. Misguided busybodies who seek to interfere with the legitimate sport of others are mounting incessant attacks, some physical, upon their sworn enemies. Political parties see this as a means to jump on the band wagon and curry votes by threatening to ban fieldsports, regardless of the fact that thousands of rural people would be thrown out of work, the gun-trade would be decimated overnight, and dogs and horses would have to be put down because there was no more work for them. Vermin species would rule the countryside, game birds and songbirds declining as a result. Nevertheless, we have a perpetual battle on our hands and it is up to everybody who uses a gun for sport, as well as to provide meat

226

A family day on the shoot

227

for his family, to take up the fight. And we can only win by uniting.

Which is why everybody who shoots should join the British Association for Shooting and Conservation (B.A.S.C.). This body, formerly the Wildfowlers' Association of Great Britain and Ireland, is active at all levels in the interests of shooting. It ensures that the sportsman's voice is heard wherever decisions are taken, whether by parliament, local government, international agencies and other statutory or non-governmental organisations which affect the shooting man. At Westminster it operates through an all-party Parliamentary Committee and maintains strong and active representation at every level. Above all, the B.A.S.C. works for the future of sporting shooting and its place in the British countryside in order that the sport can be handed down to future generations in a healthy and flourishing condition.

The B.A.S.C. has its *Codes of Practice* which set clear standards of acceptable sporting practice, a *Proficiency Award Scheme*, a *Firearms Department*, a *Legal Department* and a *Members' Shoot Advisory Service*. And in addition to all this individual members are covered for third party liability risks to the value of £1,000,000 in respect of any one accident, all inclusive for an annual ten pound subscription! Where else would you be able to buy a million pounds' worth of insurance for a tenner, and in addition receive all the other benefits which the Association has to offer, including a glossy quarterly magazine which keeps one well informed on every aspect of shooting?

Fishing

The opportunity to fish also provides the smallholder with additional fresh food for the table. I have never got round to taking up fishing, I just don't have the time. However, Angus and Gavin are keen, and after many fruitless expeditions on the banks of a local river they have now begun to catch the odd trout. Nothing is more delicious than a freshly caught trout on your plate for supper, yet another benefit of country lifestyle.

For the more enterprising smallholder who has running water on his land there is also the prospect of taking up fish-farming, either on a small scale as a subsidiary income or a much larger project on a full-time basis. I know of one farmer who started from scratch and now has five superb trout pools on his land on which he lets the fishing at five pounds per day. The fisherman is allowed to keep two trout, the rest he must put back in the water to be caught another day. That sounds to me like one better than shooting, you can't shoot a pheasant and then set it free again for next time!

228

CHAPTER TWENTY-FOUR

Vermin and Their Control

Every smallholding has its share of vermin and the purpose of this chapter is to examine the main harmful species, birds and beasts which pray on livestock, crops and animal feedstuffs, and to give the reader some idea of how to combat this menace and save himself money.

Foxes

The fox has earned itself an undeserved reputation as a lovable rogue. The public fondly believe this distant relative of the wolf to be a romantic part of the rural scene, a creature that should neither be hunted nor shot but allowed to breed unchecked. In fact, Reynard is the scourge of the poultry farmer, sheep farmer and gamekeeper. He is not as cunning as his reputation, rather wary and *persistent*. If he knows where to find a free-range bird he will lie in wait, day after day, until either he is killed or there are no birds left.

An example of the fox's lack of cunning was demonstrated to me one cold April mid-day. We were in the midst of a light snow shower when, on looking out of the window, I noticed a fox on a stubble field opposite the house, about five hundred yards away. He was sniffing about, engrossed in some scent which he had picked up. I called the family and we watched him for a while; there was no cover, I would not have given an addled egg for my chances of getting within gunshot of him. But the children were insistent so I decided to give it a go.

I loaded up with heavy goose shot and set out on what seemed to be a futile stalk. I had the advantage of a hedge until I got level with the fox but from thereon it was all open ground. I made a slight detour to get upwind, began to crawl through the stubble. I now found I had another slight advantage, the ground sloped and I was hidden from my quarry but once I reached the top of the incline Reynard was sure to see me.

A few yards further on a hare jumped up in front of me and made for the hedgerow. Obviously the fox had picked up this animal's scent but had been unable to locate the hare. Hares are masters of camouflage.

Now I was at the top of the rise; I peered cautiously over the top and saw the fox. He was still sniffing the ground to and fro, so intent on his hunting that he did not see me. I estimated the distance to be in excess of sixty yards, possibly more. Too far for a clean kill, except that I was loaded up with 1 5/8 oz of No. 1 shot and I had once witnessed a colleague perforate an oil-drum at this range. I aimed for the head and fired. The fox rolled over, flaying and kicking. I ran forward, gave him the *coup de grâce* with the second barrel.

It was unbelievable to me that I had managed to stalk this fox so easily. It was a large dog-fox, a bold animal which was not afraid to show itself in broad daylight and most certainly it would have begun taking our free-ranging birds before long.

Snaring is the most effective way of controlling foxes although I am not an advocate of the snare. There is a voluntary code of practice, apart from the legal requirements laid down in the Wildlife and Countryside Act, 1981. Self-locking snares are now illegal and only the free-running variety may be used. It is imperative that wires are inspected twice a day and are not set close to public footpaths or roads where people might be exercising their dogs.

The loop should be set small so that it catches the fox by the neck rather than round the body. It is essential to anchor the snare firmly, preferably to a hawthorn trunk in a hedge. I have always found that hedges are the best places to snare foxes. Look for the runs, particularly in snowy weather, find out where the creature goes through and put a snare there. Wear gloves when setting to avoid leaving human scent.

Always mark the position of your wires, the best way being to tie a small length of string in the hedge above the place where a snare is. Count the number of wires you put out, make sure that you check that many twice a day, and also when you come to take them up ensure that one is not left behind for surely that will be the one which will cause unnecessary suffering and get you into trouble.

Sale of fox pelts

A few years ago there was a lucrative market in fox pelts, most of which were exported to the continent. Whilst I am against exploiting creatures of the wild, foxes have to be killed so if you can make a few pounds out of the skins then it will help to reimburse you for those birds which Reynard has taken. During the boom in this trade I have had between fifteen and twenty pounds for a pelt but now the market has gone into decline and you will be lucky to get eight pounds.

Gassing

Gassing foxes is a chancey and dangerous business. You are using cyanide gas which is lethal and an accidental whiff of it could make you very ill, or worse. If you know where there is an earth containing a vixen and her cubs then don't go investigating it because at the first hint of danger the mother fox will move her young, make no mistake about that. Contact either a Ministry of Agriculture pest control officer or a gamekeeper and let them do the gassing. The procedure is to block up all the exit holes except one and then to put a spoonful of cymag powder down the remaining hole and close it up quickly. The powder, as soon as it comes into contact with the damp earth, gives off a deadly gas. Don't open up the earth until the following day, and even then stand well back. If you have been successful then generally you will find the fox and her litter dead by the exit where they have been attempting to scratch their way to freedom.

Shooting

Shooting is the most humane way of killing foxes providing it is carried out properly. This means using heavy shot and only taking foxes within range, i.e. up to thirty-five yards. Unless it is hit hard in a vital place then it will escape and die a lingering death. As much as I hate foxes I have no wish to inflict cruelty on them.

In some parts of the country 'fox-clubs' exist. These are generally unofficial groups who club together so that they can provide enough Guns, dogs and beaters to be able to drive foxes out of thick cover. Well-organised this method can be very effective, badly organised it is highly dangerous.

Certainly it reduces the fox population in dense woodlands where vermin are otherwise inaccessible. The Guns are positioned at fifty yard intervals along a woodland ride with their backs to the oncoming beaters and dogs. Hence a fox which is flushed is shot at when it is past the line of shooters, and even if two Guns fire at the same fox they are shooting away from each other.

Hunting

Hunting is not cruel as the media are always trying to claim, pandering to the anti-fieldsports brigade who resort to hysteria and distortion of the true facts. A fox is pursued by a pack of hounds and if it is caught it is invariably killed outright before being torn apart. If it goes to ground then the huntsmen dig it out and despatch it humanely. It is *not* thrown alive to the pack.

I've no objection to the Hunt on my land providing they inform me of the date and ask permission to come. If they just arrive then they are not welcome; uninvited there could be a number of complications. A hound might run into a fox wire which I have not had notice to remove, or my livestock could be frightened by the sudden intrusion of horses and hounds.

In any case, always shut your cats up during a hunt. There have been several instances reported in the press where hounds have pursued and killed a domestic cat.

Rats

Rats are the nemesis of the smallholder. Over a period of time they will do an awful lot of damage if they are allowed to establish a colony and breed unchecked. Apart from the food they eat they will spoil much more with their foulings. They steal eggs and will kill and eat chicks and poults of considerable size. I once lost a fairly large gosling to rats. They also consititute a real danger in that they will gnaw through electric wiring in a loft and perhaps start a fire. Not to mention the diseases which they will bring, the most terrible being Weil's disease (Leptospirosis) which can be fatal to humans. Also you are required by law to destroy any rats on your premises.

Your approach to rat control will be determined by whether you wish to indulge in some sport (for in spite of their despicable habits rats can give good sport to terriers, ferrets and the gun) or if you are merely interested in exterminating them in the easiest, quickest and cheapest way. Let us look at a number of methods whereby you might rid yourself of an undesirable colony of rats which have moved into your outbuildings with the onset of winter.

Ferreting

If you are out for a bit of sport with rats then there is no better way than to flush them out of their holes with ferrets. Those readers wishing to know more about ferreting and ratting might care to read my two books on the subject, *Ferreting and Trapping* and *Ratting and Rabbiting* (Nimrod Book Services).

This form of sport was at its heyday in the times when hayricks and

232

cornstacks were a common sight in nearly every farmyard. Needless to say, they were infested with rats and a group of men armed with sticks, .410s or No. 3 bore garden guns, and assisted by terriers would surround the ricks; the ferrets were put into the many holes and within a very short time bedlam broke loose. Rats scurried everywhere, were either clubbed to death, shot or killed by the dogs.

Modern farming methods heralded the end of this type of rat control although it can still be enjoyed to a lesser extent around the farmyards where rats are inhabiting the grain stores and outbuildings.

Ferrets used for this purpose should be adult ones trained against rats. The rat is a fearsome killer when cornered and a young inexperienced ferret is no match for it.

You should not combine shooting with sticks and terriers; in the melée there is always the chance of somebody or a terrier being accidentally shot. Choose one mode of attack or the other.

Flooding

Flooding can be an effective method within the confines of farm buildings. First ascertain where all the holes are and try to block them up with the exception of the one into which you will insert your hosepipe. It is a good idea to have a terrier or two at hand because invariably you will not have found every bolt hole and you need to deal with any rats which escape the deluge.

Poisoning

Poisoning is illegal except for the putting down of rat bait in covered places. You must ensure that no livestock can get at it and when you have cleared your infestation remove any surplus bait that is left. For the busy smallholder poisoning is by far the easiest and most effective method.

I always use *Neosorexa* which comes in the form of green crystals and rats and mice seem to find it preferable to any poultry foods which are left lying about. Indeed, I have known them to gnaw their way into a bag of this stuff!

Some years ago we had a colony of rats move into our turkey sheds. At night, when disturbed, they resembled a huge black serpent wriggling on the floor as they queued up to retreat into their holes. I began feeding them with Neosorexa and for the first few days they ate all that was put down without any apparent ill-effect. Then we began finding dead rats about the place and there were less to be seen by torchlight at night. And within a fortnight there wasn't a sign of a rat. The majority had died in their burrows.

Lengths of drain-piping are ideal receptacles for rat bait. Once you have baited them cover the pipes with some tin sheeting; poultry have a habit of scratching in dark corners and, anyway, the rats are bound to scatter some of the poison outside the tunnels.

Stoats, weasels and polecats

These three are bloodthirsty killers and if they find a way into your poultry sheds there will be terrible carnage. Far better to kill these vermin *before* that happens.

However, you won't be aware of their presence like you will with rats where there is evidence of food spoiling and soil excavations. These animals will hide up in an old woodpile or a hole in a bank, maybe even make their hideout deep amongst the hay bales in the barn.

The best method to combat them is to have one or two tunnel-traps set permanently. It has been illegal to use gin traps for many years now but the modern humane spring trap is just as effective. Construct a tunnel out of three lengths of wood, leaving room for the trap to spring inside it without being impeded. You don't need to bait this trap, merely to cover it with a handful of dry leaves for stoats, weasels and polecats cannot resist entering a tunnel when they can see daylight at the other end.

Site your trap along where these creatures love to run; they seldom cross open ground unless forced to do so, preferring to travel alongside stone walls, buildings, and will frequently sidle by a gatepost in a field. Traps must be inspected daily, preferably night and morning, and re-sprung every week if they have not caught or else they will rust and may not catch when eventually something crosses them.

I have already related how a polecat decimated our own flock of Silkies. Better to be safe than sorry, so set a trap first. And as a bonus you are sure to kill the odd rat in your tunnel-trap. Rats, too, like to run through tunnels.

Moles

Moles are a pest wherever cultivation takes place. You sow a neat seed-bed, cover it with netting against the attentions of birds or scratching cats, and next morning half your work is undone because a mole has travelled beneath it and pushed up unsightly heaps of soil. Or

Stoats and weasels rarely cross open ground. A gateway is the best place to trap them

else one ruins your lawns and flower borders. Good grazing land can be spoiled where there is a colony of these small subterranean creatures busily destroying good pastureland.

Up until the last war virtually every rural area had its resident mole-catcher, a man who earned his living by ridding farmland of these pests. Usually he was paid by landowners for his work and as an additional bonus he skinned and cured the pelts, for moleskins were much in demand then.

Alas the mole-catcher has gone, to be replaced by Ministry pest-officers who destroy moles with the use of strychnine-dosed worms. Often farmers can, under licence, purchase strychnine for this purpose but my advice to the novice is to leave this method strictly alone; if you want your moles poisoned then have the job done by an expert. Strychnine is a terrible poison, in truth it never dies. A creature killed by it and then eaten by another predator will spread death in a never-ending chain.

Trapping

Trapping moles requires a certain amount of skill but is not beyond the complete novice. Most country ironmongers have mole traps for sale and it is a good idea to purchase one to experiment with. You do not set traps beneath the mounds thrown up by moles but in the run between molehills. The best way is to cut out a square of turf and dig down carefully until you find the tunnel. Place the trap here, taking care that the workings are not obstructed by soil, and then replace the turf, making sure that no daylight infiltrates the run. Mark the site with a stick to facilitate inspection.

There is an old country belief that a briar placed in the run will prick the mole and that the creature will die from its wounds. Which, as far as I am concerned, is nonsense. Equally nonsensical is the method of burying an empty bottle up to its neck alongside a molehill so that the wind will hoot inside the bottle and deter the mole. I saw this method tried once; the mole showed its contempt by digging an even larger mound and half-burying the protruding milk bottle!

Mole-catching is an art, far too complex to go into detail in this brief summary. I have covered the subject at greater length in my book *Moles and their Control* (Saiga), now out of print, but many public libraries still have a copy. In this work I have covered the history of the mole, the trapper of both olden and modern times, and listed the different types of traps which are available.

There is one small consolation to be gleaned from having a mole burrowing across your land – the soil from molehills is ideal for using in the potting shed, easily gathered with a spade and a wheelbarrow and does not even need riddling! It is a worthwhile proposition when compared with the cost of a bag of sterilised soil and, in my opinion, just as good. It can be enriched, if required, by adding a little peat or well-rotted compost.

Winged vermin

Winged vermin present a threat to the small poultry farmer and to the man who grows crops. But it is essential for him to know which species are protected before he wages war on them.

All birds of prey are protected. Buzzards can be troublesome but even if they are raiding your poultry enclosures then you are not entitled to shoot them, so a local conservation officer who takes out parties of bird-watchers in this area informs me. If it is not possible to erect a netting roof over your enclosures then at least provide plenty of cover within, piles of branches for birds to hide beneath when a buzzard is in the vicinity.

You must also learn to recognise a raven from the rest of the crow tribe for this corvine is protected by law. In fact, ravens are easily identifiable by their much greater size and their distinctive throaty 'cronk'. They will do just as much damage as their numerous relatives, particularly on the sheep fields at lambing time.

The corvine problem is nationwide. Wherever you go you see rooks, magpies and jays in abundance. Not only will they take your eggs and chicks but they will also hunt the hedgerows, even in urban areas, in search of songbirds' nests. This again is something which the anti-fieldsports 'conservationist' fails to realise. *The balance of nature in this modern world can only be maintained with the help of Man.* If no vermin species were controlled then eventually only the predators would rule and multiply.

The crow tribe have been allowed to breed out of all control. There are many reasons for this but principally it is due to the reduction in the number of gamekeepers. Years ago the keeper's job was to maintain a stock of *wild* game which could only be achieved by intensive vermin control. Nowadays, with the advent of 'cheque-book' shooting, the keeper's role has changed; he has to rear as many pheasants as possible artificially, his work revolves around incubators and brooders. He has no time to spend hours lying in wait for a carrion crow to return to her nest, instead he must rear additional birds to compensate for losses by corvines. So the vermin go unchecked.

The gamekeeper is greatly restricted in his activities too. No longer does he rule the coverts, he has to contend with laws that make his job more difficult.

Corvine control

If you have the time then the gun is the best weapon to use against crows, jays and magpies. Used in conjunction with a crow and owl decoy (crows will always mob birds of prey) and the *correct* use of a crow-call, then some good shooting can often be had.

Another useful method is the cage trap. Construct a six foot by six foot strong mesh enclosure with a tapering funnel going down into it. Hard weather is the best time to use this when food is scarce, and if fed liberally with corn the crows and their relatives will drop down the funnel to feed. But they are unable to fly back out because of their wingspan! Catches must be removed daily and despatched.

It is illegal to put out poison bait in the open for crows.

For every corvine you kill it may mean a nest of eggs or a few chicks saved. It is well worth the time and trouble spent reducing your local corvine population.

Creatures which are beneficial to the smallholder

Years ago hedgehogs featured on the 'wanted' list of poultry breeders and gamekeepers. Certainly a hedgehog loves to suck an egg if he comes across a clutch but this is the exception rather than the rule.

Hedgehogs overall do far more good than harm. On a wet summer's evening our lawn has been a mass of black splodges as the slugs have emerged from their hiding places en route for the vegetable garden. And what a banquet they provide for a hungry Mister Prickles!

Hedgehogs are a bonus in any garden or smallholding.

Likewise for the organic grower ladybirds will decimate hordes of aphids. Far better than toxic sprays!

Frogs and toads, too, are welcome residents on the land. They will spend their entire lifetime hunting slugs and harmful insects.

Our role is to conserve and control, to nurture the beneficial species and keep the harmful ones down to manageable proportions. The responsibility for maintaining Nature's intended balance rests with us. To sit back, as some would have us do, and let wildlife take its own course would be destructive. The countryside as we know it would soon disappear.

CHAPTER TWENTY-FIVE

Selling Produce

Selling anything these days is not easy. To stand any chance at all one must have the right product at the right price – and a market where there is a demand. I have already covered commercial selling of organic produce which is much easier once the farmer has established his various outlets, but it is a different proposition for the smallholder.

The smallholding set alongside a main road, with ample space for cars to stop and a sign that gives the motorist enough warning (preferably in a conspicuous position fifty yards from your gate), should do a steady trade in the various seasons. Many of these customers will be people just passing through and whilst the smallholder may never see them again he can always rely on a passing trade. But the small farmer situated in a remote area has problems; he must find his trade locally. We are in the latter position, two and a half miles from the nearest village and living in a scattered community. During the summer we might see a dozen tourist's cars pass by our gate at weekends but work out the percentage of those who might be interested in a pint of goats' milk and you will realise the limitations. We need to sell around one thousand pints of milk a year to pay for the keep of our goats and anything over that is profit!

Regarding the goats' milk trade, I refer the reader to the relevant chapter on goats; he needs to advertise his products in shop windows throughout the area for a start but in order to turn his stock over, and all frozen milk should be sold in rotation, the oldest first so that none is kept for more than six months in the freezer, he needs to find a shop or supermarket who will take it in bulk regularly.

Free-range eggs are never any trouble to sell. Unless you overprice them, they will go at all times of the year. But strangely I have always had difficulty in selling duck eggs. If you have a permanent egg-sign on display it is a good idea to cover it up or take it in when you are sold out, otherwise frequent callers will be disappointed and it will be a nuisance to you.

Unless you live on the main road you could find that your eggs move slowly and therefore it is a good idea to try and build up a few regular customers, but tell them at the outset that production falls between October and February. The question we get asked most frequently during this period is 'what's gone wrong with your hens lately?'

Selling produce from the garden, though, is an inconsistent business. The first year I put an 'organic vegetable' sign outside the gate. I took it in the next day because if I had continued selling we should have had no vegetables left to see us through the winter. You must explore your market before you start growing any vegetable in quantity. Undoubtedly carrots are our best seller; we cannot sell beetroot, swedes or rhubarb simply because most Saturdays there is a produce stall in the village in aid of the church, and these can be purchased there. Lettuce will sell early in the season but once you get into June it seems that everybody has a row in their own garden or has a neighbour who has a surplus. You will have to experiment, put a card in a local shop window and be prepared to call a halt once inroads are being made into your crops.

In the beginning you must concentrate just on selling your surplus; once you have ascertained which varieties are in demand then you can grow them in greater quantities the next season.

Bear in mind that at the outset, anyway, growing and selling produce will be just a subsidiary means of earning an income. On a small scale you won't make a lot of money out of it, if you break even and have your own veg free then you will have got off to a flying start.

Vegetable customers are more time-consuming than the caller who wants a dozen eggs or a pint of goats' milk. You cannot dig or cut your crops in advance in the hope of selling them; they will wither up and be unmarketable. So, you are just in the midst of some intricate job, or perhaps earning your full-time living at home, when there is a knock on the door and somebody wants a fresh lettuce. In our case, we charge around fifteen pence for a lettuce and, depending upon crop rotation on our raised-beds, the lettuces might be in a bed up the field that year instead of in the kitchen garden next to the house. So I have to break off from whatever I'm doing and go and cut a lettuce, which will take me about ten minutes. Probably the customer wants to chat as well and that all adds up to a quarter of an hour and I've lost valuable working time in the process. I prefer to put my produce sign out during the summer holidays when I can ask one of the children to run and fetch a lettuce.

I was once asked why I didn't plough up another patch of land and grow potatoes in quantity. Good question. The answer is that the potato harvest on a bigger scale could be a time-consuming business lasting several days. Also one has to wait for a spell of dry weather and that could come at the most inconvenient time in relation to my work. I might harvest one hundred bags of potatoes which would sell at three pounds per bag. If I'm pushed for time I've got to employ somebody for the harvest which will cut the profit drastically. Then I've got to store the crop in a frost-free place which I haven't got and it would not be worthwhile building one. Then, suppose there is a glut of potatoes and they are slow selling; a third might go rotten. So, after a lot of hard work, I've ended up making a loss. Far better to grow a reasonable amount and sell a surplus if you have any.

The Inland Revenue don't like letting you get away with any perks, so on your accounts you have to state how much of your produce was for your own consumption, and you are taxed on it! This is regardless of the fact that a percentage of your crops might have rotted in the ground, you've had clubroot in the brassicas and greenfly have ruined your broad beans. It doesn't matter if it goes to waste but you have to pay if you eat it!

Of course, there are cheats in the organic trade just as there are in every other walk of life. Honesty is your best hallmark, if you stoop to buying-in chemically-grown crops to re-sell as organically-grown then you are not only deceiving genuine trusting customers but the whole object of what you are doing becomes pointless. Some of our carrot customers are patients under-going alternative treatment for cancer and they have to drink two pints of chemical-free carrot juice every day. It would be insensitive and criminal to sell them anything which was detrimental to their course of natural treatment.

The Soil Association

Mostly customers will not question your integrity but it is an added bonus to obtain the Soil Association's symbol to display at your gate. This association promotes an ecologically and economically sustainable approach to agriculture and a healthy basis to human nutrition. Organic husbandry offers the real long term option over intensive chemical farming, as already explained in this book, which is causing havoc to the land and the environment. Our health depends on the quality of our food, the plant and animal products which we eat. The quality of our food depends upon the health of the soil, a vital relationship which is crucial to the future of life on this planet. The association is pioneering ways in which the future may be made brighter, healthier and enduring.

In addition the Soil Association issue an Organic Husbandry Guidelines and Permitted List for the organic grower. This ensures that the organic smallholder trading commercially may follow these clearly defined do's and don'ts and, in due course, after having had his methods of husbandry approved by the association, receive the Soil Association registered symbol for farmers and growers.

This will almost certainly help your vegetable sales and it is a personal achievement to be granted this and to know that you are working on the right lines and fulfilling your ambitions.

The Henry Doubleday Research Association

This association will certainly benefit your husbandry. It carries out research into organic methods of horticulture and its findings are published in a quarterly newsletter which is free to members. There is a free advice service to members also. It supplies hard-to-get organic fertilizers and pesticides, access to rare vegetable and fruit varieties through the 'Finder' service and Vegetable Seed Library.

Its objects are:

1. the improvement and encouragement of horticulture generally
2. research into, and the study of, improved methods of organic farming and gardening
3. research into, and the utilisation of, Russian comfrey in connection with the foregoing objects:
4. the encouragement of research and experiment in agriculture and horticulture by, and the dissemination of knowledge of the results of such research and experiment among farmers, gardeners and schools
5. the advancement of knowledge of, and the fostering of public interest in, the benefits to be derived from the utilisation of Russian comfrey and other plants useful in organic husbandry

And if you sell organic produce the H.D.R.A. may well include you in their Organic Food Guide which is an excellent advertisment for you.

The Small Farmers' Association

You cannot afford not to be a member of this association which has the interests of the smallholder at heart. This association regards the small farm as a vital part of agriculture today. With cutbacks in agricultural advisory work there is less information available to the small farmer now than ever before. Much of the work involves the study of papers put out by the EEC, the UK Parliament and the Ministry of Agriculture, to safeguard the interests of small farmers. There is now a link between the SFA and *Home Farm* magazine, a publication which all small farmers, growers and anybody interested in husbandry should subscribe to. We have taken this magazine right from the first issue, over ten years ago, and our whole lifestyle has benefitted from it. We have had amazing results from its classified advertisment columns, selling virtually everything which we have advertised in them. In addition to this magazine, Broad Leys Publishing Company have published a 'Home Farm Source Book'; if you need to know who supplies what, it is all there within the ninety pages of indexed suppliers of everything from bees to vendors of water-power equipment. It has saved us an awful lot of time spent searching for some obscure item over the years.

Working Weekends on Organic Farms

Do you need a workman to help you with your harvest or mucking out your goat sheds but you either can't find the right man (or woman) or you can't afford to employ them? Well, here's how you can get some free help when you need it.

WWOOF is an exchange system; in return for a reasonable day's work on your farm or smallholding you provide meals and basic accommodation – a mattress on the floor will do if you do not have a spare bedroom. The idea is that you train a 'worker member' in organic farming. He gains knowledge, you gain a helping hand.

We have had some super people here working for us under this scheme. One August we had the Burgesses sleeping in our spare bedroom and the Foords camped on the front lawn in a trailer-tent. They worked hard, mucking out sheds, mulching and extending raised-beds. It was more than an employer-worker relationship and in between the chores we enjoyed some delightful walks through the surrounding countryside.

Since then Alan and Diane Burgess have sold their conventional home in Essex and made the move to Wales, where they have bought a smallholding. They found the courage to take the plunge and, the last time I heard from them, they were still trying to persuade the Foords to do likewise!

Apart from the work they have done for you, you meet some interesting people through the WWOOFer scheme. But one must enter into the true spirit of the idea and set them working on something which is applicable to organic farming, and not get them washing the car or tidying out the garage!

Selling is what your chosen way of life is all about. There is no point in producing to waste, it is immoral. However, there is one final point to bear in mind; sometimes it is more economical to produce for your own consumption than to sell. For example, just prior to last Christmas we killed and dressed all the surplus cockerels. We could have taken them to market, all twelve of them, and perhaps made fifty pounds. But, throughout the coming year we know that we should have numerous friends visiting us, usually for the day on a Sunday. Our cockerels are all sold, the game in the freezer is running low and perhaps our visitors would not appreciate vegetarian fare. So the only solution would be to buy a cockerel or chicken from the local butcher which might cost us eight pounds. So a dozen lots of visitors would cost us ninety-six pounds, less the revenue from the birds we might have taken to market. So it was more profitable in this instance to put our cockerels in the freezer in readiness for weekend visitors.

Whether you eat your produce or sell it, you will have the satisfaction of knowing that you have suceeded by your own efforts. Gone are those suburbia days when you popped down to the local supermarket to buy something out of *their* freezer!

Appendix of Useful Addresses

The Henry Doubleday Research Association, Ryton-on-Dunsmore, Coventry, CV8 3LG. Tel.: 0203-303517

The Soil Association Limited, 86–88 Colston Street, Bristol, BS1 5BB

Home Farm Magazine, Broad Leys Publishing Company, Widdington, Saffron Walden, Essex, CB11 3SP. Tel.: 0799-40922

The Small Farmers' Association, Chairman: Richard Lewis, P.O. Box 6, Ludlow, Shropshire, SY8 1ZZ

Working Weekends On Organic Farms, 19 Bradford Road, Lewes, Sussex, BN7 1RB

The Donkey Sanctuary, Sidmouth, Devon, EX10 0NU. Tel.: 03955-6391/6592

Captain D. MacLean (old varieties of potatoes), Dornock Farm, Crieff, Perthshire

Index